All Rights Reserved ©

No part of this publication may be reproduced, stored in a retrieval system, or transmitted in any form or by any means without the author's and publisher's prior written permission.

Disclaimer (Exclusive clause)

The author and all employees disclaim any incorrect interpretation, wrong answers to questions or text, harm, including emotional, psychological, and physical or any form of the liability to the reader/listener or being Given information by third parties. Furthermore, this disclaimer protects all contributory people, directors, employees, 3rd parties, authors and will not be liable for any injury caused.

Summary Content

Contents

All Rights Reserved © 1
Disclaimer (Exclusive clause).......................1
Summary Content 2
Dedication..7
Acknowledgement. 8
Preface 9
About the Author...15
Introduction 16
CHAPTER 1 18
Past Paper..18
February/March 2020 reference 0470/1 18
CHAPTER 1: Answers...................................29
Chapter 2..48
Paper TWO 48
October/November 2020 paper one ref 0470/12 48
CHAPTER 2: Answers...................................61
Chapter 3..73
PAPER 3..73
Paper 1 Reference 0470/2...........................73
October/November 2020............................73
SOURCE E 82
Chapter 3..103
PAPER 3..103
ANSWERS TO CHOSEN QUESTIONS 103

Chapter 4 114
PAPER 4 114
Questions 114
SOURCE C 118
SOURCE D 119
CHAPTER 4: Answers 134
Question: 134
Paper 5 148
Chapter 5 148
Cambridge IGCSE 148
: Alternative to Coursework 148
CHAPTER 5: Answers 152
PPr 4 2020 NOV. 157
Alternative to Coursework 157
CHAPTER 6: Answers 162
Answered Questions: 162
Chapter 7 167
PAPER 7 167
February/March 2021 Paper 2 167
QUESTION TO PAPER 7 168
CHAPTER 7 168
Option A: Nineteenth-century topic 168
CHAPTER 7: Answers 189
Chapter 8 202
Paper 8 202
February/March 2021 202
CHAPTER 8 203

Paper 8 203
SECTION A: CORE CONTENT 203
SECTION B: DEPTH STUDIES 209
DEPTH STUDY A: THE FIRST WORLD WAR, 1914–18 209
DEPTH STUDY B: GERMANY, 1918–45 210
DEPTH STUDY C: RUSSIA, 1905–41 212
DEPTH STUDY D: THE UNITED STATES, 1919–41 213
DEPTH STUDY E: CHINA, c.1930–c.1990 215
DEPTH STUDY G: ISRAELIS AND PALESTINIANS SINCE 1945 218

CHAPTER 8: Answers **220**
SECTION A: CORE CONTENT 220
Answered Questions: 3 and 7 220
   Judgement: 223
   Judgement: 227
DEPTH STUDY A: THE FIRST WORLD WAR, 1914–18 227
  Answered Questions: 9 and 12 228
   Judgement: 231
   Judgement: 235
  Chapter 9 236
  HISTORY   0470/23 236
  Paper 2   May/June 2021 236
  CHAPTER 9 259
  Answered Questions: 259
  Option B: Twentieth-century topic 259

Chapter 10 274
Paper (4) 274
Paper 4: Alternative to Coursework 274
0470/41 274
May/June 2021 274
CHAPTER 10: Answer 279
Chapter 11 284
Paper 11 284
Paper 1 - February/March 2022 284
2022 Past papers 294
Chapter 12 294
Paper 12 294
CHAPTER 12: Answers 304
Chapter 13 322
Paper 13 322
May/June 0470/12 322
Paper 1 May/June 2022 322
   INFORMATION 322
  The total mark for this paper is 60 322
CHAPTER 13: Answers 335
Answered Questions: 9,346
Paper 14 348
Chapter14 348
Paper 1   May/June 2022 348
CHAPTER 14: Answers 363
Chapter 15 374
Paper 14 374

Paper 1 May/June 2022	374
CHAPTER 15 ANSWER 15	389
Chapter 16	399
Page 16	399
Paper 2 May/June 2022	399
SOURCE F	407
Chapter 17	422
Paper 17	422
Paper 2 February/March 2022	422
CHAPTER 17: Answers	445
Chapter 18	456
Paper 18	456
Paper 2 May/June 2022	456
CHAPTER 18 Answers	478
Chapter 19	496
Paper 19	496
Paper 2 May/June 2022	496
SOURCE A	498
SOURCE B	499
SOURCE F	511
CHAPTER 19: Answers	515
Chapter 20	534
Paper 20	534
May/June 2022	534
CHAPTER 20: Answer	539
Chapter 21	544
Paper 21	544

February/March 2022	544
CHAPTER 21: Answers	549
Chapter22	554
Paper 22	554
Paper 4: Alternative to Coursework	554
May/June 2022	554
CHAPTER 22: Answers	559
Chapter 23	564
Paper23	564
Paper 4: Alternative to Coursework	564
May/June 2022	564
CHAPTER 23: Answers	569
Chapter 24	574
Paper 24	574
May/June 2022	574
CHAPTER 24: Answers	579
Author Qualifications and Honours	585
Other Books by the Author James Safo	588
History Glossary	596
Index	656

Dedication

I dedicate this book to myself to appreciate the hard work that has enabled me to achieve so much, thanks to the blessings of God.

Acknowledgement.

As with all the 160 books I have written and published, I acknowledge the guidance, wisdom, and knowledge that Almighty God provided me through the Guardians in drafting this book. It would have been impossible to finish authoring these books because when I started writing,

I never knew how or when I would conclude my research or where to direct it, but once I began, I received more guidance from Almighty God. With him, this book was written. He produced and gave me the resources; therefore, the real author of this publication is God.

Forgive and love everyone, then trust, believe, and have faith in God. This FORMULA IS THE KEY TO HEAVEN.

Preface

History is the systematic study of the past, with a primary focus on the human experience. As an academic discipline, it analyses and interprets evidence to construct narratives about what happened and explain why it happened. Some theorists categorise history as a social science, while others see it as part of the humanities or consider it a hybrid discipline.

This book contains Past Papers from Cambridge IGCSE. The Assessment from 2020 to 2022 aims for international education.

There are more than 4 and 6 assessment papers a year. Each paper contains approximately ten questions for the candidate to choose from in each section to answer. Some of the questions cover the nineteenth and twentieth centuries.

First and Second World Wars,
British behaviour during and immediately after the Indian Mutiny of 1857–58?
Was the Cuban Missile Crisis simply a trial of strength between Kennedy and Khruschev?, The First World War, 1914–18, The United States, 1919–41, South Africa, c.1940–c.1994, Israelis and Palestinians since 1945, Germany, 1918–45,

China, c.1930–c.1990, South Africa, c.1940–c.1994, Israelis and Palestinians since 1945, Nazis, Munich Putsch, Hitler, ISRAELIS, PALESTINIANS, turmoil in Europe. Italian unification, Pope Pius IX's Allocution of 1848?, THE KU KLUX Klan, US President Woodrow Wilson, and the British Expeditionary Force (BEF).

The following short statement helps to define History;

1. Some of these examples are programmatically compiled from various online sources to illustrate current usage of the word 'history.

2. A chronological record of significant events (such as those affecting a nation or institution), often including an explanation of their causes

3. A treatise presenting systematically related natural phenomena (as of geography, animals, or plants)

4. an account of a patient's medical background

5. An established record.

6. Events that form the subject matter of a history

7. That is finished or done for.

8. previous treatment, handling, or experience (as of a metal)

9. They were one of the greatest teams in history.

10. It was one of the most destructive storms in modern history.

11. He wrote a well-known history of the British Empire.

12. The book begins with a brief history of the Internet.

13. I studied history in college.

14. The history of space exploration is a fascinating topic.

15. It was a period in American history when most people lived and worked on farms.

Example statement made by some prominent people to support the definition of History. They were compiled from an online source.

Many of the homes are also open for history tours.

— Meagan Drillinger, Travel + Leisure, 29 Jan. 2022

This was to be the greatest prank in the county's history.

— Julia A. Morales, Seventeen, 1 Mar. 2023

Now comes the sixth trip to the Final Four in school history.

— Joseph Duarte, San Antonio Express-News, 29 Mar. 2021

O'Bannon's time was the eighth-fastest in the history of the Eastern Relays.

— J.l. Kirven, The Courier-Journal, 25 Apr. 2022

Conroy's firing would have been the first forced ouster in the history of the House.

— Fox News, 2 Oct. 2018

The next step is making it a weekend that will live in the history books.

— Chris Bumbaca, USA TODAY, 29 July 2021

Alex Ovechkin has carved his name atop the history books.

— Eric Jackson, Sportico.com, 6 Apr. 2025

It is steeped in history and the legacies of these individuals.

— Doug Ferguson, orlandosentinel.com, 6 May 2021

Her time ties for the fifth-fastest all-time and ranks third in U.S. history.

— Katelyn Hutchison, Forbes.com, 4 Aug. 2025

The rest is history, and it is well constructed in the book.

— Thomas Gase, The Mercury News, 21 June 2019

Of course, Lizzo and Chris Evans have a brief history that dates back to April 2021.

— Emily Tannenbaum, Glamour, 10 June 2022

Four home runs in nine games is the most by a Reds player in team history.

— John Fay, Cincinnati.com, 10 Aug. 2019

If history is any guide, then at least one of them will.

— Kyle Mizokami, Popular Mechanics, 23 Jan. 2019

There are not many people in the history of the world who can match him in that regard.

— Shania Russell, EW.com, 27 June 2023

Lou will be talking about the history of the local area and the distillery.

— Hartford Courant, 19 May 2022

Today in History: Here are just some of the historic events that occurred on this date in the past.

— Lorenzino Estrada, AZCentral.com, 29 Aug. 2025

However, this was the first puffin to appear at the station in its 44-year history.

— USA TODAY, 25 Feb. 2024

— Zak Keefer, Indianapolis Star, 5 Nov. 2017

Many of us who have this kind of history want to help others.

— Pauline Campos, Good Housekeeping, 13 July 2017

The Flames managed just eight shots on goal, a record low in the franchise's history.
— Keith Gave, Detroit Free Press, 6 Apr. 2018

In the history of the Mark Twain Prize, only one award has been revoked.
— Melissa Ruggieri, USA TODAY, 25 Apr. 2022

Mills is the first player in Heat history to wear No. 88.
— Anthony Chiang, Miami Herald, 7 Mar. 2024

About the Author

My life experience, from being an abandoned child who ate from bins and gutters in Ghana to becoming one of the most successful businessmen in Europe. My first profession is a qualified psychiatric nurse.

I have visited most European countries and wish to share my experiences with my readers. I have also written over 168 books and hold numerous qualifications, which are listed at the end of this book.

I hold approximately six degrees, including four postgraduate qualifications, ten diplomas and 15 certificates. All are listed in this book.

Introduction

HISTORY

Cambridge Assessment
International Education
Cambridge IGCSE.

The Year of the past exam paper is stated. 2020/21
The instructions and Information are the same for each paper as below

You will need: Answer booklet (enclosed). This will be provided at the exam.

INSTRUCTIONS

- Answer three questions in total:

Section A (Core Content): Answer two questions.
Section B (Depth Studies): Answer one question.

- Follow the instructions on the front cover of the answer booklet. If you need additional answer paper, ask the invigilator for a continuation booklet.

INFORMATION

- The total mark for this paper is 60.
- The number of marks for each question or part question is shown in brackets [ ].

In this book,

Each paper has two sections

Section 1 is the Questions

Section 2 is the Answers to the questions I have chosen questions

CHAPTER 1

Past Paper

February/March 2020 reference 0470/1

SECTION A: CORE CONTENT

Answer any two questions from this Section.

1   After early setbacks, Italian unification was eventually achieved.

(a)   Describe Austria's role in crushing the 1848–49 revolutions in Italy.   [4]

(b)   Why was Mazzini important to the cause of Italian unification?   [6]

(c)   Which was more important in achieving Italian unification, Cavour's diplomacy or Garibaldi's actions?

Explain your answer.   [10]

2   France, Prussia and Austria all played essential roles on the road to German unification.

(a)   Describe the crisis over Luxembourg in 1867.   [4]

(b) Why did William I appoint Bismarck as Minister-President in 1862? [6]

(c) Which was more responsible for Prussia's emergence as the dominant German power by 1866, Prussian strength or Austrian weakness? Explain your answer. [10]

3   Black Americans suffered in the USA during the nineteenth century.

(a) What did the Supreme Court decide in the Dred Scott case of 1857? [4]

(b) Why was the Fugitive Slave Act of 1850 controversial? [6]

(c) Which achieved more for black Americans, the Civil War or Reconstruction? Explain your answer. [10]

4   International agreements could increase tensions between European powers.

(a) What were the terms of the Triple Alliance? [4]

(b) Why did Austria send Serbia an ultimatum on 23 July 1914? [6]

(c) 'Britain went to war in 1914 to honour its promise to protect Belgium.' How far do you agree with this statement? Explain your answer. [10]

5   Few nations were entirely happy with the final terms of the Paris Peace Settlement.

(a)   Describe how Turkey was treated in the Treaty of Sèvres.   [4]

(b)   Why did the Treaty of Versailles have a damaging political impact on Germany up to 1923?   [6]

(c)   Who was happier with the terms of the Treaty of Versailles, Clemenceau or Wilson? Explain your answer.   [10]

6   The record of the League of Nations was mixed.

(a)   Describe how the League of Nations dealt with Upper Silesia.   [4]

(b)   Why was Haile Selassie unhappy with the way the League dealt with the Italian invasion of Abyssinia?   [6]

(c)   'The humanitarian work of the League's agencies was more important than its failure over the Japanese invasion of Manchuria.' How far do you agree with this statement? Explain your answer.   [10]

7   After the Second World War, there was friction between the USA and the USSR.

(a)   Describe how communists took over Czechoslovakia between 1945 and 1948.   [4]

(b)   Why did many Western European countries welcome the Marshall Plan?   [6]

(c)   'Stalin's foreign policy towards Europe between 1945 and 1949 was defensive.' How far do you agree with this statement? Explain your answer.   [10]

8   Relations between Iran and Iraq were poor.

(a)   Describe the Shah's programme to modernise Iran.   [4]

(b)   Why did several Western Powers support Iraq in the Iran–Iraq War?   [6]

(c)   Was Saddam Hussein right when he declared a victory for Iraq in the Iran–Iraq War? Explain your answer.   [10]

SECTION B: DEPTH STUDIES

Answer any one question from this Section.

DEPTH STUDY A: THE FIRST WORLD WAR, 1914–18

9   A stalemate quickly developed on the Western Front.

(a)   Describe the psychological problems experienced by soldiers in the trenches. [4]

(b)   Explain why Germany developed the Schlieffen Plan. [6]

(c)   How far does Belgium's reaction to German aggression explain why a stalemate developed on the Western Front? Explain your answer. [10]

10   The Battles of Verdun and the Somme were key battles in the First World War.

(a)   Describe Haig's tactics in the Battle of the Somme. [4]

(b)   Why did both sides use gas on the Western Front? [6]

(c)   'The Battle of Verdun achieved more for the Allies than the Battle of the Somme.' How far do you agree with this statement? Explain your answer. [10]

DEPTH STUDY B: GERMANY, 1918–45

11   The Nazis used both legal and illegal methods.

(a) Describe the events of the Munich Putsch. [4]

(b) Why did the Nazis do well in elections in the years 1930 to 1932? [6]

(c) Which was more critical in Hitler consolidating his power, the Enabling Act or the Night of the Long Knives? Explain your answer. [10]

12 The Nazis treated different groups in Germany very differently.

(a) Describe the activities of the Edelweiss Pirates. [4]

(b) Why did the Nazis introduce the Final Solution? [6]

(c) Which was more effective in winning over German youth, the Hitler Youth or changes to what was taught in schools? Explain your answer. [10]

DEPTH STUDY C: RUSSIA, 1905–41

13 The Tsarist regime faced many difficulties between 1905 and 1914.

(a) Describe the structure of Russian society in the countryside in the early twentieth century. [4]

(b) Why did a revolution break out in Russia in 1905? [6]

(c) How well did the Tsarist regime govern Russia between 1906 and 1914? Explain your answer. [10]

14 Stalin's reforms affected all parts of Soviet society.

(a) Describe how the Soviet authorities enforced collectivisation. [4]

(b) Why were Stalin's reforms necessary for Soviet women? [6]

(c) 'By 1941 Stalin had modernised the Soviet Union.' How far do you agree with this statement? Explain your answer. [10]

DEPTH STUDY D: THE UNITED STATES, 1919–41

15 During the 1920s, America experienced a 'boom'.

(a) Describe the new methods used by the car industry to build and sell cars. [4]

(b) Why did most farmers not benefit from the economic 'boom'? [6]

(c) 'The 1920s saw American industry doing well.' How far do you agree with this statement? Explain your answer. [10]

16 Roosevelt introduced two New Deals.

(a) Describe how the First New Deal helped farmers. [4]

(b) When he became President, why did Roosevelt first focus on the banking crisis? [6

(c) 'The Second New Deal was more important than the First.' How far do you agree with this statement? Explain your answer. [10]

DEPTH STUDY E: CHINA, c.1930–c.1990

17 The 1950s were a time of rapid change for China.

(a) Describe the work of the 'People's Courts'. [4]

(b) Why did Mao introduce the first Five-Year Plan? [6]

(c) 'By the early 1960s, Mao had achieved all his aims.' How far do you agree with this statement? Explain your answer. [10]

18 The lives of Chinese people changed under Mao's rule.

(a) Describe the experiences of minority groups under Mao. [4]

(b) Why did Mao bring the Hundred Flowers campaign to an end? [6]

(c) 'It is surprising that Mao started the Cultural Revolution.' How far do you agree with this statement? Explain your answer. [10]

19 By the 1940s, there had been many changes in South Africa.

(a) Describe the consequences of the Natives Land Act of 1913 for black South Africans. [4]

(b) Why did the South African economy develop rapidly by 1940? [6]

(c) 'Changes in South Africa brought about by the Second World War explain the victory of the National Party in the 1948 election.' How far do you

agree with this statement? Explain your answer.
[10]

20   After a long struggle, majority rule was finally achieved in South Africa.

(a)   What did Desmond Tutu contribute to the ending of apartheid?   [4]

(b)   Why did P.W. Botha's reforms fail to stop opposition?   [6]

(c)   'The transfer of power between 1989 and 1994 went well.' How far do you agree with this statement? Explain your answer.

DEPTH STUDY G: ISRAELIS AND PALESTINIANS SINCE 1945

21   At the end of the Second World War, Britain had a mandate in Palestine.

(a)   What did the United Nations' partition plan propose for the Palestinians?   [4]

(b)   Why did war break out between the Arabs and the Israelis in 1948?   [6]

(c) How surprising was the British decision to withdraw from Palestine? Explain your answer. [10]

22 The period from 1948 to 1973 was dominated by war.

(a) What were the results of the Yom Kippur War of 1973? [4]

(b) Why was the involvement of the Soviet Union in Arab–Israeli affairs important in the period 1948 to 1973? [6]

(c) Which was more important for Israel, the Suez War of 1956 or the Six-Day War of 1967? Explain your answer. [10]

CHAPTER 1: Answers

SECTION A: CORE CONTENT

Answer any two questions from this Section. Answered questions: 1, 3

1 **After early setbacks, Italian unification was eventually achieved.**

(a) **Describe Austria's role in crushing the 1848–49 revolutions in Italy.** **[4]**

Austria controlled parts of northern Italy – Lombardy and Venetia were under direct Austrian rule, giving Austria a strong position in the region. Austria defeated Italian revolutionary forces – Austrian troops under Field Marshal Radetzky crushed uprisings, especially those led by Piedmont-Sardinia.
  Austria recaptured key cities – Cities like Milan and Venice, which had rebelled, were taken back by Austrian forces.
  Austria helped restore old rulers – Austrian intervention brought back monarchs and

conservative governments that had been overthrown during the revolutions.

Austria suppressed nationalist ambitions – Its actions discouraged the spread of Italian unification and weakened the momentum of the nationalist movement.

(b)   Why was Mazzini important to the cause of Italian unification?   [6]

He inspired nationalist ideas – Mazzini strongly believed in a united, free, and republican Italy, and he spread these ideas to others through his writings and speeches.

He founded 'Young Italy' – This was a secret society that aimed to unite Italy through revolution; it attracted many young Italians to the nationalist cause.

He influenced future leaders – Although his own revolutions failed, Mazzini's ideas influenced important figures like Garibaldi and helped shape the broader unification movement.

(c)   Which was more important in achieving Italian unification, Cavour's diplomacy or

Garibaldi's actions? Explain your answer.
[10]

Cavour's diplomacy (importance) included:
He formed alliances to weaken Austria – Cavour made a key alliance with France (Napoleon III) in 1858, which helped Piedmont defeat Austria and gain Lombardy.
He modernised Piedmont – By improving the economy and army, Cavour made Piedmont strong enough to lead unification.
He used politics to unite the north – Cavour helped northern states join Piedmont through clever negotiations, especially after the Austrian defeat.
Garibaldi's actions (importance) included:
He led the military campaign in the south – Garibaldi's 1860 expedition with the "Thousand" defeated the Kingdom of the Two Sicilies.
He handed over the south to the king. After his victories, Garibaldi gave control to King Victor Emmanuel II, showing his commitment to unification.
He inspired national pride – Garibaldi became a hero to ordinary Italians, and many people came to support the unification of Italy.
Conclusion-

Both were vital, but Cavour was more important overall – Garibaldi gained the south, but without Cavour's diplomacy and leadership, Italy might not have united under one crown.

3. **Black Americans suffered in the USA during the nineteenth century.**

(a) What did the Supreme Court decide in the Dred Scott case of 1857? [4]

Dred Scott was not a citizen. The Court said that African Americans, whether enslaved or free, could not be U.S. citizens and therefore could not sue in federal court.
Living in free states did not make him free. The Court ruled that Scott's time in free territory did not change his status as an enslaved person.
Congress could not ban slavery in territories – The Court declared the Missouri Compromise unconstitutional, saying Congress had no right to stop slavery in any U.S. territory.
The decision protected enslavers – It gave more power to slaveholders and made it harder to limit the spread of slavery.

(b) **Why was the Fugitive Slave Act of 1850 controversial?** [6]

It forced people in free states to help catch escaped enslaved people – Northerners were legally required to assist in the return of runaway slaves, even if they were against slavery.

It denied rights to accused fugitives – Alleged runaway slaves could be captured without a jury trial or the chance to speak in their defence.

It encouraged the kidnapping of free Black people – Slave catchers sometimes took free African Americans and sold them into slavery, with little legal protection for the victims.

It angered abolitionists and increased resistance. Many Northerners saw the law as immoral and began helping enslaved people escape through the Underground Railroad.

It deepened the North–South divide. The law made slavery a national issue, not just a Southern one, increasing tensions between free and enslaved persons in the states.

(c) **Which achieved more for black Americans, the Civil War or Reconstruction? Explain your answer.** [10]

Achievements of the Civil War:

Ended slavery (13th Amendment) – The Civil War led to the abolition of slavery in 1865, freeing nearly 4 million enslaved people.

Gave hope for equality – Many Black Americans believed the end of the war would bring freedom, rights, and a better life.

Allowed Black men to serve in the army – Over 180,000 Black men fought for the Union, showing their loyalty and bravery.

Achievements of Reconstruction:

Gave legal rights (14th and 15th Amendments) – Black Americans were granted citizenship and the right to vote.

More political power – During Reconstruction, some Black men were elected to local, state, and even national offices.

Education and land – New schools and some land reforms provided Black Americans with better opportunities, albeit limited.

Judgement:

Reconstruction achieved more in terms of rights and equality. While the Civil War ended slavery,

Reconstruction gave Black Americans political and legal rights, even if many were later taken away in the South.

SECTION B: DEPTH STUDIES

Answer any one question from this Section.
Answered Questions: 9,11, and 14

DEPTH STUDY A: THE FIRST WORLD WAR, 1914–18

9. A stalemate quickly developed on the Western Front.

a. Describe the psychological problems experienced by soldiers in the trenches. [4]

Shell shock
A condition caused by constant loud explosions and stress, leading to shaking, confusion, and inability to speak or move properly.

Anxiety and panic attacks
Soldiers often lived in fear of sudden death, which caused extreme nervousness and breakdowns.
Sleep problems and nightmares – The constant danger and stress led to insomnia and terrifying dreams about the battlefield.

Depression and emotional numbness.
Many soldiers became emotionally shut down or hopeless due to the horrors they saw daily.

b. **Explain why Germany developed the Schlieffen Plan.** **[6]**

To avoid fighting a war on two fronts, Germany feared being attacked from both the west by France and the east by Russia, so it planned to defeat France quickly before turning to Russia.

To counter the alliance system, France and Russia formed an alliance, which led Germany to expect both to go to war together. The plan was designed to deal with both enemies efficiently.

Because Russia would take longer to prepare, Germany believed Russia would take weeks to mobilise its army, giving them time to defeat France first.

To invade France through Belgium, Germany sought to bypass France's strong defences along the border, so the plan involved invading France through neutral Belgium to catch them off guard.

To achieve a quick victory, Germany sought a swift and decisive war to avoid a lengthy and costly conflict, especially since it was not as well-resourced as Britain or Russia.

c. **How far does Belgium's reaction to German aggression explain why a stalemate developed on the Western Front? Explain your answer.** [10]

Belgium's Reaction was important in causing a stalemate because:

Belgium resisted the German invasion strongly – despite being smaller and less equipped, Belgian forces fought hard and slowed down the German army's planned rapid advance.

Delayed German timetable – The resistance in Belgium disrupted the Schlieffen Plan, which depended on a rapid sweep through Belgium to defeat France quickly.

Gave time for the Allies to prepare – The delay allowed British and French forces more time to mobilise and set up defences, which helped stop the German advance at battles like the Marne.

Other Reasons for the stalemate:

French and British resistance – The Allies fought fiercely to defend France, especially around Paris and the Marne River, halting the Germans' advance further west.

Geography and trenches
Once both sides dug trenches for protection, it became challenging for either side to advance, resulting in a protracted stalemate.

New technology and weapons;
Machine guns, artillery, and barbed wire favoured defence over attack, making it difficult to break through enemy lines.

Failure of the Schlieffen Plan;
Germany's original plan underestimated the time required and the resistance it would face, making a swift victory impossible.
Logistical problems – Supplying large armies over long distances slowed down attacks and made offensives harder to maintain.

Judgement:
Belgium's reaction was vital because it delayed the German advance; however, the stalemate also resulted from the strong Allied defence, new military technology, trench warfare, and the failure of German plans. So, Belgium's resistance was a key factor, but not the only one.

DEPTH STUDY B: GERMANY, 1918–45

11. **The Nazis used both legal and illegal methods.**

a. **Describe the events of the Munich Putsch. [4Hitler and the Nazi Party attempted a takeover in Munich.**

In November 1923, Hitler and about 600 supporters tried to seize power by marching into Munich.

They aimed to overthrow the Weimar government – Hitler planned to force the Bavarian government to join him in a national revolution.

The police stopped the march. When Hitler and his followers marched through the streets, they were confronted by police and soldiers.

The Putsch failed, and Hitler was arrested. The march ended in a brief gunfight, several people died, and Hitler was captured and later put on trial.

b. **Why did the Nazis do well in elections in the years 1930 to 1932?** [6]

The Great Depression caused economic hardship. Many Germans were unemployed and desperate, so they turned to the Nazis, who promised jobs and financial recovery.

Weakness of the Weimar government – People lost faith in the democratic government because it seemed unable to solve Germany's problems.

Effective Nazi propaganda – The Nazis used speeches, rallies, posters, and radio to spread their message widely and attract supporters.

Hitler's strong leadership – Hitler was seen as a confident and influential leader who promised to restore Germany's greatness.

Fear of communism – Many middle-class and wealthy Germans supported the Nazis because they were afraid of a communist takeover.

Promises of nationalism and pride – The Nazis promised to reject the Treaty of Versailles and rebuild Germany's power, which appealed to many voters.

c. **Which was more critical in Hitler consolidating his power, the Enabling Act or the Night of the Long Knives? Explain your answer.** [10]

Importance of the Enabling Act:

Gave Hitler legal power to make laws – It allowed Hitler to pass laws without the Reichstag's approval for four years.

Ended democracy in Germany – The Act effectively destroyed the Weimar Constitution and gave Hitler dictatorship powers.

Allowed banning of opposition parties – Hitler could now legally outlaw other political parties, making the Nazi Party the only one allowed.

Helped control the government – With the Enabling Act, Hitler was able to exert complete control over the entire government, unchecked and unbalanced.

Importance of the Night of the Long Knives:

Eliminated internal threats – Hitler ordered the murder of Ernst Röhm and other leaders of the SA who threatened his power.

Gained support of the army – By removing the SA's leadership, Hitler reassured the German military, which saw the SA as a rival.

Consolidated control over the Nazi Party – It removed rivals within his own party and showed Hitler's power was absolute.

Intimidated other opponents – The killings sent a message that opposition to Hitler would not be tolerated.

Judgement:

While the Night of the Long Knives removed internal enemies and secured the army's loyalty, the Enabling Act was more important because it gave Hitler the legal authority to rule without limits. Without the Enabling Act, Hitler could not have made his dictatorship official.

14. Stalin's reforms affected all parts of Soviet society.

(a) Describe how the Soviet authorities enforced collectivisation. [4]

Forced peasants to give up their land and join collective farms – The government compelled peasants to combine their farms into large, state-controlled farms known as collectives.

Used propaganda and pressure – Authorities encouraged peasants to support collectivisation and labelled those who resisted as enemies or "kulaks."

Harsh punishments for resistance – Peasants who refused to join or resisted were arrested, deported to labour camps, or even executed.

Confiscated grain and livestock – The government seized food and animals from peasants to feed cities and export for financial gain, resulting in hardship in rural areas.

(b) Why were Stalin's reforms necessary for Soviet women? [6]

Improved access to education and work – Stalin's policies encouraged women to join the workforce and attend schools and universities.

Legal equality – Women were granted equal rights under the law, including the right to vote and hold jobs.

Support for working mothers – The government provides childcare facilities, such as nurseries and kindergartens, to help women balance their work and family responsibilities.

Changes in family law – Divorce became easier to obtain, and abortion was legalised, giving women more control over their lives.

Increased political participation – Some women gained positions in the Communist Party and government, increasing their influence.

Encouraged women to contribute to industrial growth – Women were seen as necessary for the country's industrialisation and rebuilding efforts.

(c) **'By 1941 Stalin had modernised the Soviet Union.' How far do you agree with this statement? Explain your answer.** [10]

Arguments agreeing that Stalin had modernised the Soviet Union:

Rapid industrial growth – Stalin's Five-Year Plans significantly increased industrial production, particularly in heavy industries such as steel, coal, and machinery.

Improved infrastructure – New factories, railways, and power plants were built, helping to modernise the economy.

Urbanisation – Many people moved to cities for work, which altered the country's social and economic structure.

Increased military strength – By 1941, the Soviet Union had developed modern weapons and a stronger army, preparing for war.

Education and literacy – Stalin improved education and literacy, creating a more skilled workforce.

Arguments against the idea that Stalin had fully modernised the Soviet Union:

Agriculture was still backwards. Collectivisation led to famine and low farm productivity, resulting in the countryside not being modernised as quickly as the cities.

Poor living standards for many – Despite industrial growth, many workers lived in harsh conditions with low wages and inadequate housing.

Economic problems and inefficiency – The command economy faced issues such as waste, poor-quality goods, and shortages.

Repression and fear – The brutal political system and purges created fear and hindered creativity and innovation.

Uneven development – Some parts of the Soviet Union remained underdeveloped and impoverished compared to the industrial centres.

Judgement:

Stalin had modernised the Soviet Union in many important ways, especially in industry and military power. However, modernisation was incomplete because agriculture lagged, and many people's lives remained complex. The economy also suffered from inefficiency and political repression.

Chapter 2

Paper TWO

October/November 2020 paper one ref 0470/12

Same instruction as above

QUESTIONS
CHAPTER 2
SECTION A: CORE CONTENT

Answer any two questions from this Section.

1   1848 was a year of great upheaval in Europe.

(a)   Describe events in Sicily in January 1848. [4]

(b)   Why did violence erupt in Paris in June 1848? [6]

(c)   How far do you agree that the 1848 revolutions were a failure? Explain your answer. [10]

2   The path to Italian unification was not smooth.

(a)   Describe the role of Pope Pius IX in the 1848–49 revolutions. [4]

(b)   Why was Italy not unified by 1861? [6]

(c)   'France played a more important role than Austria in events leading to the unification of Italy.' How far do you agree with this statement? Explain your answer. [10]

3   Britain expanded its empire in the nineteenth century.

(a) Describe Lugard's ideas about how Britain should govern its African colonies. [4]
(b) Why was Britain interested in China? [6]
(c) 'Natural disasters were the main reason for the Boxer Rising.' How far do you agree with this statement? Explain your answer. [10]

4   The years before 1914 were characterised by tension in Europe.

(a) Describe Germany's war preparations by 1914. [4]
(b) Why did the Alliance System fail to prevent war? [6]
(c) How far do you agree that Morocco was the most crucial cause of tension before 1914? Explain your answer. [10]

5   The Versailles settlement had different consequences for different countries.

(a) What was the purpose of the 'war guilt' clause? [4]
(b) Why were plebiscites included in the peace settlement? [6]

(c) How far do you agree that Clemenceau achieved his aims at Versailles? Explain your answer.
[10]

6 Hitler's foreign policy involved Germany in developments in Europe.

(a) Describe Germany's involvement in the Spanish Civil War. [4]

(b) Why was taking control of Czechoslovakia important to Hitler? [6]

(c) How surprising was it that Britain and France pursued a policy of appeasement? Explain your answer. [10]

7 The USA and USSR contributed to increased tensions in Europe after 1945.

(a) Describe the Communist takeover of Czechoslovakia in 1948. [4]

(b) Why was the Berlin Blockade lifted in May 1949? [6]

(c) How far do you agree that Truman was to blame for the Cold War? Explain your answer. [10]

8   Iraq's involvement in the war had many consequences.

(a)   What was the impact of the Iran-Iraq war on Iraqi civilians?   [4]

(b)   Why did Saddam Hussein's regime survive the First Gulf War?   [6]

(c)   'Oil was the most important cause of the dispute between Iraq and Kuwait.' How far do you agree with this statement? Explain your answer.   [10]

SECTION B: DEPTH STUDIES

Answer any one question from this Section.

DEPTH STUDY A:
THE FIRST WORLD WAR, 1914–18

9   The stalemate on the Western Front was hard to break.

(a)   Describe events on the Western Front on 1 July 1916.   [4]

(b)   Why were conditions in the trenches unhealthy for soldiers?   [6]

(c) How far do you agree that new technology was used effectively in the First World War? Explain your answer. [10]

10 Germany's fortunes changed in 1918.

(a) Describe the situation facing German forces at the start of 1918. [4]

(b) Why were the mutinies at Kiel and Wilhelmshaven important? [6]

(c) 'The British naval blockade was the main reason for the defeat of Germany.' How far do you agree with this statement? Explain your answer. [10]

DEPTH STUDY B: GERMANY, 1918–45

11 Many factors contributed to Hitler's rise to power.

(a) What was the 25 Point Programme? [4]

(b) Why was Goebbels important to Hitler? [6]

(c) 'Electoral success was the most important factor in Hitler becoming Chancellor.' How far do you agree with this statement? Explain your answer. [10]

12 The Nazi regime aimed to change society and the economy.

(a) What were the Nazis' views on the role of women in society? [4]

(b) Why did the Nazis aim to achieve autarky? [6]

(c) 'The policy of Total War had a greater impact on German civilians than any other aspect of the Second World War.' How far do you agree with this statement? Explain your answer. [10]

DEPTH STUDY C: RUSSIA, 1905–41

13 The Tsar ruled by autocratic means.

(a) What was it like for Russian peasants by 1905? [4]

(b) Why was the October Manifesto introduced? [6]

(c) How far would you agree that the Tsar was firmly in control of Russia at the start of 1914? Explain your answer. [10]

14 Stalin was determined to gain and keep control over the USSR.

(a) What did Lenin say about Stalin and Trotsky in his Political Testament? [4]

(b) Why was Lenin's funeral meaningful in the power struggle? [6]

(c) 'Stalin's personality cult was his most effective means of control.' How far do you agree with this statement? Explain your answer. [10]

DEPTH STUDY D: THE UNITED STATES, 1919–41

15 The 1920s brought changes in American society.

(a) What was a 'flapper'? [4]

(b) Why did the 1920s become known as the Jazz Age? [6]

(c) 'Prohibition failed because it encouraged violence.' How far do you agree with this statement? Explain your answer. [10]

16 The Wall Street Crash had political and social consequences.

(a) What was the Bonus March? [4]

(b) Why did 'buying on the margin' contribute to the Wall Street Crash? [6]

(c) How surprised are you that Hoover was known as the 'do nothing' President? Explain your answer. [10]

DEPTH STUDY E: CHINA, c.1930–c.1990

17   Mao changed the economy and society in China.

(a)   Describe Communist treatment of the landlords.   [4]

(b)   Why did Mao embark on the Great Leap Forward?   [6]

(c)   How far do you agree that Mao's attempts at social reform were a success? Explain your answer.   [10]

18   China's relationships with other countries have fluctuated over the years.

(a)   What did China gain from its relationship with the USSR in the 1950s?   [4]

(b)   Why was there tension between China and India in the 1960s?   [6]

(c) How far do you agree that trade was the main reason for China's improved foreign relations in the 1980s? Explain your answer. [10]

DEPTH STUDY F: SOUTH AFRICA, c.1940–c.1994

19 In the 1950s and 1960s, the apartheid system was strengthened.

(a) In what ways did Afrikaners benefit from apartheid? [4]

(b) Why was the Pan Africanist Congress (PAC) formed? [6]

(c) 'The Bantu Education Act (1953) did more to reinforce apartheid than any other legislation.' How far do you agree with this statement? Explain your answer. [10]

20 The 1990s brought the end of apartheid in South Africa.

(a) Describe Mandela's aims for South Africa on becoming President. [4]

(b) Why did Botha's constitutional reforms fail to improve relations between non-whites and the government? [6]

(c) How far did de Klerk's policies to end apartheid have the backing of white South Africans? Explain your answer. [10]

DEPTH STUDY G: ISRAELIS AND PALESTINIANS SINCE 1945

21 External involvement in the Middle East has had significant consequences.

(a) Describe Moshe Dayan's role in the Six-Day War. [4]

(b) Why did the Soviet Union become involved in the Middle East? [6]

(c) How far do you agree that Egypt gained the most from the Suez crisis of 1956? Explain your answer. [10]

22 The United Nations (UN) faced many challenges in its role in the Middle East.

(a) Describe the role of the UN in Lebanon. [4]

(b) Why did some groups working for Palestinian liberation become more militant from the 1980s? [6]

(c) How far do you agree that the UN achieved little in its involvement in the Middle East? Explain your answer. [10]

ANSWERS TO CHOSEN QUESTIONS

CHAPTER 2: Answers

SECTION A: CORE CONTENT

Answer any two questions from this Section.

Answered Questions: 2, 4

2. The path to Italian unification was not smooth.

a) **Describe the role of Pope Pius IX in the 1848–49 revolutions.** [4]

- Initially, Pope Pius IX seemed supportive of reform. When he became pope in 1846, he was popular because he promised some liberal changes.
- He supported the idea of Italian unity at first. Early on, he showed some sympathy for Italian nationalism and reformers.
- He later opposed the revolutions – When the 1848 revolutions started, especially the war against Austria, he withdrew his support.

- Pope led the Papal States against revolutionaries – He called for help from French troops to protect the Papal States and crushed the revolutionary movements in Rome.

b) **Why was Italy not unified by 1861?** [6]

- Different regions had different rulers and governments – Italy was divided into many separate states, such as the Kingdom of the Two Sicilies, the Papal States, and the Kingdom of Sardinia.
- The Pope opposed unification – The Pope controlled the Papal States and did not want to lose his power or authority over central Italy.
- Foreign powers-controlled parts of Italy – Austria controlled northern regions like Lombardy and Venetia, and wanted to keep its influence.
- Lack of support from some Italians – Not all Italians wanted unification; some were loyal to their local rulers or feared change.
- Differences in political ideas and methods – Some wanted a republic (like Mazzini), others supported a monarchy (like Cavour), causing divisions.

- Wars and conflicts slowed progress – Ongoing wars with Austria and other conflicts delayed the process of unification.

c) **'France played a more important role than Austria in events leading to the unification of Italy.' How far do you agree with this statement? Explain your answer.**
[10]

Arguments agreeing that France played a more critical role:

- France helped Piedmont in wars against Austria – Napoleon III of France supported Cavour and sent troops to help defeat Austria in the Second Italian War of Independence (1859).
- French military victories weakened Austrian control – Battles like Magenta and Solferino forced Austria to give up Lombardy.
- French troops protected the Papal States – France's army defended the Pope and prevented Rome from joining Italy until 1870, influencing the pace of unification.
- French diplomacy influenced Italy's future – France's support was crucial for Piedmont's rise and the eventual unification under Victor Emmanuel II.

Arguments that Austria played a more critical role:
- Austria was the main foreign power blocking unification – Austria controlled large parts of northern Italy and opposed Italian nationalism.
- Austria's repression caused resentment – Harsh Austrian rule in places like Lombardy and Venetia increased Italian desire for unification and independence.
- Austrian defeats shaped unification events – Austria's losses in 1848 and 1859 weakened its hold on Italy and opened the way for unification.
- Austria's presence kept Italy divided for a long time – Without Austria's influence, Italian unification might have happened sooner.

Judgement:
- France played a vital role by supporting Piedmont and fighting Austria, which directly helped unification. However, Austria's control and opposition were the main obstacles that had to be overcome. So, both countries were important but in different ways: Austria was the barrier to unification, and France was a key helper in breaking that barrier.

4. **The years before 1914 were characterised by tension in Europe.**

a) Describe Germany's war preparations by 1914. [4]

- Germany built a large and well-trained army – By 1914, Germany had one of the strongest armies in Europe with well-trained soldiers ready for war.
- The German navy was expanded – Germany increased the size of its navy to challenge British naval power.
- The Schlieffen Plan was developed – Germany prepared a detailed military plan to quickly defeat France by attacking through Belgium before turning to fight Russia.
- Germany stockpiled weapons and supplies – The country made sure it had enough guns, ammunition, and equipment for a long war.

b) Why did the Alliance System fail to prevent war? [6]

- Alliances created two opposing sides – The system divided Europe into two main groups: the Triple Alliance (Germany, Austria-Hungary, Italy) and the Triple Entente (France, Russia, Britain).

- Tensions increased because of rivalries – Countries felt more confident and aggressive because they had powerful allies to back them up.
- Small conflicts escalated quickly – When Austria declared war on Serbia, alliances caused other countries to join, turning a local fight into a bigger war.
- Lack of communication and trust – Countries did not fully trust each other, which made diplomatic solutions harder and increased suspicion.
- Rigid military plans tied to alliances – Plans like Germany's Schlieffen Plan assumed alliances would lead to a quick war, making diplomacy less likely.
- Countries felt forced to support allies – Once one country was attacked, others had to join because of their treaty obligations, making it hard to stop the conflict.

c) **How far do you agree that Morocco was the most crucial cause of tension before 1914? Explain your answer.**
[10]

Arguments agreeing that Morocco was the most important cause:
- Morocco crises increased tension between Germany and France – Germany challenged France's influence in Morocco in 1905 and again in 1911, causing serious conflicts.
- The crises tested alliances – The crises strengthened the partnership between France and Britain (Entente Cordiale) as they worked together against Germany's actions.
- Germany's aggressive stance alarmed other powers – Germany's attempts to block French control made other countries see Germany as a threat.
- The Moroccan crisis almost led to war; The tensions created by these events brought Europe close to military conflict several times.

Arguments disagreeing that Morocco was the most important cause:
- Other causes were more serious and long-lasting – Rivalry over the Balkans and the assassination of Archduke Franz Ferdinand were more immediate causes of war.
- The Alliance System created deep divisions – The complex web of alliances increased suspicion and made any conflict likely to involve many countries.

- Arms race and militarism increased fear – The build-up of armies and navies made countries ready for war and less willing to compromise.
- Imperial rivalries beyond Morocco also caused tension – Competition over colonies in Africa and Asia was widespread, not limited to Morocco.

Judgement:
- The Moroccan crises were vital because they increased tensions and tested alliances, but other factors like Balkan rivalries, the alliance system, and militarism were also crucial. Therefore, Morocco was a key cause but not the only or most important cause of tension before 1914.

SECTION B: DEPTH STUDIES

Answer any one question from this Section.
DEPTH STUDY B: GERMANY, 1918–45

Answered Questions: 11

11 Many factors contributed to Hitler's rise to power.

a) What was the 25 Point Programme? [4]

- The 25 Point Programme was a list of political goals announced by the Nazi Party in 1920.
- It outlined what the Nazis wanted to achieve in Germany, including national unity and strong leadership.
- The programme called for the exclusion of Jews from German society and citizenship.
- It also demanded the overthrow of the Treaty of Versailles and the expansion of German territory.

b) **Why was Goebbels important to Hitler? [6]**

- Goebbels was Hitler's Minister of Propaganda – He controlled all the messages that the Nazi Party shared with the German people.
- He helped build Hitler's image – Goebbels made Hitler look strong, trustworthy, and Germany's best hope.
- He used newspapers, radio, films, and rallies – Goebbels spread Nazi ideas through many forms of media to reach a broad audience.
- He encouraged hatred of the Jews and other enemies – Goebbels' propaganda increased support for Nazi policies by promoting anti-Semitic ideas.
- He organised large, emotional rallies – These events inspired loyalty and excitement among Nazi supporters.
- Goebbels kept the Nazi Party united; His propaganda helped maintain morale and enthusiasm within the party, especially during hard times.

c) **'Electoral success was the most important factor in Hitler becoming Chancellor.'**

How far do you agree with this statement? Explain your answer. **[10]**

Arguments agreeing that electoral success was most important:

- The Nazi Party's rise in elections gave Hitler political legitimacy. By 1932, the Nazis were the largest party in the Reichstag with about 37% of the vote.
- Electoral success made it clear that Hitler had widespread support.

This pressured other politicians and President Hindenburg to consider him as Chancellor.

- Nazi popularity showed that democracy was fragile – The failure of moderate parties to control the situation helped Hitler's rise.

Arguments disagreeing that electoral success was most important:

- Backroom political deals were crucial – Hitler was appointed Chancellor because conservative politicians like Franz von Papen thought they could control him.
- The role of President Hindenburg was key – Hindenburg's decision to appoint Hitler was influenced by political pressure, not just election results.

- Economic problems and fear of communism helped Hitler. The Great Depression and the fear of a communist takeover made many elites support Hitler despite his extremist views.
- Violence and intimidation by the SA also helped the Nazis. This created fear and weakened opposition, influencing political decisions beyond just votes.

Judgement:
- Electoral success was critical because it gave Hitler legitimacy and showed public support. However, political deals, Hindenburg's choices, economic crisis, and fear of communism were equally significant. Therefore, electoral success was one of several key factors, but not the only or most important reason Hitler became Chancellor of Germany.

Chapter 3

PAPER 3

Paper 1 Reference 0470/2

October/November 2020

Same instruction as above

CHAPTER 3

Option A: Nineteenth-century topic
WAS JOHN BROWN A HERO OR A VILLAIN?

Study the Background Information and the sources carefully, and then answer all the questions.

Background Information

John Brown learned his abolitionist views from his father. In 1855, he went to Kansas to oppose pro-slavery forces and, in 1856, led an attack on the pro-slavery settlement at Pottawatomie Creek, where five men were hacked to death.

In 1859, Brown turned his attention to Virginia, a slave-owning state. He rented a farmhouse and started to gather rifles, gunpowder and swords. On 16 October, he led a group of armed men in an attack on the federal arsenal at Harpers Ferry. He planned to use the twenty thousand weapons in the arsenal to equip enslaved people who, he hoped, would rise in rebellion against slavery. Brown managed to gain control of the armoury, but on 18 October, ninety US Marines arrived, and Brown and his men were soon either captured or killed.

Brown was charged with treason against the state of Virginia, tried and hanged.

Reactions to Brown's actions and execution have often been extreme, both at the time and since. He has been represented as both a hero and a villain.

SOURCE A

John Brown, a mad visionary, hit on a deadly plan. The enslaved people, he thought, might be persuaded to rebel against their enslavers if Northern sympathisers would provide them with weapons. He therefore proposed to descend on a suitable spot in the South, launch a revolt and, as the enslaved people flocked to join him, organise them into an army. It was a ridiculous fantasy, well illustrating Brown's insanity, the abolitionists' ignorance of the South and their growing tolerance of bloodshed and treason. Brown easily raised money in the North, and he and eighteen followers descended on the federal arsenal at Harpers Ferry. He was dealt with without difficulty by the US Army. Brown's handful of men was soon forced to surrender, and Brown himself was taken to Richmond, tried and hanged.

Brown thrilled New England. Abolitionist clergy welcomed the slave rebellion, which they thought Brown's actions would stimulate. Their ravings drowned the numerous Northern voices which condemned Brown as a criminal. The impressions made on the South were deep. Here at last was the nightmare come true: the abolitionist appeal to the enslaved people to rebel. John Brown's raid thus marks the point of no return: it began the uncoiling of a terrible chain of events leading to rebellion and war.

From a history book published in 1985.

SOURCE B

John Brown left a permanent mark on American history. His raid at Harpers Ferry resulted in both reverence and revulsion. It was a pivotal moment in American history, marking a shift away from compromise and toward war. When Brown and his small army of twenty-one men took over the federal arsenal and rifle factory, it was the fulfilment of a pledge to God to increase hostility toward slavery. Brown was a religious man who, with every drop of his honest blood, hated slavery and dedicated himself to eradicating it by any means necessary. To his mind, his duty was clear, and he never faltered.

Expecting enslaved people to join them, Brown and his men waited in the armoury while the townspeople surrounded the building. Gunfire was exchanged, and eight of Brown's men were killed or captured. Brown was wounded in the attack and taken to jail at Charlestown. The bravest man and most self-sacrificing soul in American history was hanged at Charlestown in December 1859. He set an example of moral courage and of single-hearted devotion to an ideal for all men and for all ages.

From a recent account of the raid at Harpers Ferry.

SOURCE C

Did John Brown draw his sword against slavery and thereby lose his life in vain? To this I answer ten thousand times, No! No man fails who so grandly gives himself to a righteous cause. No man could fail who, when on his way to be executed, could so forget himself as to stop and kiss a little child, one of the hated race for whom he was to die.

Did John Brown fail? John Brown began the war that ended slavery. Let us look over places for which this honour is claimed. We shall find not Carolina, but Virginia, not Fort Sumter, but Harpers Ferry, and the arsenal began the war that ended American slavery and made this free Republic. Until this blow was struck, the prospect for freedom was dim, shadowy and uncertain.

From a speech in Harpers Ferry by Frederick Douglass, 30 May 1881. Douglass was an ex-slave and a leading abolitionist.

SOURCE D

Brown and his bandits made a desperate onslaught on the persons and property of the people of Virginia. It is a matter of great regret that the cowardly villains who sent them on their desperate venture cannot grace the same gallows from which they will swing. We feel angry at the tone of the Northern newspapers. Are treason, murder and robbery less hateful? Would insurrection and house burning have been less dreadful, because, according to the New York Times, Brown was courageous and convinced of the rightfulness of his acts? This would mean that because Brown glories in what he has done, his life should be spared. Isn't the New York Times ashamed of itself for pandering to the depraved sympathy of the city in which it is located?

Brown denies that he planned a slave insurrection. What then were the swords for? Did he not intend the swords and other weapons to be used by the enslaved people in resistance to the masters? We have concluded that if the South is to maintain her rights, her property, and the lives of her citizens, she must rely upon herself and not look North for aid or sympathy.

From a newspaper, published in Richmond, Virginia, November 1859.

SOURCE E

An illustration called 'The Last Moments of John Brown' was published in Philadelphia in 1885. It shows Brown leaving jail on his way to his execution. The artist has shown Brown kissing a black child, as described at the time in a Northern newspaper. However, most accounts say that only. Soldiers were present when Brown left the jail.

SOURCE F

A mural entitled 'Tragic Prelude', from the late 1930s. It shows John Brown in Kansas during the 1850s. The book in his hand is the Bible. A prelude is an event that is an introduction to something more important.

SOURCE G

I deny everything except what I have always admitted, the plan to free the enslaved people. I intended to act as I did last winter when I went into Missouri, enslaved people without the firing of a gun and took them to Canada. I never did intend murder or treason, or the destruction of property, or to excite enslaved people to rebellion or to make insurrection.

Had I acted on behalf of the rich and powerful, every man in this court would have deemed it an act worthy of reward rather than punishment. The Bible teaches me to 'Remember them that are in bonds.' I endeavoured to act up to that instruction on behalf of God's despised poor. If it is deemed necessary that I should lose my life for justice and mingle my blood with the blood of millions in this slave country whose rights are disregarded by the wicked, cruel and unjust laws, I submit.

John Brown's speech to the court after he had been told his sentence, 2 November 1859.

SOURCE H

John Brown dies today! As Republicans, maintaining as we do that no one in the North has a right to interfere with slavery, we cannot say that he suffers unlawfully. The man's heroism, which is as great as a martyr's, and his constancy to his convictions have led to sympathy on his behalf throughout the North, but nowhere is the opinion supported that he should not be answerable for his act. As long as we are part of the Union, we cannot join the opposition to the punishment that the infatuated older man will suffer. When the right of a Sovereign State to inflict punishment for breaking its laws is questioned, disunion is being advocated. For that, we are not prepared.

To our more radical readers, these views will be unacceptable. When the fanatical action of the South dissolves the ties that hold North and South together, then we may have reason to support any means, including force, to emancipate every human being on American soil. Until then, we have a firm belief that the execution of Brown will hasten the downfall of the accursed system against which he waged war.

From a Republican newspaper published in Chicago, Illinois, 2 December 1859.

Now answer all the following questions. You may use any of the sources to help you answer the questions, in addition to those sources which you are told to use. When answering the questions, use your knowledge of the topic to help you interpret and evaluate the sources.

1   Study Sources A and B.

How far do these two sources agree? Explain your answer using details of the sources.   [7]

2   Study Sources C and D.

Does Source D prove that Douglass (Source C) was wrong? Explain your answer using details of the sources and your knowledge. [8]

3   Study Sources E and F.

How similar are these two illustrations? Explain your answer using details of the sources and your knowledge.   [8]

4   Study Source G.

How valuable would this source be to a historian studying John Brown and the raid on Harpers Ferry? Explain your answer using details of the source and your knowledge. [7]

5   Study Source H.

Are you surprised by this source? Explain your answer using details of the source and your knowledge. [8]

6   **Study all the sources.**

How far do these sources provide convincing evidence that John Brown was a hero? Use the sources to explain your answer. [12]

Option B: Twentieth-century topic

HOW FAR WAS Khruschev successful IN THE CUBAN MISSILE CRISIS?

Study the Background Information and the sources carefully, and then answer all the questions.

Background Information

On 14 October 1962, an American U-2 reconnaissance plane obtained photographic evidence of Soviet missile sites in Cuba. This led to the Cuban Missile Crisis. The crisis was resolved at the end of October when Khrushchev agreed to remove the missiles and Kennedy decided not to invade Cuba. Kennedy also secretly agreed to remove American missiles from Turkey.

Did Khrushchev achieve what he wanted by placing missiles in Cuba? Any answer to this question needs to take into account his motives in putting the missiles there in the first place. Was he merely trying to protect Cuba from the USA, or was he planning to attack the USA? Was it an attempt to strengthen the Soviet Union's overall military position in relation to the West? Some have suggested that the Soviet Union was trying to defend its position as the world leader of Communism against its rival, China.

By the end of the crisis, it appeared to many people that Khrushchev had backed down and been humiliated. However, was this really the case?

SOURCE A

Khrushchev was able to claim a victory over the missile crisis. He argued that Kennedy had now promised not to invade Cuba, so the continued existence of a socialist Cuba in the Soviet sphere of influence was guaranteed. This is clearly significant, especially if you accept the view that this was the main reason that Khrushchev put missiles in Cuba in the first place. Khrushchev must also be given credit for being prepared to back down in the face of nuclear war, especially when so many saw his handling of the crisis as a humiliation for the Soviet Union. However, the Soviet military was furious. They had to accept a hasty withdrawal from Cuba, as well as the ultimate humiliation of having US officials count the missiles as they were removed.

Castro was also furious with Khrushchev. He was not consulted on the final deal regarding the missiles or the withdrawal of Soviet bomber planes and troops that had been sent to aid the Cuban army. In the following months, Khrushchev had to rebuild his relations with Castro and prevent a Chinese-Cuban alliance from developing.

From a history book published in 2008.

SOURCE B

Khrushchev backed down because he had information that the US bombing of Cuba could begin in three to four days. On 28 October, as US officials prepared to strike on 30 October, Khrushchev accepted Kennedy's offer. Khrushchev decided to withdraw the missiles without consulting Castro. He knew that if he did, the Cuban leader would disagree. A furious Castro therefore refused to allow UN inspectors into his country to observe the missiles' dismantling, and then at first refused to return Soviet long-range bombers.

Contrary to what was believed, Kennedy did not give absolute assurances that the United States would not invade Cuba. In a letter to Khrushchev, his no-invasion pledge depended on Cuba committing no aggressive acts against any Western nation. This was a huge loophole.

These events angered the Chinese and widened the Chinese-Russian split to the edge of a complete breakdown. The Chinese called Khrushchev foolish for putting the missiles into Cuba and cowardly for removing them. The crisis

had not enhanced the Soviet leader's personal power within the communist bloc. His decline opened new opportunities for the Soviet satellites in Eastern Europe to regain more autonomy.
From a history book published in 1997.

SOURCE C

A cartoon published in an American newspaper, 29 October 1962. The figure on the right represents Khrushchev

SOURCE D

MEMORANDUM FOR THE PRESIDENT

The speech should emphasise that our success in Cuba does not prove that force can solve all problems. Significant steps have been taken to lift the threat of war. This has been made possible by the unity of the American people and by Khrushchev's belated recognition that his adventure was a dangerous miscalculation, which was bringing the world close to war. The events of the last weeks have fully exposed Castro, and we are confident that the forces of change will take care of his regime more effectively than an invasion could.

If we had not acted, we would have allowed a drastic revision of the world balance of power. Our use of force was effective because the Communists knew that they were in the wrong and could not justify their actions to the world.

From a report written by Arthur Schlesinger, 29 October 1962. He is advising Kennedy on a speech he was due to make to the American people. Schlesinger was a senior adviser to the President.

SOURCE E

The United States' reactionary forces have been doing everything to overthrow Cuba's revolutionary government and restore their domination there. Revolutionary Cuba was compelled to take all measures to strengthen its defence, and an agreement was reached to station Soviet missiles in Cuba. Our only aim was to defend Cuba. All talk that Cuba was being converted into a base for an attack on the USA was a vicious lie.

The President of the United States declared that if we agreed to remove these weapons, the United States would not invade Cuba. We had shipped weapons to Cuba precisely to prevent such aggression against Cuba. Which side won? One may say that sanity and the cause of peace ultimately prevailed. The Soviet Union has not only exposed the US imperialist intrigues against Cuba, but when Cuba was threatened, we sent weapons and people ready to fight shoulder to shoulder with the Cuban people.

From a speech by Khrushchev to the Supreme Soviet (the Parliament of the USSR), 12 December 1962.

SOURCE F

SOURCE G

The main point about the crisis is that it has guaranteed the existence of a Socialist Cuba. If Cuba had not undergone this ordeal, the Americans would likely have organised an invasion. Now that the tension has reached its climax and we have exchanged commitments with the American government, it will be challenging for them to interfere. If the United States were to invade now, the Soviet Union would have the right to retaliate in kind. We have secured the existence of a Socialist Cuba for at least another two years while Kennedy is President, and he may be in office for another six years. To make it through six years in this day and age is no small thing. Moreover, six years from now, the balance of power in the world will have probably shifted – and shifted in our favour, in favour of Socialism!

A letter from Khrushchev to Castro was sent immediately after the crisis.

Now answer all the following questions.

You may use any of the sources to help you answer the questions, in addition to those sources which you are told to use. When answering the questions, use your knowledge of the topic to help you interpret and evaluate the sources.

1   Study Sources A and B.

How far do these two sources agree? Explain your answer using details of the sources.   [7]

2   Study Source C.

Why was this cartoon published on 29 October 1962? Explain your answer using details of the source and your knowledge.   [8]

3   Study Sources D and E.

How far does Source D make Source E surprising? Explain your answer using details of the sources and your knowledge.   [8]

4   Study Source F.

What is the cartoonist's message? Explain your answer using details of the source and your knowledge. [8]

5   Study Source G.

How far does this source prove that Khrushchev's motive in the Missile Crisis was to protect Cuba? Explain your answer using details of the source and your knowledge. [7]

6   Study all the sources.

How far do these sources provide convincing evidence that the Cuban Missile Crisis was a success for Khrushchev? Use the sources to explain your answer. [12]

Chapter 3

PAPER 3

ANSWERS TO CHOSEN QUESTIONS

CHAPTER 3: RESPONSE
Option B: Twentieth-century topic

1. Study Sources A and B.

How far do these two sources agree? Explain your answer using details of the sources. [7]

Areas of Agreement:
- Both sources agree that Khrushchev backed down and withdrew the missiles from Cuba
- Both acknowledge that Castro was furious with Khrushchev for not consulting him about the withdrawal
- Both sources agree that the crisis damaged Khrushchev's relationships with allies (Castro and China)

- Both mention that the Soviet military/officials were unhappy with the outcome
- Both agree that Khrushchev could claim some success through Kennedy's promise not to invade Cuba

Areas of Disagreement:
- On Khrushchev's success: Source A suggests Khrushchev "was able to claim a victory" and achieved his primary goal of protecting Cuba. Source B is more critical, stating the crisis "had not enhanced the Soviet leader's personal power"
- On Kennedy's guarantees: Source A implies Kennedy's promise not to invade Cuba was solid. Source B reveals Kennedy's pledge had a "huge loophole" - it depended on Cuba not committing aggressive acts
- Overall assessment: Source A gives Khrushchev credit for avoiding nuclear war, while Source B emphasises his decline and the "complete breakdown" with China

In conclusion, the sources agree on the basic facts but differ significantly in their assessment of whether Khrushchev achieved success through the crisis.

2. **Study Source C.**

Why was this cartoon published on 29 October 1962? Explain your answer using details of the source and your knowledge.
[8]

This cartoon was published on October 29, 1962, the day after Khrushchev announced the withdrawal of Soviet missiles from Cuba.
Cartoonist's Purpose:
- Celebrate American victory: The cartoon shows Khrushchev in retreat, suggesting the US had won the confrontation
- Mock Soviet weakness: Khrushchev is depicted as backing down, reinforcing the American narrative that the Soviets had been humiliated
- Reassure the American public: After days of nuclear tension, the cartoon provided relief by showing the threat was over
- Political commentary: Published in an American newspaper, it reflected and shaped public opinion about the crisis resolution

Visual Analysis: Khrushchev appears to be retreating or withdrawing, which aligns with the American perception that the Soviet leader had been forced to back down under pressure.

Historical Context: Americans needed reassurance after the terrifying prospect of nuclear war. This cartoon helped frame the resolution as an American diplomatic victory rather than a mutual compromise.

3. Study Sources D and E.

How far does Source D make Source E surprising? Explain your answer using details of the sources and your knowledge. [8]

Source D in the American perspective presents the crisis as:
- A clear American victory ("our success in Cuba")
- Khrushchev's "dangerous miscalculation"
- Communists being "in the wrong"
- Effective use of American force

Source E in Khrushchev's perspective claims:
- The Soviet Union was defending Cuba from US aggression
- The weapons were sent to prevent an American invasion
- "Sanity and the cause of peace" won

- Soviet Union exposed "US imperialist intrigues"

Source D makes Source E moderately surprising because:

Predictable Elements:
- It is expected that each leader would present their side positively
- Both are clearly propaganda pieces for domestic audiences
- The contradictory narratives reflect Cold War tensions

Surprising Elements:
- The complete reversal of who was the aggressor
- Khrushchev's confident claim of victory despite clearly backing down
- The boldness of Khrushchev's assertion that the Soviet Union was purely defensive

In conclusion, while some disagreement is expected, the complete contradiction in who achieved victory and who was the aggressor makes Source E somewhat surprising, given Source D's confident American narrative.

4. Study Source F.

What is the cartoonist's message? Explain your answer using details of the source and your knowledge.
[8]

- Crisis Resolution- Published the day after the crisis ended, likely celebrating the peaceful resolution
- American Success- Probably depicted the outcome favorably for the United States
- Relief from Tension- After coming close to nuclear war, the cartoon likely expressed relief
- Commentary on Leadership- May have commented on how Kennedy and/or Khrushchev handled the crisis

5. Study Source G.

How far does this source prove that Khrushchev's motive in the Missile Crisis was to protect Cuba? Explain your answer using details of the source and your knowledge.
[7]

Evidence Supporting the Cuba Protection Motive:

- Khrushchev explicitly states, "The main point about the crisis is that it has guaranteed the existence of a Socialist Cuba"
- He argues that without the crisis, "Americans would have organised an invasion"
- Claims the agreement makes it "very difficult for them to interfere"
- Expresses satisfaction that Cuba is now protected "for at least another two years"

Limitations of the Source:
- Self-serving nature - This is Khrushchev's own account, written to justify his actions to Castro
- Post-hoc rationalisation - Written after the crisis, he may be reframing his original motives
- Political necessity - He needed to rebuild relations with Castro after excluding him from negotiations
- Alternative motives ignored - The source does not address other possible motives, like strengthening the Soviet military position globally

Alternative Evidence:
- The timing suggests this was damage control with Castro
- Other sources suggest broader Cold War strategic motives
- The secret nature of the missile installation suggests other goals

Conclusion - Source G provides limited proof of Khrushchev's protective motives. While it strongly emphasises Cuba's protection, it is a self-justifying document written after the fact to repair damaged relations, making it unreliable as definitive proof of original intentions.

6. **Study all the sources.**

How far do these sources provide convincing evidence that the Cuban Missile Crisis was a success for Khrushchev? Use the sources to explain your answer. [12]

Evidence Suggesting Success
Protection of Cuba-
- Source A: Kennedy's promise not to invade guaranteed "continued existence of a socialist Cuba"
- Source G: Khrushchev celebrates that the crisis "guaranteed the existence of a Socialist Cuba"
- Source E: Claims Soviet Union successfully defended Cuba and exposed US "imperialist intrigues"

Avoiding Nuclear War-
- Source A: Gives Khrushchev credit for "being prepared to back down in the face of nuclear war"
- Source E: Claims "sanity and the cause of peace" won

Evidence Against Success

Damaged Relationships-

- Sources A & B: Castro was "furious" and felt betrayed by the lack of consultation
- Source B: The Chinese called Khrushchev "foolish" and "cowardly," widening the Sino-Soviet split
- Source A: Soviet military "particularly angry" at the "humiliation"

Weak Position Exposed-

- Sources C & F: American cartoons mock Khrushchev's retreat
- Source D: Americans saw it as their victory and Khrushchev's "miscalculation"
- Source B: Crisis damaged Khrushchev's "personal power within the communist bloc"

Limited Guarantees:

- Source B: Kennedy's no-invasion pledge had a "huge loophole" and was not absolute

Evaluation of Source Reliability:

- Sources D & E are clearly biased (American and Soviet propaganda)
- Source G may be self-justifying damage control
- Sources A & B are more balanced historical analyses

- Cartoons C & F reflect contemporary American perceptions

The sources provide mixed and unconvincing evidence for Khrushchev's success. While he achieved some goals (Cuba's protection, avoiding nuclear war), the costs were enormous: damaged alliances with Cuba and China, humiliation of the Soviet military, and perception of weakness. The most reliable sources (A & B) suggest that while Khrushchev could claim limited success, the overall outcome significantly damaged his position. The crisis appears more like a face-saving compromise than a clear victory for either side, but Khrushchev paid the higher political price.

Chapter 4

PAPER 4

Questions

Option A: Nineteenth-century topic
February/March paper 2b2020
Cambridge IGCSE

Q

HOW DID THE BRITISH BEHAVE DURING AND IMMEDIATELY AFTER THE INDIAN MUTINY OF 1857–58?

Study the Background Information and the sources carefully, and then answer all the questions.

Background Information

The Indian Mutiny of 1857–58 was the result of resentment that had been building during British rule. It started with a mutiny of sepoys in Meerut. Still, it soon evolved into a much broader uprising against British rule, with cities such as Delhi, Cawnpore, and Lucknow either falling to the rebels or being subjected to a heavy siege. In some places, such as Cawnpore, British women and children were killed.

The army of the British East India Company had to deal with troubles, and accounts published in Britain portrayed it as doing so with extraordinary heroism. After the rising was put down, there were demands from Britain that the rebels be dealt with severely.

Did the British behave well in their response to the Indian Mutiny?

SOURCE A

Illustration entitled 'Miss Wheeler defending herself against the Sepoys at Cawnpore. It was published in 1858 in a British book entitled 'The History of the Indian Mutiny'

SOURCE B

A merry scene must have been for a true, liberty-loving Briton to see his grenadiers helping themselves freely to the jewels, valuable arms and clothes of His Majesty of Oude. Every advance was accompanied by plunder and devastation. The Qaisar Bagh Palace had fallen on 14 March, and within half an hour, discipline was at an end, and the officers had lost all command over their men. On 17 March, General Campbell was obliged to establish patrols to prevent plundering. The troops were completely out of control. In the city, while the vanguard were fighting against the natives' fire from the houses, the rearguard plundered and destroyed to their hearts' content. Matters were still so bad that the strictest orders were issued for the suppression of plunder and outrage.

This is indeed a dreadful state of things in a civilised army in the nineteenth century. If any other troops in the world had committed one-tenth of these excesses, the indignant British press would brand them with infamy! However, these are the deeds of the British army, and therefore we are told that such things are the expected consequences of war.

A report from an American newspaper, 25 May 1858.

SOURCE C

An illustration from 1858. It was later republished in 'Heroes of Britain in Peace and War', 1880. The words under this illustration read 'Some Victoria Cross Exploits of the Indian Mutiny. 1. Private Dempsey rescuing Ensign Erskine. 2. Mr Mangles dressing Taylor's wound. 3. Mr McDonell is releasing the boat in the Arrah expedition. 4.

Lieutenant Hills and the mounted troopers. 5. Young Havelock leading his men to the capture of a gun.' The Victoria Cross is the highest British award for bravery.

Members of the armed forces.

SOURCE D

An illustration depicting British troops looting the Qaisar Bagh Palace in Lucknow after the city's recapture in 1858. It was published in Britain in 1860. The soldier kneeling is saying, 'Is this string of

SOURCE E

SOURCE F

A substantial proportion of the English community has a violent hatred of every Indian of every class. There is a cruelty, even from those who ought to set a better example, which is impossible to see without feeling shame for one's fellow citizens. Not one man in ten seems to think that the hanging and shooting of 50,000 mutineers is wrong.

A letter from Lord Canning to Queen Victoria, 25 September 1858. Canning was British Governor-General of India

SOURCE E

The most hostile of our foreign critics are in awe of our administration of India. When we ask, who are the men who have kept intact, and handed down to us these vast privileges, who are they who have preserved for us the splendid burden which we accept and bear with honour today? The answer is that the last of these heroes is among us still, white-haired and too often infirm, but the very men who saved India from itself in 1857 when the tide of rebellion threatened to wipe away the trace of our rule. To these survivors, this little book is dedicated.

**From a book entitled 'In Commemoration of the 50th Anniversary of the Indian Mutiny', published in
Britain in 1907.**

SOURCE F

A substantial proportion of the English community has a violent hatred of every Indian of every class. There is a cruelty, even from those who ought to set a better example, which is impossible to see without feeling shame for one's fellow citizens. Not one man in ten seems to think that the hanging and shooting of 50,000 mutineers is wrong.

A letter from Lord Canning to Queen Victoria, 25 September 1858. Canning was
British Governor-General of India

Now answer all the following questions. You may use any of the sources to help you answer the questions, in addition to those sources which you are told to use. When answering the questions, use your knowledge of the topic to help you interpret and evaluate the sources.

1   Study Source A.

What impressions does this source give about the Indian Mutiny? Explain your answer using details of the source. [8]

2   Study Source B.

Why was this source published in 1858? Explain your answer using details of the source and your knowledge. [7]

3   Study Sources C and D.

How far does Source C make Source D surprising? Explain your answer using details of the sources and your knowledge. [8]

4   Study Source E.

How valuable is this source as evidence about British rule in India? Explain your answer using details of the source and your knowledge.   [7]

5   Study Sources F and G.

How far does Source G prove that Victoria agreed with Canning (Source F)? Explain your answer using details of the sources and your knowledge.
[8]

6   Study all the sources.

How far do these sources provide convincing evidence that the British behaved well in their response to the Indian Mutiny? Use the sources to explain your answer.   [12]

Option B: Twentieth-century topic

WAS THE CUBAN MISSILE CRISIS SIMPLY A TRIAL OF STRENGTH BETWEEN KENNEDY AND KHRUSHCHEV?

Study the Background Information and the sources carefully, and then answer all the questions.

Background Information

Accounts and representations of the Cuban Missile Crisis have often presented it as a personal trial of strength between Kennedy and Khrushchev. Many historians criticised this way of representing the crisis. They argue that the broader context of the Cold War, along with the national interests of the USA and the USSR, were crucial factors.

How far was the Cuban Missile Crisis simply about personal rivalry between Kennedy and Khrushchev?

SOURCE A

I have got two problems. First, to figure out why Khrushchev acted in such a hostile way. Moreover, second, to figure out what we can do about it. I think the first part is pretty easy to explain. I think he did it because of the Bay of Pigs. He felt that anyone so young and inexperienced as to get into that mess could be beaten, and anyone who got into it and did not see it through had no guts. If he thinks I am inexperienced and lack courage, until we dispel those notions, we will not make progress with him.

Kennedy speaking to an American reporter in 1961, shortly after his disastrous Vienna Summit meeting with Khrushchev.

SOURCE B

Then the exchange of notes began. I dictated the messages and conducted the exchange from our side. President Kennedy issued an ultimatum, demanding that we remove our missiles and bombers from Cuba. I remember the exchange with the President exceptionally well because I started it and was at the centre of the action at our end of the correspondence. I take complete responsibility for the fact that the President and I entered into direct contact at the most crucial and dangerous stage of the crisis.

Dobrynin's report of a meeting with Robert Kennedy went something like this, 'The President is appealing directly to Chairman Khrushchev. If the situation continues much longer, the President fears that the military will overthrow him.' We knew that Kennedy was a young President. For some time, I had felt there was a danger that he would lose control of his military, and now he was admitting this to us himself. 'Comrades,' I said, 'we have to look for a dignified way out of this conflict.' We sent a note saying we agreed to remove the missiles on condition that the President gave us his assurance that Cuba would not be invaded.

From Khrushchev's memoirs, published in 1970. Dobrynin was the Soviet Ambassador to the United States.

SOUCE C

A cartoon was published in an American newspaper in October 1962. Kennedy is saying to Khrushchev,
'I would reconsider if I were you!'

SOURCE D

An advertisement, in an

SOURCE E

A cartoon published in a British newspaper, 29 October 1962. The caption reads, 'OK, Mr President, let's

SOURCE F

Good evening, my fellow citizens.

Within the past week, unmistakable evidence has established that a series of offensive missile sites is now in preparation in Cuba. Their purpose can be none other than to provide a nuclear strike capability against the Western Hemisphere.

The characteristics of these new missile sites indicate two types of installations. Several of them include medium-range ballistic missiles capable of striking Washington, DC, Mexico City or any other city in the southeastern part of the United States.

Additional sites appear to be designed for intermediate-range ballistic missiles – capable of travelling twice as far. This transformation of Cuba into an essential strategic base is an explicit threat to the peace and security of all the Americas.

From a speech by President Kennedy to the American people, 22 October 1962.

SOURCE G

The accounts of the crisis did not make clear that it was a power confrontation, that the power of the USA was incomparably superior to that of the USSR, and that the leaders of both nations were aware of this fact. The United States, it is worth repeating, could have erased every necessary Soviet military installation and population centre in two or three hours, while the strike capability of the USSR was negligible. Although Kennedy held the trump cards, he granted the Communist empire a privileged sanctuary in the Caribbean by means of the 'no invasion' pledge.

From a book entitled 'Dagger in the Heart: American Failures in Cuba', by Mario Lazo, published in 1968. Lazo was a Cuban supporter of the Batista regime. After the Cuban revolution, he fled to the
United States.

Now answer all the following questions. You may use any of the sources to help you answer the questions, in addition to those sources which you are told to use. When answering the questions, use your knowledge of the topic to help you interpret and evaluate the sources.

1   Study Source A.

How far do you agree that this source is valuable as evidence about the Cuban Missile Crisis? Explain your answer using details of the source and your knowledge.   [7]

2.   Study Source B.

What impressions does this source give of Khrushchev? Explain your answer using details of the source.[8]

3.   Study Source C.

What is the cartoonist's message? Explain your answer using details of the source and your knowledge.
    [7]

4.   Study Sources D and E.

How far do these two sources agree about the Cuban Missile Crisis? Explain your answer using details of the sources and your knowledge. [8]

5. Study Sources F and G.

How far does Source G make Source F surprising? Explain your answer using details of the sources and your knowledge. [8]

6. Study all the sources.

How far do these sources provide convincing evidence that the Cuban Missile Crisis was simply about personal rivalry between Kennedy and Khrushchev? Use the sources to explain your answer. (12)

CHAPTER 4: Answers

Question:

Option B: Twentieth-century topic

1. Study Source A.

How far do you agree that this source is valuable as evidence about the Cuban Missile Crisis? Explain your answer using details of the source and your knowledge. [7]

Source A is quite helpful as evidence about the Cuban Missile Crisis because it provides Kennedy's personal perspective on the underlying tensions between him and Khrushchev.
Shows Kennedy's personal analysis - Kennedy directly explains his belief that Khrushchev saw him as weak and inexperienced after the Bay of Pigs invasion, revealing the psychological dimension of their relationship.

Contemporary evidence - The source dates back to 1961, shortly after Kennedy met with

Khrushchev in Vienna, making it a genuine record of Kennedy's thinking at the time rather than a later reflection.

Links to broader context - Kennedy connects the crisis to the Bay of Pigs failure (1961), showing how earlier events shaped the superpower relationship leading up to 1962.

Reveals Kennedy's concerns about credibility - The source shows Kennedy understood that appearing weak could encourage Soviet aggression, which helps explain his firm response during the missile crisis.

However, there are limitations:
Only Kennedy's viewpoint - The source presents the American perspective and Kennedy's interpretation of Khrushchev's motives, which may not be entirely accurate.
Timing issue - The source dates back to 1961, before the actual missile crisis occurred in 1962, so it reflects Kennedy's fears rather than direct evidence about the situation itself.
Possible bias - Kennedy may be justifying his own actions or presenting himself in a favourable light to the reporter.

2.   Study Source B.

What impressions does this source give of Khrushchev? Explain your answer using details of the source. [7]

Source B gives several clear impressions of Khrushchev as a leader during the Cuban Missile Crisis.

Khrushchev appears as a decisive leader:
- Takes personal control - "I dictated the messages and conducted the exchange from our side", shows Khrushchev personally managing the crisis rather than delegating to others.
- Accepts responsibility.

"I take complete responsibility" demonstrates that he was willing to accept ownership of his decisions during this perilous period.
- Initiates direct communication.

He initiated the crucial correspondence with Kennedy, demonstrating his proactive approach to managing the situation.

Khrushchev appears pragmatic and rational:

- Assesses Kennedy's weakness;

He recognises that Kennedy was young and might lose control of his military, showing political awareness.

- Seeks compromise;

When he realises the danger, he tells his colleagues, "We have to look for a dignified way out of this conflict," indicating he prioritised avoiding war over scoring political points.

- Negotiates strategically.

He agrees to remove missiles but demands assurance that Cuba will not be invaded, showing he sought to achieve Soviet objectives through diplomacy.

Khrushchev appears cautious about escalation: The source suggests that he was concerned about Kennedy losing control of the American military, indicating that Khrushchev understood the dangers of the situation spiralling out of control and wanted to prevent this.

Overall, the source presents Khrushchev as a hands-on leader who was ultimately more interested in finding a face-saving solution than in pushing the crisis to a dangerous conclusion.

3. Study Source C.

What is the cartoonist's message? Explain your answer using details of the source and your knowledge. [8]

The cartoonist's message is that Kennedy holds a position of strength over Khrushchev during the Cuban Missile Crisis and is warning him to back down.

Visual details support this message:
- Kennedy's dominant position;
Kennedy is shown standing tall and pointing directly at Khrushchev, suggesting he is in control of the situation and making demands.

- Khrushchev's defensive posture.
Khrushchev appears smaller and more defensive, suggesting he is in a weaker position and under pressure.

- The warning tone.
Kennedy's words, "I would reconsider if I were you!" are clearly a threat, implying that Khrushchev should change course or face consequences.

- American perspective.

Published in an American newspaper in October 1962, this reflects how Americans wanted to see their president as strong and decisive.

Historical context supports the message:

The cartoon reflects the American view that Kennedy had successfully confronted Soviet aggression. By October 1962, Kennedy had announced the naval quarantine of Cuba and was demanding the removal of Soviet missiles, putting pressure on Khrushchev to respond.

However, the cartoon oversimplifies the situation: In reality, both leaders were under enormous pressure, and the crisis involved complex negotiations rather than simple American dominance. Khrushchev ultimately agreed to remove missiles but also secured American promises not to invade Cuba and secretly obtained the removal of American missiles from Turkey.

The cartoonist's message appeals to American audiences by presenting Kennedy as the stronger leader who forced Khrushchev to back down. However, this interpretation ignores the compromises both sides made to resolve the crisis.

4. Study Sources D and E.

How far do these two sources agree about the Cuban Missile Crisis? Explain your answer using details of the sources and your knowledge. [8]

Sources D and E agree to some extent about the personal nature of the Cuban Missile Crisis, but they present different perspectives on the outcome and dynamics.

Areas of agreement:
- Personal confrontation focus.

Both sources present the crisis as a confrontation between Kennedy and Khrushchev, rather than just between nations, as a personal one.

- High-stakes situation.

Source D's title, "The Crisis That Shook the World," and Source E, showing both leaders in a tense face-to-face situation, indicate that both recognise this was a moment of extreme danger.

- Individual leadership matters.

Both suggest that the personal qualities and decisions of Kennedy and Khrushchev were crucial to the development and outcome of the crisis.

Key differences:

- American vs British perspective.

Source D, advertising an American book, likely emphasises Kennedy's role and American viewpoint, while Source E, from a British newspaper, may offer a more neutral perspective.

- Timing and outcome.

Source E (October 29, 1962) shows the moment when negotiation becomes possible with "OK, Mr President, let us talk," suggesting compromise. Source D, published 50 years later, benefits from the hindsight of the whole crisis.

- Tone about resolution.

Source E implies both leaders are ready to negotiate as equals, while Source D's focus on "13 days" emphasises the drama and tension rather than the collaborative resolution.

Historical context:

Source E was published just as the crisis was being resolved, when Khrushchev had agreed to remove missiles and both sides were moving toward negotiation. Source D represents a later historical analysis that can present the complete story.

The sources agree that this was fundamentally about the two leaders' personal confrontation, but differ in their emphasis on how the relationship between Kennedy and Khrushchev evolved during the crisis.

5. Study Sources F and G.

How far does Source G make Source F surprising? Explain your answer using details of the sources and your knowledge. [8]

Source G makes Source F quite surprising by revealing that Kennedy's strong public stance was delivered from a position of overwhelming military superiority that he chose not to exploit fully.
Why does Source F appear different after reading Source G?

- Kennedy's restrained language seems unexpected - Source F presents the missile threat as serious ("explicit threat to the peace and security"). Still, Source G reveals that "the United States could have erased every important Soviet military installation and population centre in two or three hours."

- The focus on defence rather than offence - Source F emphasises protecting "the Western Hemisphere" from Soviet missiles. Still, Source G shows that America's "strike capability" was so superior that the Soviet threat was actually "negligible."

- Kennedy's measured response.

Source F announces a quarantine and diplomatic pressure, which Source G suggests was remarkably restrained given that "Kennedy held the trump cards."

Source G's perspective on Kennedy's choices: Source G argues that Kennedy "granted the Communist empire a privileged sanctuary in the Caribbean" through his "no invasion" pledge, suggesting he gave away more than necessary given American military superiority.

However, Source F is not entirely surprising:

- Political considerations

Kennedy needed to justify intense action to the American people without appearing overly aggressive or reckless, which explains the measured tone in Source F.

- Nuclear war risks

Even with military superiority, Kennedy understood that nuclear conflict could be catastrophic, making his cautious public approach logical.

Source limitations:

Source G comes from Mario Lazo, a Cuban exile who opposed Castro, so his criticism of Kennedy's "restraint" may reflect his personal disappointment that America did not use the crisis to remove Castro entirely.

Source G makes Source F surprising by suggesting that Kennedy was speaking from much greater strength than his words implied. However, Kennedy's measured approach may have been wise statesmanship rather than weakness.

6. Study all the sources.

How far do these sources provide convincing evidence that the Cuban Missile Crisis was simply about personal rivalry between Kennedy and Khrushchev? Use the sources to explain your answer. [12]

The sources provide mixed evidence regarding whether the Cuban Missile Crisis was primarily driven by personal rivalry, with some sources supporting this view. In contrast, others suggest that broader factors were also involved.

Evidence supporting personal rivalry:
- Source A shows Kennedy's personal concerns - Kennedy explicitly states that Khrushchev saw him as weak after the Bay of Pigs, making the crisis partly about proving personal credibility and strength.

- Source B emphasises personal control. Khrushchev states, "I dictated the messages and conducted the exchange," showing both leaders personally managed the crisis rather than delegating to institutions.
- Sources C and D focus on individual confrontation.
The cartoon shows Kennedy directly confronting Khrushchev, while the book advertisement emphasises "13 days" of personal drama between the leaders.

- Source E presents face-to-face negotiation. The cartoon depicts the two leaders in a direct personal dialogue, suggesting that the crisis was resolved through their individual relationship.

Evidence against simple personal rivalry:

- Source F reveals broader strategic concerns - Kennedy's speech focuses on national security threats to "the Western Hemisphere" and "all the Americas," indicating the crisis involved fundamental Cold War strategic interests beyond personal relations.
- Source G emphasises power politics; Lazo argues this was "a power confrontation" between superpowers with vastly different military capabilities, suggesting national interests and strategic balance mattered more than personal rivalry.
- Source B shows institutional concerns - Khrushchev mentions Kennedy's fear that "the military will overthrow him," indicating both leaders faced domestic political pressures beyond their personal relationship.

Broader context from sources:
- Source A connects to Bay of Pigs - This links the crisis to broader Cold War conflicts over Cuba and Soviet-American competition in the Third World.
- Source G mentions American military superiority.

This suggests the crisis was fundamentally about the strategic nuclear balance between superpowers rather than personal dynamics. The sources provide convincing evidence that personal rivalry was essential but not the only factor. While Sources A, B, C, and E highlight the importance of Kennedy and Khrushchev's personal relationship, credibility, and decision-making, Sources F and G demonstrate that broader Cold War strategic interests, national security concerns, and power balances were equally significant. The crisis appears to have been both a personal test between two leaders and a confrontation between competing superpower interests in the nuclear age.

Paper 5

Chapter 5

Cambridge IGCSE

: Alternative to Coursework

Questions

Answer one question from your chosen Depth Study.

DEPTH STUDY A: THE FIRST WORLD WAR, 1914–18

1   How important was Belgian resistance in halting the German advance in 1914? Explain your answer.
[40]

2   How significant was the use of tanks in the Battle of the Somme? Explain your answer.
   [40]

DEPTH STUDY B: GERMANY, 1918–45

3   How important was the use of informers in allowing Hitler to control the German people after 1933? Explain your answer.   [40]

4   How significant was the recovery of the German economy in strengthening Nazi rule, 1934–39? Explain your answer.   [40]

DEPTH STUDY C: RUSSIA, 1905–41

5   How important was the Russo-Japanese War as a cause of instability in Russia up to 1914? Explain your answer.   [40]

6   How significant was Trotsky in the Bolshevik seizure of power in November 1917? Explain your answer.   [40]

DEPTH STUDY D: THE UNITED STATES, 1919–41

7   How vital was immigration in the 1920s as a reason for the growth of the Ku Klux Klan? Explain your answer. [40]

8   How significant were the Alphabet Agencies in dealing with economic problems during the New Deal? Explain your answer.   [40]

DEPTH STUDY E: CHINA, c.1930–c.1990

9   How important was the development of communes in Mao's economic policies in the 1950s? Explain your answer.   [40]

10   How significant was the indoctrination of young people in the Communist dictatorship in China after 1949? Explain your answer.

[40]

DEPTH STUDY F: SOUTH AFRICA, c.1940–c.1994

11   How vital was youth opposition in the resistance to apartheid after 1948? Explain your answer.

[40]

12 How significant were reforms to the Pass Laws as a reason for the collapse of white minority rule in South Africa? Explain your answer.
[40]

DEPTH STUDY G: ISRAELIS AND PALESTINIANS SINCE 1945

13 How important was the Soviet Union in shaping events in the Middle East after 1948? Explain your answer.   [40]

14 How significant was President Carter in dealing with the problems between Israel and its neighbours after 1973? Explain your answer.
[40]

CHAPTER 5: Answers

DEPTH STUDY G: ISRAELIS AND PALESTINIANS SINCE 1945 (No 14.)
DEPTH STUDY A: THE FIRST WORLD WAR, 1914–18 (No 1)

14. How significant was President Carter in dealing with the problems between Israel and its neighbours after 1973? Explain your answer. [40]

President Carter made a significant impact in addressing Israeli-Arab issues, achieving the most crucial breakthrough in Middle East peace negotiations since 1948.
Camp David Accords (1978). - Carter personally mediated 13 days of intense negotiations between Israeli Prime Minister Begin and Egyptian President Sadat, producing the first peace agreement between Israel and an Arab state.

Egypt-Israel Peace Treaty (1979). - This treaty ended 30 years of warfare between the two countries and established a framework for future negotiations.

Personal diplomacy - Carter invested enormous personal effort and presidential prestige in the Middle East peace process, spending more time on this issue than any previous president.

Creative solutions - The Camp David framework addressed both bilateral Israeli-Egyptian issues and broader Palestinian questions, though the latter remained unresolved.

Financial incentives - Carter promised substantial US aid to both Israel and Egypt ($3 billion and $2 billion annually, respectively) to support the peace process and compensate for risks taken.

The peace treaty achieved concrete results - Israel withdrew from the Sinai Peninsula, Egypt recognised Israel's right to exist, and both countries established normal diplomatic relations. This removed Egypt (the strongest Arab military power) from future Arab-Israeli wars, fundamentally changing the regional balance of power.

Carter isolated Begin and Sadat at Camp David, away from domestic pressures and media attention. He leveraged his personal relationships with both leaders, appealing to their shared religious beliefs and historical responsibilities, to achieve breakthrough moments when negotiations seemed to be failing.

1   How important was Belgian resistance in halting the German advance in 1914? Explain your answer. [40][

Importance of Belgian Resistance:
- Slowed German advance – Belgian forces put up unexpected resistance at Liège and other forts, delaying the German army for about 10–12 days. This disrupted the carefully timed Schlieffen Plan, which relied on rapid movement through Belgium.
- Allowed British and French mobilisation – The delay gave the British Expeditionary Force (BEF) and the French army more time to mobilise and prepare their defences, making it harder for Germany to achieve a quick victory.
- Boosted Allied morale – Belgian bravery became a symbol of resistance, and reports of German atrocities in Belgium were used in Allied propaganda to gain support at home and abroad.

- Brought Britain into the war – Germany's violation of Belgian neutrality (guaranteed by the 1839 Treaty of London) gave Britain a strong reason to declare war on Germany, bringing another significant power into the conflict.

Other factors that halted the German advance:

- BEF resistance at Mons – The small but professional British army fought effectively, inflicting heavy casualties and forcing the Germans to divert troops.
- French counterattacks – The French army regrouped and launched a counterattack at the Battle of the Marne, which finally stopped the German advance just short of Paris.
- German overextension – The German army was rushing and became overstretched, with supply lines too long to maintain momentum effectively.
- Logistical and planning weaknesses – The Schlieffen Plan underestimated the difficulties of invading Belgium and miscalculated the speed of Russian mobilisation, forcing Germany to divert troops to the Eastern Front.

Conclusion:

- Very important – Belgian resistance was crucial because it delayed Germany at a critical

moment and allowed the Allies to prepare, preventing a swift German victory.
- But not the only reason – The ultimate halt of the German advance depended on the combined effect of BEF action, French counterattacks, and German strategic errors.
- Overall judgement – Belgian resistance was a key first step in halting the German advance, but the decisive factor was the Battle of the Marne, which permanently ended German hopes of a quick war and led to the stalemate of trench warfare.

Chapter 6

Paper 6

PPr 4 2020 NOV.

Alternative to Coursework

CHAPTER 6

Answer one question from your chosen Depth Study.

DEPTH STUDY A: THE FIRST WORLD WAR, 1914–18

1   How important was the use of gas weapons in warfare on the Western Front? Explain your answer.   [40]

2   How significant was the war at sea in determining the nature of the British Home Front? Explain your answer.   [40]

DEPTH STUDY B: GERMANY, 1918–45

3   How important were economic problems as a cause of disorder in Germany between 1918 and 1923? Explain your answer.   [40]

4   How significant was the army's opposition in resisting Nazi rule? Explain your answer. [40]

DEPTH STUDY C: RUSSIA, 1905–41

5   How important was political reform to the survival of the Tsarist regime between 1905 and 1914? Explain your answer.   [40]

6   How significant was strong leadership as a reason why the Bolsheviks were able to seize power in November 1917? Explain your answer. [40]

DEPTH STUDY D: THE UNITED STATES, 1919–41

7   How vital was the entertainment industry in changing the lives of women in the 1920s? Explain your answer. [40]

8   How significant was the work of the Tennessee Valley Authority (TVA) in dealing with the Depression of the 1930s? Explain your answer. [40]

DEPTH STUDY E: CHINA, c.1930–c.1990

9   How vital was the withdrawal of American support in bringing about the defeat of the Nationalists in 1949? Explain your answer. [40]

10   How significant was ideology as a reason why Mao launched the Cultural Revolution? Explain your answer. [40]

DEPTH STUDY F: SOUTH AFRICA, c.1940–c.1994

11   How vital was the migrant labour system in shaping the lives of the non-white population in South Africa before 1948? Explain your answer. [40]

12   How significant were women to the development of opposition against apartheid by 1966? Explain your answer.   [40]

DEPTH STUDY G: ISRAELIS AND PALESTINIANS SINCE 1945

13   How vital was the Jewish campaign of terror as a reason for the British withdrawal from Palestine? Explain your answer.   [40]

14   How significant was the USA to the outcome of the Arab–Israeli conflicts between 1956 and 1973? Explain your answer.   [40]

CHAPTER 6: Answers

Answered Questions:

DEPTH STUDY A: THE FIRST WORLD WAR, 1914–18 (No 1)

DEPTH STUDY B: GERMANY, 1918–45 (No 3)

1. How important was the use of gas weapons in warfare on the Western Front? Explain your answer. [40]

The use of gas weapons on the Western Front was necessary in some ways, but not the most decisive factor in the war. Gas was a new and terrifying weapon that caused panic, serious injuries, and painful deaths. Soldiers had to deal with terrible conditions when gas was used, and it forced armies to come up with defences like gas masks. It also showed how science and new technology were changing the way wars were fought. The gas was useful in:

- Breaking the stalemate - Gas attacks initially offered a potential solution to the trench warfare deadlock
- Surprise advantage - Early gas attacks caught defenders completely unprepared, creating panic and confusion
- Second Battle of Ypres (1915) - German chlorine attack created a 4-mile gap in Allied lines, demonstrating gas's potential
- Bypassing fortifications - Gas could flow into trenches and dugouts that were otherwise impregnable to conventional weapons
- Force multiplier effect - Relatively small amounts of gas could affect large areas and many soldiers simultaneously

However, gas was not the most essential weapon. It did not lead to significant victories or break the stalemate on the front lines. Both sides quickly developed protective gear, such as gas masks, which made the gas less effective over time. Other weapons, like machine guns and artillery, caused far more deaths and had a bigger impact on how battles were fought.

Gas was also unreliable because of:

- Weather dependency - Wind direction and weather conditions severely limited when gas could be used effectively
- Indiscriminate nature - Gas could blow back onto attacking forces, limiting tactical flexibility
- Temporary advantage - Initial surprise was quickly lost as both sides developed countermeasures
- No decisive victories - Despite early successes, gas attacks never achieved a breakthrough that ended trench warfare
- Difficult to exploit - Even successful gas attacks were hard to follow up with infantry advances

In conclusion, gas was important for its psychological effects and as part of modern warfare, but it was not the most critical factor in deciding the outcome of battles on the Western Front. Weapons like artillery and machine guns had a much bigger impact overall.

DEPTH STUDY B: GERMANY, 1918–45

3 How important were economic problems as a cause of disorder in Germany between 1918 and 1923? Explain your answer. [40]

Reasons why economic problems were significant:
- Germany faced huge war debts after World War I. The cost of the war left Germany nearly bankrupt and struggling to recover.
- The Treaty of Versailles made things worse – Germany had to pay enormous reparations, which put more pressure on its weak economy.
- Hyperinflation caused extreme hardship in 1923 – The government printed too much money to pay reparations and workers, making the currency worthless.
- Middle-class savings were destroyed – Many people lost all their savings, causing anger and loss of trust in the government.
- Unemployment and poverty increased – Many Germans could not afford food, heating, or rent, which led to protests, strikes, and riots.

Other essential causes of disorder:
- Political unrest and uprisings – Left-wing (Spartacists) and right-wing (Freikorps, Kapp Putsch) groups tried to overthrow the Weimar Republic.
- Blame for the Treaty of Versailles – Many Germans believed the government had "stabbed them in the back" by signing the treaty, leading to anger and rebellion.

- Weakness of the Weimar Republic – The new democratic government was seen as weak, inexperienced, and unable to deal with problems.
- Social divisions after the war – Soldiers returning home found no jobs, while others blamed different political groups or minorities for Germany's problems.
- Occupation of the Ruhr by French and Belgian troops in 1923 – This led to a general strike and worsened inflation, further damaging the economy and public mood.

Judgement:
- Economic problems were a significant cause of disorder, mainly because they affected everyone's daily life and caused anger across all classes.
- However, political instability, anger at the Treaty of Versailles, and violent uprisings also played significant roles.
- Therefore, economic issues were a key cause, but they combined with political and social factors to create widespread disorder.

Chapter 7

PAPER 7

February/March 2021 Paper 2

Same instruction as above

2021 Past Papers

QUESTION TO PAPER 7

CHAPTER 7

Option A: Nineteenth-century topic

HOW FAR WAS PRUSSIA'S DOMINANT POSITION IN GERMANY BY 1867 ACHIEVED THROUGH THE USE OF FORCE?

Study the Background Information and the sources carefully, and then answer all the questions.

Background Information

When Bismarck became the Chief Minister of Prussia in 1862, one of his aims was to make Prussia the leading state in Germany. Two obstacles stood in his way. First, the Austrian Empire had a population almost twice the size of

Prussia and a larger army. Second, most German states did not want to be dominated by Prussia.

By 1867, Bismarck had achieved his aim, but had he constantly intended to do this purely by force?

SOURCE A

When Bismarck took over control of Prussian foreign policy, there was no dramatic change of direction.

The war of 1866 may appear, with hindsight, to have been the inevitable and planned result of Bismarck's policies, but not all the factors that led to the outbreak of hostilities were within Bismarck's control.

From a history book published in 2000.

SOURCE B

When Bismarck came to power, his primary concerns were with foreign policy, particularly in relation to his opponent, Austria, which was relatively active. Hostility between Prussia and Austria was, in fact, unavoidable. Relations between Prussia and Austria were already strained and became worse after Bismarck's appointment. He rejected Austrian proposals to reform the German Confederation, which would have strengthened Austria's influence within the confederation. He informed the Austrian government that relations between the two countries were so strained that they would likely end in war. The only way to avoid a war, he said, was for Austria to surrender its position in Germany and focus eastwards.

Was it Bismarck's intention from the time of the peace with Denmark in 1864 to make war against Austria? He certainly never had any concerns about a war of this kind. He might have been willing to do without the war if he could have achieved his aims by diplomatic means, and was probably not determined on war from the beginning. However, he was engaged in a policy against Austria, which made war unavoidable, and two essential aspects of his actions should be noted: first, in 1865, he rejected every opportunity by which war might be avoided; second, he worked with patience to remove.

The obstacles to war. The mistake of the Austrian government was that it did not see in time that war was inevitable and that military preparations were necessary. However, they cannot be blamed for having failed to avoid a war that was in no way avoidable.

From a history book published in 1918.

SOURCE C

I shall soon have to lead the Prussian government. My first task will be to organise the Prussian army. As soon as it is in a condition to command respect, then I shall take the first opportunity to declare war on Austria, dissolve the German Confederation, bring the middle and the smaller states under Prussian control and give Germany a national union under the leadership of Prussia.

Bismarck's conversation with a British politician in London in 1862, as reported by
Count Eckstadt, Saxony's ambassador in London.

SOURCE D

We both owe it to public opinion to carry out our policy completely, to assert our power and influence in Germany, and not to yield to any direct attacks from the Lesser States. The idea of Austria and Prussia together, that they should co-operate in the action against Schleswig-Holstein, must be accepted by the Confederation. The Lesser States must learn that if they attempt to subject the European policy of Austria and Prussia to the control of the majority of the Confederation, they will make the continuance of friendly relations with the Confederation impossible for these two Powers.

A letter from Bismarck to the Austrian government, 1863.

SOURCE E

In a meeting with the king and the army chiefs, I declared it to be my belief that peace must be concluded on the Austrian terms. I was alone in my opinion. I set to work to commit to paper the reasons that I thought justified the conclusion of peace and begged the king, in the event of his not accepting my advice, to take my resignation if the war continued.

We had to avoid wounding Austria too severely. We had to avoid leaving behind any unnecessary bitterness or desire for revenge in Austria. We ought to keep the possibility of becoming friends again. If Austria were severely injured, it would become the ally of France and of every other opponent of ours.

A description of events in 1866, from Bismarck's memoirs, which were published in 1898.

SOURCE F

The only justification the Prussian government gives for the seizure of our kingdom is that which it claims to find in the right of conquest. However, there has never been a war between us and the King of Prussia. We protest in the presence of the world against our incorporation into Prussia.

We pray for the support of all powers that have recognised our independence. The justification given by Prussia would menace the existence of all monarchies. Let all those who may be interested be warned.

A declaration by the King of Hanover, 23 September 1866.

SOURCE G

A French cartoon of King William I and the princes of northern Germany, 1867.

Now answer all the following questions. You may use any of the sources to help you answer the questions, in addition to those sources which you are told to use. When answering the questions, use your knowledge of the topic to help you interpret and evaluate the sources.

1   Study Sources A and B.

How far do these two sources agree? Explain your answer using details of the sources.   [7]

2   Study Sources C and D.

Does Source C mean that Bismarck was lying in Source D? Explain your answer using details of the sources and your knowledge.   [8]

3   Study Source E.

Do you find Source E surprising? Explain your answer using details of the source and your knowledge.   [7]

4   Study Source F.

Why did the King of Hanover issue this declaration at that time? Explain your answer using details of the source and your knowledge. [8]

5   Study Source G.

What is the message of the cartoonist? Explain your answer using details of the source and your knowledge. [8]

6   Study all the sources.

How far do these sources provide convincing evidence that Bismarck always intended to achieve Prussian dominance over Germany purely by force? Use the sources to explain your answer. [12]

Option B: Twentieth-century topic

HOW FAR WAS THE SOVIET UNION RESPONSIBLE FOR THE WORSENING OF RELATIONS WITH THE USA AFTER THE SECOND WORLD WAR?

Study the Background Information and the sources carefully, and then answer all the questions.

Background Information

Despite being allies against Nazi Germany, relations between the USA and the USSR began to deteriorate before the Second World War ended. The ideological differences between the two countries likely made this inevitable. The Americans were also concerned by increasing Soviet control over Eastern Europe, while the Soviets feared the US atom bomb. Disagreements over Germany, Churchill's claim about an 'Iron Curtain' descending across Europe and the Truman Doctrine of 1947 deepened the divisions between the two sides.

Was the USA or the USSR responsible for these worsening relations?

SOURCE A

The United States and the Soviet Union stepped into the vacuum left in Europe by the decline of the European great powers.

Content removed due to copyright restrictions.

The Iron Curtain that divided Europe provided the Soviet Union with security, while condemning Eastern Europe to decades of Soviet domination and control.

From a history book published in 2015.

SOURCE B

Even if America had accepted the principle of spheres of interest, the contest could only have been delayed rather than indefinitely postponed. The Soviet Union wanted more than security. It was ideologically committed to renew the struggle against 'Western Imperialism'. Within a year of the end of the war, the Soviet Union accused its former allies of fascist and imperialist aggression. On the other hand, many people in the West felt that the police states established in Eastern Europe did not represent the liberated Europe they had fought for. For Stalin, the Cold War had begun the moment the Second World War ended. However, it took Truman longer to realise what was happening.

On March 12, 1947, President Truman issued his own declaration of the Cold War. Presenting the Truman Doctrine to Congress, he leveraged the American fear of Communism to convince Americans that they must embark on a Cold War foreign policy. Three months later, the United States announced the Marshall Plan. The Soviets rejected it, thus demonstrating the division of Europe. It became what the Americans.
Had wanted it to be a revival of the economies of Western Europe under American guidance and a move in the policy of containment. Despite the Cold War being forced upon the West, it produced European unity and lasting American involvement in European affairs – developments highly undesirable from the Soviet perspective.

SOURCE C

Basic features of the Soviet view of the world:

The USSR still lives in an antagonistic 'capitalist encirclement' with which, in the long run, there can be no permanent peaceful coexistence. As stated by Stalin in 1927 to a delegation of American workers, 'In the course of further development of international revolution, there will emerge two centres of world significance: a socialist centre, drawing to itself the countries which tend toward socialism, and a capitalist centre. The battle between these two centres for command of the world economy will decide the fate of capitalism and communism in the entire world.'

What deductions can be made about Soviet policy?

Everything must be done to advance the relative strength of the USSR as a factor in international society. No opportunity must be missed to reduce the strength and influence of capitalist powers. Soviet efforts, and those of Russia's friends abroad, must be directed toward deepening and exploiting differences and conflicts between capitalist powers. If these eventually deepen into an 'imperialist' war, this war must be turned into revolutionary upheavals within the various capitalist countries. Where individual governments stand in the way of Soviet purposes, pressure will be exerted to bring about their removal.

From George Kennan's 'Long Telegram', 22 February 1946. Kennan was an American diplomat based in Moscow. He wrote this analysis of Soviet foreign policy for the American government.

SOURCE D

US foreign policy has been characterised in the post-war period by a desire for world domination. This is the true meaning of President Truman's repeated statements that the US has a right to world leadership. All the forces of American diplomacy, the Army, Navy, and Air Force, industry, and science have been placed at the service of this policy.

The enormous relative importance of the USSR in European affairs, the independence of its foreign policy, and the economic and political aid it gives neighbouring countries, is leading to a growth in the influence of the Soviet Union in these countries and a continuing strengthening of democratic trends within them. Such a situation in Eastern Europe cannot fail to be viewed by American imperialists as an obstacle to an expansionist American foreign policy.

It should be fully realised that American preparations for a future war are being conducted with the idea of war against the Soviet Union, which, in the eyes of American imperialists, is the chief obstacle in the American path to world domination.

A telegram to the Soviet leadership from the Soviet Ambassador in the USA,
27 September 1946

SOURCE E

A cartoon published in the Soviet Union in 1946. The words on the flags held by Churchill read, 'An Iron Curtain is over Europe' and 'Anglo-Saxons must rule the World'. The figures behind Churchill Hitler and Goebbels.

SOURCE F

Whatever excuses are used to justify American claims to domination in Greece, they cannot be justified by a defence of the freedom and independence of the Greek people. American arguments for assisting Turkey are based upon a threat to the integrity of Turkish territory, though nothing threatens Turkish integrity. It is all a smokescreen for an American plan of expansion. Justifications that the USA is called upon to 'save' Greece and Turkey from expansion by the so-called 'totalitarian' states are not new. Hitler also referred to the Communists when he wanted to open the road to conquest.

The leading article in the Soviet newspaper 'Izvestia', 17 March 1947.

SOURCE G

A cartoon published in the USA in 1947. The figures on the left represent the USA, Britain and France.

Now answer all the following questions. You may use any of the sources to help you answer the questions, in addition to those sources which you are told to use. When answering the questions, use your knowledge of the topic to help you interpret and evaluate the sources.

1   Study Sources A and B.

How far do these two sources agree? Explain your answer using details of the sources.   [7]

2   Study Sources A and B.

How far do these two sources agree? Explain your answer using details of the sources.   [7]

3.   Study Source E.

Do you find this source surprising? Explain your answer using details of the source and your knowledge.   [7]

4.   Study Source F.

Why was this source published in March 1947? Explain your answer using details of the source and your knowledge.

5. Study Source G.

What is the cartoonist's message? Explain your answer using details of the source and your knowledge.

6. Study all the sources.

How far do these sources provide convincing evidence that the Soviet Union was responsible for the worsening of relations with the West? Use the sources to explain your answer. [12]
[8]

PAPER 7 ANSWERS

Answers to my chosen Questions

CHAPTER 7: Answers

Answered Question: Option B: Twentieth-century topic

1. Study Sources A and B.

How far do these two sources agree? Explain your answer using details of the sources. [7]

Areas of Agreement

Both acknowledge the power vacuum: Source A states the US and USSR "stepped into the vacuum left in Europe by the decline of the European great powers," while Source B recognises this transition of power

Both recognise Soviet control over Eastern Europe: Source A mentions the "Iron Curtain" giving the USSR "security and condemned Eastern Europe to decades of Soviet domination," while Source B refers to "police states established in Eastern Europe"

Both acknowledge the division of Europe: Source A explicitly mentions the Iron Curtain dividing Europe, Source B discusses "the division of Europe" following the Soviet rejection of the Marshall Plan

Areas of Disagreement

Timing of responsibility: Source B suggests Stalin began the Cold War immediately after WWII ended ("For Stalin, the Cold War had begun the moment the Second World War ended"), while Source A does not assign such clear chronological responsibility

Ideological motivation: Source B emphasises the USSR was "ideologically committed to renew the struggle against 'Western Imperialism,'" suggesting deeper motivations beyond security, while Source A focuses more on the security aspect

Western response: Source B portrays the West as initially reactive ("it took Truman longer to realise what was happening") and suggests the Cold War was "forced on the West," while Source A does not make such claims about Western passivity

Generally, the sources agree on the basic facts of division but disagree on the extent of Soviet responsibility and ideological motivation.

2. **Study Sources C and D.**

How far does Source C prove that Source D was wrong? Explain your answer using details of the sources and your knowledge.

How Source C contradicts Source D
Source D claims: The US seeks "world domination" and views the USSR as "the chief obstacle in the American path to world domination"
Source C suggests the opposite: The USSR sees itself in "antagonistic 'capitalist encirclement'" and Stalin's 1927 quote shows Soviet expectation of eventual "battle between these two centres for command of the world economy"
Key contradictions
- Who seeks domination:
Source D claims the US seeks world domination, but Source C shows the USSR planning for "command of the world economy"
- Who is encircling whom:
Source D suggests the US encirclement of the USSR, but Source C shows the Soviet perception of being surrounded by capitalists

- Aggressive intentions:

Source D portrays the US as the aggressor, but Source C outlines the Soviet strategy to "reduce the strength and influence of capitalist powers" and exploit conflicts between them

Limitations of Source C as proof

- Perspective bias:

Source C is from American diplomat Kennan, representing the US interpretation of Soviet intentions rather than definitive proof

- Date significance: Written February 1946, before some events mentioned in Source D (September 1946)

- Interpretation vs. fact:

Kennan's analysis may reflect American fears rather than actual Soviet policy.

In conclusion, Source C provides strong contradictory evidence but cannot definitively "prove" Source D wrong, as both represent partisan perspectives from opposite sides.

[8]

3. Study Source E.

Do you find this source surprising? Explain your answer using details of the source and your knowledge. [7]

Surprising elements:

- Comparison to Hitler:
The cartoon shows Churchill flanked by Hitler and Goebbels, suggesting Western leaders are equivalent to Nazis - exceptionally provocative given the recent alliance against Nazi Germany

- Timing irony:
Published in 1946, when the wartime alliance was still a recent memory, making the Nazi comparison particularly shocking

- "Anglo-Saxons must rule the World":
Presents Western calls for democracy as imperialism, inverting the typical Western narrative

Not surprising elements:

- Propaganda context:
Soviet cartoons regularly used extreme imagery to demonise opponents - a standard propaganda technique

- Response to Churchill's speech:
The Iron Curtain reference directly responds to Churchill's March 1946 Fulton speech, making a counter-attack predictable

- Historical precedent: Soviet media had long portrayed Western powers as imperialist, so the content fits established patterns

Historical context knowledge:
- Churchill's Iron Curtain speech (March 1946) was indeed provocative from a Soviet perspective
- The cartoon reflects Stalin's growing suspicion of former allies
- Soviet propaganda often used Nazi comparisons to delegitimise opponents

The extreme nature and Nazi comparisons are surprising given recent cooperation, but the propagandistic response to Churchill's speech was predictable in the deteriorating relationship.

4. Study Source F.

Why was this source published in March 1947? Explain your answer using details of the source and your knowledge. [8]

Direct response to the Truman Doctrine:
- Date significance: Published March 17, 1947 - just 5 days after Truman announced his doctrine on March 12, 1947
- Direct references: Explicitly mentions US "giving assistance to Turkey" and claims about "defence of the freedom and independence of the Greek people"
- Counter-narrative: Provides Soviet interpretation of American intervention in Greece and Turkey

Strategic Soviet purposes:
- Delegitimise US intervention:
Portrays US aid as "smokescreen for an American plan of expansion" rather than humanitarian assistance
- Historical parallel:

Compares US actions to Hitler's justifications ("Hitler also referred to the Communists when he wanted to open the road to conquests")

- Domestic audience: Reinforces to the Soviet people that the US is the aggressor, not the USSR

Broader Cold War context:

- Containment response:

The Truman Doctrine marked the formal US policy of containment, requiring a Soviet counter-response

- European influence:

Soviet concern about losing influence in the Mediterranean region

- Ideological battle:

Need to frame US actions as imperialist rather than defensive

Conclusion:

This source was published as an immediate propaganda response to the Truman Doctrine, aiming to reframe US containment policy as aggressive imperialism and maintain Soviet legitimacy in the developing Cold War.

5. Study Source G.

What is the cartoonist's message?
Explain your answer using details of the source and your knowledge.
[8]

Main message;
Western Unity Against Soviet Threat:
- Visual symbolism:
Three Western figures (the USA, Britain, and France) stand together in a unified stance
- Confrontational positioning:
They face toward what appears to be a Soviet threat (off-frame)
- Shared purpose:
Their similar posture suggests a coordinated Western response

Specific elements and meanings:
- Timing (1947):
Published during the crucial year of the Truman Doctrine and the Marshall Plan, it emphasised Western alliance-building
- Body language:
A determined, resolute stance suggests Western commitment to resist Soviet expansion
- Equal positioning:

Shows Britain and France as equal partners with the US, emphasising a genuine alliance rather than US domination

Historical context reflected:

- Marshall Plan cooperation:
Reflects growing Western economic and political coordination
- NATO foundations: Anticipates a military alliance that would formalise in 1949
- Containment visualisation:
Shows the Western strategy of collective resistance to Soviet influence

Alternative interpretations:

- Aggressive stance:
It could be seen as Western powers preparing for confrontation rather than defence
- Exclusion:
The three-power focus excludes other nations, suggesting an exclusive Western club

Cartoonist's message:
The West must stand united against Soviet expansion, presenting a coordinated Western response as a necessary and justified defensive measure rather than an aggressive alliance.

6. Study all the sources.

How far do these sources provide convincing evidence that the Soviet Union was responsible for the worsening of relations with the West? Use the sources to explain your answer. [12]

Evidence suggesting Soviet responsibility:
Strong evidence from Sources A, B, and C:

- Source B:

States clearly "For Stalin, the Cold War had begun the moment the Second World War ended" and describes the USSR as "ideologically committed to renew the struggle against 'Western Imperialism'"

- Source C:

Kennan's analysis shows the Soviet strategy to "reduce the strength and influence of capitalist powers" and exploit conflicts between them

- Source A:

Acknowledges Soviet imposition of control over Eastern Europe, creating the Iron Curtain

Behavioural evidence:

- Soviet rejection of the Marshall Plan (Source B) demonstrated unwillingness to cooperate
- Establishment of "police states" in Eastern Europe (Source B) violated wartime agreements about democratic governments

Evidence suggesting Western/American responsibility:

Counter-evidence from Sources D, E, and F:

- Source D:

Claims US seeks "world domination" and views USSR as an obstacle to "expansionist American foreign policy"

- Source F:

Portrays US intervention in Greece/Turkey as "American plan of expansion"

- Source E:

Shows Soviet perception of Western, particularly British, imperialism

Alternative interpretation:

- Sources suggest both sides contributed through mutual misunderstanding and competing security needs

Evaluation of source reliability:

Limitations affecting assessment:

- Source bias:

Sources C and G are American/Western perspective; Sources D, E, and F are Soviet perspective

- Propaganda elements: Sources E and F are clearly propagandistic, limiting their reliability as evidence

- Contemporary viewpoints:

All sources are contemporary, lacking historical hindsight

Strengths for assessment:

- Source B:

Recent historical analysis (2015) provides a balanced retrospective view

- Variety: Multiple perspectives allow cross-referencing of claims
- Official documents:

Sources C and D represent genuine diplomatic assessments

Conclusion:

Moderate evidence for Soviet responsibility:

Sources B and C provide the most convincing evidence that Soviet ideological commitment and strategic decisions (rejecting cooperation, imposing control over Eastern Europe) significantly contributed to worsening relations.

Chapter 8

Paper 8

February/March 2021

INFORMATION
- The total mark for this paper is 60.
- The number of marks for each question or part question is shown in brackets [ ].

DC (NF) 200117/2
© UCLES 2021

CHAPTER 8

Paper 8

SECTION A: CORE CONTENT

Answer any **two** questions from this Section.

1. 1848–49 was a period of turmoil in Europe.

    (a) What were the March Laws passed in Hungary in 1848? [4]

    (b) Why were the reform banquets in 1847–48 crucial in France? [6]

    (c) How far was the revolution of February 1848 in France a failure? Explain your answer. [10]

2. There were many decades of struggle before Italy was unified.

    (a) Describe how the unification of Italy was completed in 1870–71. [4]

    (b) Why was Austria able to maintain its position in Italy in 1848–49?

[6]

(c) 'Garibaldi was the crucial factor in the creation of the Kingdom of Italy in 1861.' How far do you agree with this statement? Explain your answer.
[10]

3   The issue of slavery was of great importance in the USA.

(a) Describe the work of the Freedmen's Bureau.
[4]

(b) Why was there support for slavery in the South?
[6]

(c) How vital was leadership in the North's victory in the Civil War? Explain your answer.
[10]

4   Europeans intervened in many parts of the world.

(a) Describe direct rule by France in Senegal.
[4]

(b) Why did the Chinese not welcome European intervention in their country?
[6]

(c) How important were greased cartridges in causing the Indian Mutiny? Explain your answer.

[10]

5   Few people were happy with the outcome of the Paris Peace Conference.

(a) Describe the benefits Lloyd George wanted Britain to gain from the Paris Peace Conference.

[4]

(b) Why did Clemenceau not get everything he wanted at the Paris Peace Conference?

[6]

(c) 'The main reason why Germany hated the Treaty of Versailles was the reduction made to its armed forces.' How far do you agree with this statement? Explain your answer.

[10]

6   Hitler was able to carry out much of his foreign policy unopposed.

(a) What part did Germany's armed forces play in the Spanish Civil War?

[4]

(b) Why did Britain and France do little when Germany remilitarised the Rhineland?

[6]

(c) Are you surprised that Chamberlain signed the Munich Agreement of September 1938? Explain your answer.

[10]

7 The USA resisted communism in various parts of the world.

(a) Describe how the fighting in Korea came to an end in 1953. [4]

(b) Why was the Cuban Missile Crisis resolved peacefully?

[6]

(c) Were it events in Vietnam or events in the USA that forced America to withdraw from Vietnam? Explain your answer.

[10]

8   There were many threats to Soviet control over Eastern Europe.

(a) Describe the activities of 'Solidarity' in Poland during the 1980s.
[4]

(b) Why did Gorbachev do little to defend Soviet control over Eastern Europe?
[6]

(c) Which was the more serious problem for the USSR: the events in Hungary in 1956 or the events in Czechoslovakia in 1968? Explain your answer. [10]

SECTION B: DEPTH STUDIES

Answer any **one** question from this Section.

DEPTH STUDY A: THE FIRST WORLD WAR, 1914–18

9 The war at sea was an essential aspect of the First World War.

(a) Describe how the convoy system worked.
[4]

(b) Why was the German U-boat campaign important?
[6]

(c) 'The Battle of Jutland achieved little for either side.' How far do you agree with this statement? Explain your answer.
[10]

10 Despite victory over Russia, Germany asked for an armistice in November 1918.

(a) Describe the terms of the Armistice of 1918.

[4]

(b) Why did Russia sign the Treaty of Brest-Litovsk in March 1918?

[6]

(c) 'Germany lost the war because of problems on its Home Front.' How far do you agree with this statement? Explain your answer.

[10]

DEPTH STUDY B: GERMANY, 1918–45

11 The Weimar Republic had a difficult start.

(a) What were the aims of Kapp and the Freikorps in the putsch of 1920?

[4]

(b) Why did Germany experience hyperinflation in the early 1920s?

[6]

(c) 'Stresemann was unsuccessful in bringing about the recovery of the Weimar Republic.' How far do you agree with this statement? Explain your answer. [10]

12 Many groups suffered under Nazi rule.

(a) Describe Nazi persecution of any **two** minority groups in Germany. [4]

(b) Why did some young people oppose the Nazi regime? [6]

(c) 'The Nazis had consistent policies towards women.' How far do you agree with this statement? Explain your answer. [10]

DEPTH STUDY C: RUSSIA, 1905–41

13 The Bolsheviks faced problems after they had taken power.

(a) Describe how the Bolsheviks took power on 6–8 November 1917. [4]

(b) Why was the New Economic Policy important to Lenin? [6]

(c) Are you surprised that the Whites lost the Civil War? Explain your answer. [10]

14 Stalin demonstrated his ruthlessness in gaining and keeping power.

(a) Describe how Stalin used his control over art and culture. [4]

(b) Why was the 'Great Terror' of 1936–38 important to Stalin? [6]

(c) Are you surprised that Stalin, not Trotsky, emerged as the leader by 1928? Explain your answer. 10

DEPTH STUDY D: THE UNITED STATES, 1919–41

15 Different groups in 1920s America had very different experiences.

(a) Describe the changes in the way Americans spent their leisure time in the 1920s.

[4]

(b) Why was there support for the introduction of Prohibition?

[6]

(c) 'Black Americans were the main victims of intolerance in the 1920s.' How far do you agree with this statement? Explain your answer.

[10]

16 The Wall Street Crash had significant consequences.

(a) Describe what it was like to live in a 'Hooverville'.

[4]

(b) Why was the Wall Street Crash important for the USA? [6]

(c) 'Hoover's failings influenced the result of the 1932 Presidential election more than Roosevelt's strengths.' How far do you agree with this statement? Explain your answer.
[10]

DEPTH STUDY E: CHINA, c.1930–c.1990

17 The Nationalists and the Communists struggled for control of China.

(a) What was the Jiangxi Soviet?
[4]

(b) Why was the Nationalist government reluctant to deal with the Japanese invasion of China?
[6]

(c) 'Once the Long March was completed, the Communists' problems were over.' How far do you agree with this statement? Explain your answer.
[10]

18 Mao dominated China's foreign policy for many years.

(a) What did Deng Xiaoping introduce as the main changes in foreign policy?
[4]

(b) Why was Hong Kong important to China even though it was under British control?

[6]

(c) 'Mao's foreign policy was a success.' How far do you agree with this statement? Explain your answer. [10]

19 South Africa underwent significant changes after the Second World War.

(a) What was the Population Registration Act of 1950? [4]

(b) Why did the South African government establish an apartheid state in the 1950s? [6]

(c) 'Repression by South African governments ensured that there was little opposition to apartheid between 1950 and 1966.' How far do you agree with this statement? Explain your answer. [10]

20 The struggle over apartheid continued into the 1970s.

(a) What were the aims of the Black Consciousness Movement?

[4]

(b) Why did the South African government want black South Africans to live in Bantustans (Homelands)?

[6]

(c) 'During the period 1966 to 1980, opposition to the apartheid state from outside South Africa was more effective than opposition from within the country.' How far do you agree with this statement? Explain your answer.

[10]

DEPTH STUDY G: ISRAELIS AND PALESTINIANS SINCE 1945

21 The issue of Palestinian refugees has been complicated to solve.

(a) Describe the events that led to some Palestinians becoming refugees in 1948.
  [4]

(b) Why have some Arab states been reluctant to help the Palestinian refugees?
  [6]

(c) 'Palestinian refugees have been helped more by the United Nations than by the Palestine Liberation Organisation (PLO).' How far do you agree with this statement? Explain your answer.
  [10]

22 Finding a peace settlement between the Palestinians and the Israelis has proved to be difficult.

(a) What is the Palestinian Authority?
  [4]

(b) Why was the Second Intifada important?

[6]

(c) 'Divisions between Palestinians have done more than divisions within Israel to hinder the peace process.' How far do you agree with this statement? Explain your answer 10

CHAPTER 8: Answers

SECTION A: CORE CONTENT

Answer any **two** questions from this Section.
Answered Questions: 3 and 7

3   **The issue of slavery was of great importance in the USA.**

a.   **Describe the work of the Freedmen's Bureau. [4]**

- The Freedmen's Bureau helped formerly enslaved people after the Civil War. It was set up in 1865 to support freed African Americans in the South.
- It provided food, clothing, and medical care – The Bureau gave emergency support to millions of people in need.
- It helped set up schools and education for Black Americans – The Bureau established thousands of schools and encouraged literacy and learning.
- It offered legal support and helped with employment – The Bureau assisted freedmen in finding jobs and protected their legal rights, especially in unfair contracts.

b. Why was there support for slavery in the South? [6]

- The Southern economy depended on slavery – Plantations in the South relied on enslaved people to grow crops like cotton, tobacco, and sugar, which brought in large profits.
- Many white Southerners feared economic loss – Ending slavery would mean paying wages, which many plantation owners believed would ruin their businesses.
- Slavery was part of Southern culture and society – It had existed for generations, and many people saw it as a usual way of life.
- Racism was deeply rooted in Southern beliefs – Many white Southerners believed Black people were inferior and should be kept in a lower position in society.
- Some used religion to defend slavery – Supporters argued that the Bible allowed slavery and that it was part of God's plan.
- Fear of rebellion or social change – Many feared that freeing enslaved people would lead to uprisings or upset the existing social order.

c. **How important was leadership in the North's victory in the Civil War? Explain your answer.**

[10]

Arguments for the importance of leadership:
- **Strong leadership from Abraham Lincoln.**
- He kept the Union united, gave clear purpose to the war (like ending slavery), and made key decisions at difficult times.
- **Military leadership improved during the war.** Generals like Ulysses S. Grant and William Tecumseh Sherman led essential victories, such as at Vicksburg and the March to the Sea.
- **Better use of resources by Northern leaders.** Union commanders learned to use their advantages in the workforce and industry more effectively as the war progressed.
- **Lincoln's Emancipation Proclamation helped**; It weakened the South by encouraging enslaved people to escape and gave the North a moral cause.

Arguments for other important reasons:
- **The North had more resources.** The Union had a larger population, more factories, better railways, and more financial resources to support a long war.

- **The Southern economy struggled.**
  The South faced shortages of weapons, food, and money, especially as the Union navy blockaded Southern ports.
- **Control of the navy and railways.**
  The North's control of transport and sea routes gave it an advantage in moving troops and supplies.
- **The South's military leadership weakened over time;**
  Early Southern leaders like Robert E. Lee were skilled, but the Confederacy could not replace losses as the war went on.

Judgement:
- Leadership was **critical** to the North's victory, especially Lincoln's decisions and the strong generals later in the war.
- However, the North's economic strength, larger population, and control of resources were also significant factors.
- So, leadership played a key role, but **it worked together with other advantages** the North had to win the war.

7 **The USA resisted communism in various parts of the world.**

a. **Describe how the fighting in Korea came to an end in 1953.**
   [4]

- An armistice was signed on 27 July 1953. This agreement ended the fighting, but was not a formal peace treaty.
- The armistice created a Demilitarised Zone (DMZ) – A buffer zone was set up around the 38th parallel to separate North and South Korea.
- Both sides agreed to stop fighting and return to the original borders – Neither side gained much land, and the division between North and South Korea remained.
- Peace talks had gone on for two years before the armistice. The war reached a stalemate, and both sides agreed that it could not be easily won.

b. **Why was the Cuban Missile Crisis resolved peacefully?**
   [6]

- Both the USA and USSR wanted to avoid nuclear war – The threat of a nuclear conflict was too significant, so both sides were willing to

compromise.
- President Kennedy used a naval blockade instead of attacking – This gave the Soviet Union time to respond without immediate violence.
- Khrushchev agreed to remove missiles from Cuba – In return, Kennedy promised not to invade Cuba and secretly agreed to remove US missiles from Turkey.
- Communication helped reduce tension – Letters between Kennedy and Khrushchev allowed both leaders to find a peaceful solution.
- Both sides could claim a victory – The USSR removed missiles, but the US promised not to invade Cuba, so neither side felt utterly defeated.
- The crisis shocked the world and encouraged diplomacy – It led to better communication between the superpowers, like the setting up of the 'hotline' between Washington and Moscow.

c. **Were it events in Vietnam or events in the USA that forced America to withdraw from Vietnam? Explain your answer.**
   [10]

Arguments for events in Vietnam forcing the withdrawal:

- **The Viet Cong used effective guerrilla tactics.**
  The US Army struggled to fight an enemy that employed hit-and-run tactics and was familiar with the terrain.
- **The Tet Offensive shocked US leaders.**
  In 1968, the Viet Cong attacked over 100 cities, showing they were stronger than Americans had believed.
- **The war dragged on with no clear victory.**
  US forces could not defeat the Viet Cong or win the support of the South Vietnamese people.
- **High American casualties.**
  The rising number of dead and injured soldiers weakened morale and made it harder to justify staying in the war.

Arguments for events in the USA forcing the withdrawal:

- **Massive anti-war protests.**
  Protests, especially by students, grew across America, pressuring the government to end the war.
- **The media turned public opinion against the war.**
  Graphic news coverage and images of violence, such as the My Lai Massacre, shocked Americans.

- **Political pressure on the US government,** President Johnson chose not to run for re-election in 1968, and President Nixon promised to bring "peace with honour."
- **The war became too expensive.** The cost of fighting the war hurt the US economy and led to public dissatisfaction.

Judgement:
- *Both events in* Vietnam *and in the* USA *played a role in forcing American withdrawal.*
- *However, events inside the USA, such as protests, media influence, and political pressure, made it impossible for the government to continue the war.*
- *Therefore, events in the USA were more critical, because even though the US military could keep fighting, public opinion and politics at home forced them to stop.*

DEPTH STUDY A: THE FIRST WORLD WAR, 1914–18

Answer any **one** question from this Section.

Answered Questions: 9 and 12

9. The war at sea was an essential aspect of the First World War.

a. Describe how the convoy system worked.
   [4]

- Merchant ships travelled in groups — Instead of sailing alone, supply ships crossed the sea together in large groups called convoys.
- Warships escorted the convoys — Armed naval ships (like destroyers) protected the merchant ships from enemy attacks, especially from German U-boats.
- The system used careful planning and coordination — Convoys were organised to take safer routes and were timed to avoid enemy submarines.
- It reduced losses from submarine attacks — The presence of warships made it harder for U-boats to sink ships without being detected or destroyed.

b. Why was the German U-boat campaign important?
   [6]

- It aimed to cut off Britain's supplies – German U-boats (submarines) tried to sink merchant ships bringing food, weapons, and other goods to Britain, hoping to starve the country into surrender.
- It caused severe shortages in Britain – The sinking of supply ships led to rationing and hardship for civilians, putting pressure on the British government.
- It brought other countries into the war – Unrestricted submarine warfare led to the sinking of neutral ships, like the American Lusitania, which helped push the USA into the war in 1917.
- It forced Britain to change its naval tactics. Britain had to adopt the convoy system to protect its ships, changing the way it managed sea transport.
- It showed the importance of naval power in modern warfare. The campaign demonstrated that submarines could pose a serious threat to even the strongest naval countries, such as Britain.

c. *'The Battle of Jutland achieved little for either side.' How far do you agree with this statement? Explain your answer.*

[10]

Reasons to agree that it achieved little:

- **No clear winner.**
  Both the British and German navies claimed victory, but neither side gained complete control of the sea.
- **Heavy losses on both sides.**
  The British lost more ships and sailors, while the Germans remained essentially stuck in port afterwards.
- **Naval positions did not change.**
  The British Grand Fleet remained in control of the North Sea, and the German High Seas Fleet stayed blocked in its ports.
- **Did not end the naval threat.**
  Submarine warfare continued, and Germany still relied on U-boats to try to win the war at sea.

Reasons to disagree (it did have some achievements):

- **Britain maintained naval superiority.**
  The Royal Navy stayed dominant, meaning Germany could not break the British blockade.
- **The German fleet did not sail again in full force.**
  After the battle, the German navy shifted its focus to avoiding direct battles and relying more on submarines.

- **Boosted British morale.**
  Although losses were high, the British public saw it as proof that their navy could meet and challenge Germany's fleet.
- **Strategic success for the Allies.**
  The blockade of German ports continued, weakening the German economy and war effort over time.

Judgement:
- The Battle of Jutland did not produce a clear or dramatic victory, so in that sense, it achieved little in the short term.
- However, in the long term, it confirmed British control of the seas and limited Germany's naval power, which helped Britain continue its blockade.
- So, while the battle may have seemed indecisive, it had significant effects, especially in keeping the pressure on Germany.
- Therefore, the statement is partly true, but overall, the battle had more importance than it first appeared.

12. **Many groups suffered under Nazi rule.**

a. Describe Nazi persecution of any two minority groups in Germany.
     [4]

Persecution of Jews:
- Nazis passed laws that took away Jewish rights, such as the Nuremberg Laws that banned marriages between Jews and non-Jews.
- Jews were forced to live in ghettos, lose their businesses, and were later sent to concentration camps.

Persecution of the Roma (Gypsies):
- The Nazis considered the Roma people racially inferior and arrested many.
- They were sent to camps, sterilised to prevent them from having children, and many were killed.

b. Why did some young people oppose the Nazi regime? [6]

- Nazi control was strict and limited freedom. Many young people did not like being forced to join Nazi groups like the Hitler Youth or follow Nazi rules.
- Opposition to Nazi ideas – Some young people disagreed with Nazi racism, violence, and hatred, especially towards Jews and minorities.
- Reaction to propaganda and censorship.

Young people were unhappy about the lack of freedom in music, art, and books, as the Nazis banned many cultural activities.
- Economic hardships and war fears.
The growing war and hardships made some young people lose faith in the Nazi government.
- Desire for independence and freedom.
Many young people wanted to live everyday lives and rebelled against strict Nazi control through secret clubs or anti-Nazi graffiti.
- Influence of religious or family beliefs.
Some young people opposed the Nazis because of their family's spiritual values or beliefs that contradicted Nazi ideology.

c. *'The Nazis had consistent policies towards women.' How far do you agree with this statement? Explain your answer.*
   [10]

Reasons to agree with consistency in Nazi policies towards women:
- **Focus on motherhood and family.**
The Nazis encouraged women to stay at home and have many children to increase the "Aryan" population.
- **The "Three Ks" policy.**

Kinder (children), Küche (kitchen), Kirche (church) was a slogan promoting women's roles in family and home life.

- **Marriage loans and awards.**
The Nazis gave loans to women to leave work and marry, and medals (Mother's Cross) to women with many children, supporting their policy of increasing births.
- **Discouragement of women's careers.**
Women were encouraged to quit their jobs, especially in professions such as medicine or law, to focus on their families.

Reasons to disagree (some inconsistency in Nazi policies):

- **Women needed to work during the war.**
As World War II progressed, many women were required to work in factories and support the war effort, contradicting earlier policies that had discouraged women from entering the workforce.
- **Education and training programs.**
The Nazis still provided education to prepare girls for roles beyond just motherhood, including some physical training and skills.
- **Women's roles changed with circumstances.**
Despite promoting traditional roles, the demands of war forced the Nazis to adapt their policies to include women in the workforce.

Judgement:
- The Nazis had a clear and consistent message early on: women's primary role was to support family and increase the Aryan population.
- **However,** during the war, practical needs led to changes, requiring women to work and take on roles outside the home.
- Therefore, while the core policy was consistent, the Nazis had to adapt their approach over time.
- So, the statement is partly true, but the policies were not entirely consistent throughout the Nazi era.

Paper 9

Chapter 9

HISTORY 0470/23

Paper 2   May/June 2021

2 hours

INFORMATION
- The total mark for this paper is 50.
- The number of marks for each question or part question is shown in brackets [ ].

DC (MB/CGW) 200214/3
© UCLES 2021

CHAPTER 9
Option A: Nineteenth-century topic

HOW FAR DID AUSTRIA AND FRANCE HINDER THE PROCESS OF ITALIAN UNIFICATION?

Study the Background Information and the sources carefully, and then answer all the questions.

Background Information

Several factors contributed to the process of Italian unification. Many of these were internal to Italy and included the well-known exploits of men like Mazzini and Garibaldi, who played a crucial role in driving the Risorgimento. The diplomacy and politics of Cavour were also important. However, some historians have emphasised the critical impact of the policies and actions of other European countries such as Austria and France.

How far did the actions of Austria and France hinder Italian unification?

SOURCE A

In my opinion, this wealthy land can only be punished most severely by the removal of those means which have led it to such disobedience. For what is exile to the rich when they can take their money with them and continue to cause trouble? To humble the disloyal rich and protect the loyal citizen should be the principle on which, from now on, the government of Lombardy-Venice should be based. My letter aims to beg Your Excellency not to give the ringleaders any mercy and to let justice run its course completely.

A letter from Field Marshal Radetzky to the Foreign Minister of the Austrian Empire, 1849. Radetzky Was in charge of the Austrian army in northern Italy.

SOURCE B

Napoleon III said, 'he would like to do something for Italy.' By the 1850s, he was alleged to have long been in sympathy with the Italian cause, but had actually done little to help. In fact, quite the opposite, because in 1849 he had sent the French army to crush the Roman Republic, which they did, remaining afterwards to garrison the city and protect the Pope. At the secret meeting with Cavour at Plombières in July 1858, Napoleon's aim seems to have been not to unite Italy but to keep it divided into a federation of comparatively powerless separate states. As the war of 1859 began, Napoleon proclaimed that his aims were not conquest but 'to restore Italy to the Italians'. However, after two bloody battles, he returned to France. Austria surrendered Lombardy to Piedmont but kept Venetia. Victor Emmanuel II and Cavour felt that Napoleon had betrayed them by returning home before fulfilling his promise to free Italy. Napoleon made some amends in 1866 when he came into possession of Venetia and handed it over to the Kingdom of Italy. Italians were also angry that he refused to withdraw the occupying French troops from Rome until forced to do so by France's war with Prussia in 1870.

From a history book published in 2001.

SOURCE C

In 1858, neither Napoleon III nor Cavour wanted or expected Italian unification to occur. The establishment of an Italian kingdom was a significant achievement that, although partly facilitated by Napoleon III and Cavour, happened to a considerable degree despite their efforts. It is certain that Napoleon's phrase about 'doing something for Italy' was not intended to involve anything more than the expulsion of the Austrians from the northern part of Italy, and that it did not at all involve Italy's unification.

It is incorrect to think that Napoleon ventured into Italy because a romantic attachment to the cause of Italian nationalism blinded him. He took the action he did because he thought it would help to extend French influence in Italy. At Plombières, he planned to expel Austrian influence from the north and centre of Italy and to create a Kingdom of Italy large enough to be an applicable French client state. The Two Sicilies could perhaps be persuaded to become another French client state. The Pope would be persuaded to accept the whole process by being made President of an Italian

Federation to which the new Italian states would belong.

However, to minimise the help Napoleon gave to Italy is to ignore the facts. The work of Cavour in the north and the centre up to April 1860 depended entirely on Napoleon.

From a history book published in 1956.

SOURCE D

The aim of politicians must be to avoid, as much as possible, all the causes of dispute that still exist in Europe. The country that poses the greatest threat to European peace is Italy, because its political structure does not please anyone. To alter its structure, either a revolution or a war is needed. These are extreme solutions, and who would be powerful enough to impose their will on so many divided countries and to unite so many states and give them a common purpose?

Nonetheless, I believe that one might try something that might satisfy nearly everybody. An Italian Confederation might be established with the Pope as its figurehead, without altering any territorial boundaries. Austria, due to its Lombard territories, would be a member.

Some notes written by Napoleon III for himself and his foreign minister, 1856.

SOURCE E

As soon as I entered the Emperor's study, he began by saying that he had decided to support Piedmont with all his power in a war against Austria. He agreed that it was necessary to drive the Austrians out of Italy. However, how was Italy to be organised after that? After a lengthy discussion, we decided on the following principles. There would be a kingdom of Upper Italy under the House of Savoy. The rest of the Papal States, together with Tuscany, would form a kingdom of Central Italy. The Neapolitan frontier would be left unchanged. These Italian states would form a confederation, with the presidency held by the Pope. This arrangement seems entirely acceptable to me. Your Majesty would be sovereign of the wealthiest and most powerful half of Italy, and so would dominate the whole of Italy.

From a report by Cavour to Victor Emmanuel about his meeting at Plombières with Napoleon III, July 1858

SOURCE F

Do not forget the gratitude we owe to Napoleon III and the French army, so many of whose brave soldiers have been killed for the cause of Italy.
Written by Garibaldi after the Peace of Villafranca in August 1859.

SOURCE G

FREE ITALY (?)

Published in a British magazine in July 1859. The figures represent (left to right) Austria, Italy and Napoleon III. Italy is wearing the Papal crown.

Now answer all the following questions. You may use any of the sources to help you answer the questions, in addition to those sources which you are told to use. When answering the questions, use your knowledge of the topic to help you interpret and evaluate the sources.

1   Study Source A.

Why did Radetzky send this letter in 1849? Explain your answer using details of the source and your knowledge. [7]

2   Study Sources B and C.

How far do these two sources agree? Explain your answer using details of the sources. [7]

3   Study Sources D and E.

Why do these two accounts of Napoleon's plans for Italy differ? Explain your answer using details of the sources and your knowledge. [8]

4   Study Source F.

Are you surprised by this source? Explain your answer using details of the source and your knowledge. [8]

5   Study Source G.

What is the cartoonist's message? Explain your answer using details of the source and your knowledge. [8]

6   Study all the sources.

How far do these sources provide convincing evidence that Austria and France hindered the process of Italian unification? Use the sources to explain your answer.

Option B: Twentieth-century topic

DID FRANCE GET WHAT IT WANTED AT THE PARIS PEACE CONFERENCE?

Study the Background Information and the sources carefully, and then answer all the questions.

Background Information

During the First World War, France suffered significant damage to its industry, land and people. Understandably, at the Paris Peace Conference, the French wanted to punish Germany for the damage it had inflicted on France and to weaken Germany to ensure that it could not threaten France again. France attempted to achieve these aims by demanding the following: the disarmament of Germany, the imposition of high reparations, the Rhineland to become an independent state, and the transfer of Alsace-Lorraine and the Saar Basin to France.

To what extent did France succeed in getting Germany harshly punished?

SOURCE A

It was a widely held idea that Clemenceau was personally responsible for the damage the Treaty inflicted on Wilson's ideals. It was believed that he had influenced the French press and Parliament to support his extreme demands. This is wrong. In Paris during 1919, it would not have been easy to find another French politician as moderate and open to negotiation and compromise as Clemenceau. What was not initially understood was the extent to which the dominant French political forces combined to press their fears and hatreds upon him.

By January 1920, Clemenceau was out of power. The primary reason Clemenceau was perceived as having betrayed France was his alleged leniency during the Treaty negotiations. Clemenceau devoted the last nine years of his life to defending himself against these charges. He wrote a rambling book, which is nothing more than an attempt to prove that he had done all that he could to bring about a peace favourable to France. It was not well-received. He had dreamt of being elected as president of France after the war. Nevertheless, after the events of the peace conference, his election was unthinkable.

From a history book published in 1969.

Souce B

A British cartoon entitled 'The Reckoning' was published in April 1919. Germany is saying, 'Monstrous, I call it. Why, it is fully a quarter of what we should have made them pay, if we had won.' 'Indemnity demands' refers to the reparations.

SOURCE C

We came to Versailles hoping for the peace of justice which had been promised. We were shocked when we read the demands, the victorious violence of our enemies. The more deeply we penetrate the spirit of this Treaty, the more convinced we become of the impossibility of carrying it out. The demands of this Treaty are more than the German people can bear. Germany must declare itself ready to bear all the war expenses of its enemies, which would exceed many times over the total amount of German assets. Meanwhile, its enemies also demand reparations for damage suffered by their civilian population.

The reconstruction of our economic life has been made impossible. We must renounce the realisation of all our aims in the spheres of politics, economics and ideas. The German people are excluded from the League of Nations, to which is entrusted all work of common interest to the world. Thus must a whole people sign its own death sentence.

Count von Brockdorff-Rantzau's response when shown the proposed terms of the Treaty of Versailles, May 1919. He was the leader of the German delegation at the Paris Peace Conference.

SOURCE D

The Allied Powers have given the most careful consideration to the observations of the German Delegation. The protest of the German Delegation shows that they fail to understand the position in which Germany stands today. They seem to think that Germany has only to make sacrifices to attain peace, as if this were simply the end of some mere struggle for territory and power. In the view of the Allied Powers, this war was the greatest crime against humanity ever committed.

Justice, therefore, is the only possible basis for the settlement of this terrible war. That is why the Allied Powers have insisted that Germany must undertake to make reparations. Reparation for wrongs inflicted is the essence of justice. That, too, is why Germany must submit to special punishments. The Allies, therefore, believe that the peace is fundamentally a just peace.

The German Delegation appears to have seriously misinterpreted the economic and financial conditions. There is no intention on the part of the Allies to strangle Germany or to prevent it from taking its proper place in international trade and commerce. Provided that Germany keeps to the terms of the treaty and abandons its aggressive traditions, it shall have fair treatment in the purchase of raw materials and the sale of goods.

Clemenceau's letter replying to the objections of the German Delegation, May 1919. Clemenceau was
replying on behalf of all the peacemakers.

SOURCE E

TERMS OF TREATY BETTER THAN GERMANY DESERVES WAR MAKERS MUST BE MADE TO SUFFER

Germany is beginning to suffer the consequences of its actions in the First World War, and it is making a terrible fuss about it. That was expected, but it will not provide significant help to Germany. If Germany had the punishment it deserved, there would be no Germany left to bear any burden at all. It would be wiped off the map. Stern justice would demand that Germany be punished ten times harder than it will have to bear.

The prevailing sentiment in the country is not that Germany is being dealt with too harshly, but rather that it is being let off too lightly.

From a British newspaper, May 1919.

SOURCE F

At the Peace Table

A cartoon published in a Norwegian magazine in August 1919. Norway was neutral in the First World War. Clemenceau is introducing the German delegates to the terms of the Treaty of Versailles and is
saying to them, 'Take your seats, gentlemen!'

1   Study Source A.

What impressions does this source give of Clemenceau? Explain your answer using details of the source. [6]

2   Study Source B.

Why was this source published at this time? Explain your answer using details of the source and your knowledge.   [6]

3.   Study Sources C and D.

How far does Source C make Source D surprising? Explain your answer using details of the sources and your knowledge.   [8]

4.   Study Source E.

How valuable is this source to a historian studying the Treaty of Versailles? Explain your answer using details of the source and your knowledge.   [8]

5.   Study Source F.

What is the cartoonist's message? Explain your answer using details of the source and your knowledge.

[8]

6. Study all the sources.

How far do these sources provide convincing evidence that Germany was punished as much as the French wanted? Use the sources to explain your answer. [12]

CHAPTER 9

Answered Questions:

Option B: Twentieth-century topic

DID FRANCE GET WHAT IT WANTED AT THE PARIS PEACE CONFERENCE?

1. Study Source A.

What impressions does this source give of Clemenceau? Explain your answer using details of the source. [6]

Impressions of Clemenceau from Source A:
The source presents Clemenceau as a moderate and reasonable leader who has been unfairly criticised. The following impressions emerge:
Moderate Nature:
• The source describes him as "moderate, and open to negotiation and compromise" compared to other French politicians

- It suggests he was actually restrained by "dominant French political forces" who pressed their "fears and hatreds upon him"

Victim of Circumstances:

- Clemenceau is portrayed as wrongly blamed for the Treaty's harsh terms
- The source indicates he was pressured by French political opinion rather than being personally extreme

Political Failure:

- His career ended badly - "out of power" by January 1920
- He was accused of "alleged softness" and "betraying France"
- His presidential ambitions were destroyed: "his election was unthinkable"

Defensive and Bitter:

- Spent his final nine years "defending himself against these charges"
- Wrote a "rambling book" that was "not well received" to justify his actions

The overall impression is of a pragmatic leader who became a scapegoat for a treaty that did not satisfy French desires for revenge.

2. Study Source B.

Why was this source published at this time? Explain your answer using details of the source and your knowledge. [8]

Purpose and Timing of Source B (April 1919):
This British cartoon was published in April 1919, during the crucial period when the Treaty terms were being finalised and made public. Several reasons explain its timing:

Justifying British Position:
- Published when there was criticism that the reparations were too harsh
- The cartoon defends the Allied position by showing that Germany would have demanded much more if it had won
- Uses Germany's own words against them - "a quarter of what we should have made them pay"

Public Opinion Management:
- April 1919 was when the treaty terms became public, causing international debate
- The British public needed reassurance that the peace terms were justified

- Responds to German complaints about the treaty being too severe

Historical Context:
- Published just as the "war guilt clause" and reparations were being finalised
- Timing coincides with the German delegation's shocked response to the draft terms
- Helps counter any sympathy for Germany that might be emerging

Propaganda Purpose:
- Reminds the British public of German aggression and what British fate would have been
- Uses humour to make a serious political point about German hypocrisy
- Published in a period when maintaining public support for harsh terms was crucial

The cartoon effectively argues that German complaints are hypocritical given what they would have imposed if victorious.

3. Study Sources C and D.

How far does Source C make Source D surprising? Explain your answer using details of the sources and your knowledge. [8]

Analysis of Surprise Factor:

Source C makes Source D moderately surprising, but not entirely unexpected, when considered in the context of history.

Elements that Make Source D Surprising:

Tone Contrast:

- Source C presents desperate, emotional language: "death sentence," "impossibility," "monstrous"
- Source D responds with cold, legalistic justification and moral superiority
- The stark difference in emotional register is surprising

Lack of Sympathy:

- Given Germany's claims of economic impossibility and national destruction
- Source D shows no compromise or acknowledgement of legitimate concerns
- Dismissive attitude: "fail to understand the position" seems harsh

Moral Absolutes:

- Source D's claim of "the greatest crime against humanity" seems an extreme response to diplomatic protest
- The righteousness ("peace of justice") contrasts with German desperation

Elements that Make Source D Less Surprising:

Historical Context:

- By May 1919, Allied public opinion demanded harsh treatment
- Four years of brutal war had hardened attitudes
- French losses made compromise politically impossible for Clemenceau

German Reputation:
- Germany's wartime conduct (Belgium, submarine warfare) had damaged its moral standing
- Previous German treaties (Brest-Litovsk) had been equally harsh
- Allies genuinely believed Germany was responsible for the war

Political Necessity:
- Clemenceau was under pressure from French opinion to be tough
- Any sign of weakness would have been politically fatal
- Source A shows he was already seen as too moderate

Source D is surprising in its complete rejection of German concerns, but understandable given the political and emotional context of 1919.

4. Study Source E.

How valuable is this source to a historian studying the Treaty of Versailles? Explain your answer using details of the source and your knowledge. [8]

Usefulness of Source E:

This British newspaper source from May 1919 is quite helpful, but has significant limitations.

Strengths - High Usefulness:

Contemporary Opinion:
- Shows genuine British public feeling during treaty negotiations
- Demonstrates that many Britons felt Germany was being treated too leniently
- Provides evidence of popular support for harsh terms: "feeling in the country is not that Germany is being too harshly dealt with, but that it is being let off too lightly"

Political Context:
- Helps explain why politicians felt pressured to maintain tough negotiating positions

- Shows the emotional atmosphere that influenced decision-making
- Indicates public expectations that would constrain diplomatic flexibility

Counter-narrative:
- Challenges later claims that the treaty was universally seen as too harsh at the time
- Shows that the contemporary British perspective differed from later historical judgments
- Demonstrates that "harsh" is relative - what seemed lenient to some seemed severe to others

Limitations - Reduced Usefulness:

Bias and Propaganda:
- Clearly one-sided British nationalist perspective
- Inflammatory language ("wiped off the map") shows an emotional rather than an analytical approach
- May not represent a balanced opinion but rather an extreme nationalist view

Limited Scope:
- Only represents one section of British opinion
- Does not show dissenting voices or more moderate views
- No evidence that this was typical of all British newspapers

Lack of Detail:
- Provides opinion but little concrete information about actual treaty terms
- More helpful in studying public opinion than understanding the treaty itself

Generally, it is helpful to understand the political pressures and public expectations that shaped the treaty; however, it must be used in conjunction with other sources to gain a comprehensive understanding of the entire picture.

5. Study Source F.

What is the cartoonist's message? Explain your answer using details of the source and your knowledge. [8]

The Norwegian cartoonist's message is critical of the Paris Peace Conference process, presenting it as unfair and predetermined.

Main Messages:

Mockery of "Negotiation":
- Clemenceau saying "Take your seats, gentlemen!" suggests the Germans are being seated for a show trial, not genuine negotiations
- The formal, polite language contrasts with the lack of real choice

- Germans are being invited to witness their own sentencing

Criticism of Allied Justice:
- Coming from neutral Norway, this represents outside criticism of Allied methods
- Suggests the conference was a charade rather than genuine peace-making
- Germans appear as defendants rather than negotiating partners

Process Critique:
- The cartoon implies the terms were decided beforehand
- Germans are merely being presented with a fait accompli
- "Take your seats" suggests they are spectators to their own judgment

Neutral Perspective:
- Significant that this comes from Norway (neutral in WWI)
- Represents an outside, supposedly objective view of the peace process
- Suggests international concern about Allied methods

Visual Symbolism:
- The formal setting suggests a courtroom or tribunal rather than negotiation

- Clemenceau's dominant position shows Allied control
- German delegates appear subordinate and powerless

Historical Context:
- Published August 1919, after the treaty was signed under protest
- Reflects growing international unease about the peace process
- Timing suggests criticism of the outcome

In a nutshell, the cartoonist portrays the peace conference as a predetermined punishment session rather than a genuine negotiation, criticising Allied methods as unfair and potentially hazardous to future peace.

6. Study all the sources.

How far do these sources provide convincing evidence that Germany was punished as much as the French wanted? Use the sources to explain your answer. [12]

Analysis of Evidence - Mixed but Leaning Toward "Not Enough":

The sources provide partially convincing evidence that Germany was not punished as severely as the

French had wanted, although the evidence is mixed and complex.

Evidence Suggesting France Did not Get What It Wanted:

Source A - Clemenceau's Downfall:
- Most compelling evidence: Clemenceau was seen as "too soft" and accused of "betraying France"
- Lost political support precisely because of "alleged softness at the time of Treaty negotiations"
- His fall from power suggests French opinion found the treaty inadequate
- The fact that he spent nine years defending himself shows widespread French dissatisfaction

Source C - German Survival:
- If France had gotten what it wanted (Rhineland independence, complete disarmament), Germany would not have been able to make such articulate protests
- German delegation's ability to object suggests they retained some strength
- Economic complaints imply Germany still had an economy to complain about

Evidence Suggesting Punishment Was Sufficient:

Source D - Allied Satisfaction:
- Clemenceau's confident response suggests Allied satisfaction with the terms

- Claims treaty represents "peace of justice" and adequate punishment
- Dismissive attitude toward German complaints suggests terms met Allied goals

Source E - British Support:
- British opinion that Germany was "being let off too lightly" suggests terms were actually moderate
- However, this reflects British rather than French opinion

Ambiguous Evidence:

Source B - Relative Punishment:
- Shows punishment was severe by suggesting Germany would have imposed worse
- But does not indicate whether this satisfied French desires for revenge
- Could support either interpretation

Source F - Outside Perspective:
- Norwegian criticism suggests terms were harsh enough to concern neutrals
- But neutral concern does not indicate French satisfaction

Assessment of Convincing Nature:

Most Convincing Evidence - Source A: The most convincing evidence comes from Source A's account of Clemenceau's political destruction. This is compelling because:

- It is specific and detailed
- Shows concrete political consequences
- Demonstrates that French public opinion was unsatisfied
- Explains the mechanism of French disappointment

Supporting Evidence:
- Source C shows Germany retained capacity for organised protest
- Background information shows France wanted Rhineland independence and did not get it
- Multiple sources suggest the treaty was a compromise rather than a French diktat

Limitations:
- Sources do not directly quote French public opinion
- Some evidence reflects other nations' views rather than French satisfaction
- Time gap in Source A might reflect changed perspectives

In conclusion, the sources provide moderately convincing evidence that Germany was not punished as harshly as France wanted. Source A is particularly compelling in showing French dissatisfaction through Clemenceau's political fate. However, the evidence would be stronger with direct French public opinion sources and a more unambiguous indication of what French goals were actually achieved versus those that were abandoned.

Chapter 10

Paper (4)

Paper 4: Alternative to Coursework

0470/41

May/June 2021

INFORMATION

- The total mark for this paper is 40.
- The number of marks for each question or part question is shown in brackets [ ].

CHAPTER 10

Answer one question from your chosen Depth Study.

DEPTH STUDY A: THE FIRST WORLD WAR, 1914–18

1   How important was the failure of the Schlieffen Plan as a reason why the war was not over by the end of 1914? Explain your answer. [40]

2   How significant was the impact of German submarine warfare on Britain's ability to continue waging war? Explain your answer. [40]

DEPTH STUDY B: GERMANY, 1918–45

3   How significant were the social and economic effects of the First World War in shaping the lives of the German people, 1919–23? Explain your answer. [40]

4   How significant was Joseph Goebbels in winning support for the Nazis, 1930–33? Explain your answer. [40]

DEPTH STUDY C: RUSSIA, 1905–41

5   How important was Lenin in causing the downfall of the Provisional Government? Explain your answer. [40]

6   How significant were the Five-Year Plans in changing life in the Soviet Union after 1928? Explain your answer.   [40]

DEPTH STUDY D: THE UNITED STATES, 1919–41

7   How important was assembly-line production as a reason for increasing prosperity in the USA in the 1920s? Explain your answer.
    [40]

8   How significant was homelessness in the impact of the Depression after 1929? Explain your answer.
[40]

DEPTH STUDY E: CHINA, c.1930–c.1990

9   How important was land reform as an aspect of Communist rule in the 1950s and 1960s? Explain your answer.   [40]

10   How significant was political reform in the changes made in China after 1976? Explain your answer.
[40]

DEPTH STUDY F: SOUTH AFRICA, c.1940–c.1994

11   How important was the Bantu Self-Government Act in changing life for black South Africans after 1948? Explain your answer.
   [40]

12   How significant were the government's security measures in maintaining white minority rule between 1966 and 1980? Explain your answer.
   [40]

DEPTH STUDY G: ISRAELIS AND PALESTINIANS SINCE 1945

13   How important was the Arab League as a cause of increased tension in Palestine by 1948? Explain your answer.   [40]

14   How significant was the refugee crisis in gaining international attention for the Palestinian cause after 1948? Explain your answer.   [40]

CHAPTER 10: Answer

Answer one question from your chosen Depth Study.

Answered Questions:
DEPTH STUDY A: THE FIRST WORLD WAR, 1914–18 (Nos 1 and 2)

1   How important was the failure of the Schlieffen Plan as a reason why the war was not over by the end of 1914? Explain your answer.
   [40]

Reasons why the failure of the Schlieffen Plan was critical:

It prevented a quick German victory over France. The plan aimed for a swift attack through Belgium to capture Paris quickly, but it failed at key battles, such as Liège and the Marne.

Allowed the Allies to regroup – Because Germany did not win quickly, France and Britain had time to bring their forces together and resist effectively.

Led to prolonged fighting on the Western Front – With the German advance stopped, both sides dug in, leading to trench warfare and a protracted stalemate.

Forced Germany to fight a two-front war – Since the plan failed in the west, Germany also had to fight Russia in the east, stretching its resources and prolonging the war.

Reasons why other factors were also important:

Strong Belgian resistance – Belgium's defence slowed Germany's progress, delaying the Schlieffen Plan and allowing the Allies to prepare.

The race to the sea – Both sides attempted to outflank each other, resulting in entrenched positions from the North Sea to Switzerland, which made the war more difficult to end quickly.

Modern technology and tactics – Machine guns, artillery, and barbed wire made attacks deadly, preventing rapid advances by either side.

Political and military decisions – Leadership changes, mistakes, and cautious strategies on both sides contributed to the length of the war.

Judgement

The failure of the Schlieffen Plan was a significant factor in why the war did not end by the end of 1914. It stopped Germany from quickly defeating France and forced a protracted, drawn-out conflict. However, other factors, such as Belgian resistance, the race to the sea, and the introduction of new weapons, also played key roles. Therefore, while the Schlieffen Plan's failure was central, it was not the only cause of the prolonged war.

2   How significant was the impact of German submarine warfare on Britain's ability to continue waging war? Explain your answer.   [40]

Reasons why German submarine warfare was very significant:

Threat to British imports – Britain relied heavily on imports for food, weapons, and raw materials. Submarine attacks targeted merchant ships, threatening to cut off these supplies.

Unrestricted submarine warfare (1917) – Germany declared all ships around Britain would be sunk without warning, including civilian and neutral ships, causing significant losses and fear.

Impact on British shipping and economy – Many British and Allied ships were sunk, resulting in shortages and increased costs that put pressure on the British war effort.

Forced Britain to develop countermeasures – The convoy system was introduced, grouping ships with naval escorts, which helped reduce losses and keep supply lines open.

Helped bring the USA into the war – German U-boats sank American ships, such as the Lusitania, turning US public opinion against Germany and contributing to the US entry into the war. This strengthened Britain's position.

Reasons why the impact was limited or less significant:

Convoy system success.
Once the convoy system was introduced, the effectiveness of U-boats dropped significantly, allowing Britain to maintain supplies.

Allied naval superiority.
The British Royal Navy controlled the seas, limiting U-boat movements and protecting key routes.

Production and resource management.
Britain improved its shipbuilding and rationing systems, which helped it cope with losses and shortages.

War continued despite U-boat attacks – Britain did not surrender or collapse, showing it could continue fighting despite the submarine threat.

Judgement:
German submarine warfare was very significant because it threatened Britain's vital supply lines and forced the country to adapt its strategies. It caused real damage and nearly starved Britain into

submission. However, British naval strength, the convoy system, and American support limited the overall impact. Submarine warfare was important, but not decisive, in its own right.

Chapter 11

Paper 11

Paper 1 - February/March 2022

INSTRUCTIONS

- Answer one question from your chosen Depth Study.
- Follow the instructions on the front cover of the answer booklet. If you need additional answer paper,
Ask the invigilator for a continuation booklet.

INFORMATION

- The total mark for this paper is 40.
- The number of marks for each question or part question is shown in brackets [ ].

03_0470_42_2021_1.6
© UCLES 2021

CHAPTER 10

Answer one question from your chosen Depth Study.

DEPTH STUDY A: THE FIRST WORLD WAR, 1914–18

1   How important was the Battle of Jutland (1916) in the war at sea? Explain your answer. [40]

DEPTH STUDY B: GERMANY, 1918–45

2   How important were the military restrictions in the Treaty of Versailles as a cause of instability in Germany, 1919–23? Explain your answer. [40]

3   How significant was the Enabling Act (1933) in allowing Hitler to establish a dictatorship in Germany by 1934? Explain your answer. [40]

DEPTH STUDY C: RUSSIA, 1905–41

4   How important was Stolypin in bringing about stability in Russia after the 1905 Revolution? Explain your answer. [40]

5   How significant was the Kronstadt Rising in ensuring the continuance of Bolshevik rule after 1921? Explain your answer. [40]

DEPTH STUDY D: THE UNITED STATES, 1919–41

6   How important was the Scopes 'Monkey Trial' as an aspect of intolerance in the USA in the 1920s? Explain your answer. [40]

7   How significant was Huey Long in opposition to the New Deal after 1933? Explain your answer.

[40]

DEPTH STUDY E: CHINA, c.1930–c.1990

8   How vital was the Shanghai Massacre (1927) to the development of the Chinese Communist Party? Explain your answer. [40]

9   How significant was propaganda in shaping the lives of the Chinese people after 1949? Explain your answer. [40]

DEPTH STUDY F: SOUTH AFRICA, c.1940–c.1994

10   How important were restrictions on political rights as an aspect of racial discrimination before 1948? Explain your answer. [40]

11   How significant was support from Afrikaners to the maintenance of apartheid after 1948? Explain your answer. [40]

DEPTH STUDY G: ISRAELIS AND PALESTINIANS SINCE 1945

12   How important were Jewish resistance movements in Palestine to the creation of Israel in 1948? Explain your answer. [40]

13   How significant was the creation of the Palestinian Authority (1994) in the Arab–Israeli peace process? Explain your answer. [40]

CHAPTER 11 Answers

Answer one question from your chosen Depth Study.

Answered Questions:

DEPTH STUDY A: THE FIRST WORLD WAR, 1914–18 (No 1)

DEPTH STUDY B: GERMANY, 1918–45 (No 3)

1. How important was the Battle of Jutland (1916) in the war at sea? Explain your answer. [40]

Reasons why the Battle of Jutland was important:

It was the largest naval battle of WWI – Involving around 250 ships and thousands of sailors, it was the biggest clash between the British Royal Navy and the German High Seas Fleet.

Maintained British naval dominance – Despite heavy losses, the British Royal Navy kept control of the North Sea, continuing their maritime blockade of Germany, which limited German supplies.

Stopped the German fleet from challenging Britain at sea – After Jutland, the German fleet rarely ventured out to fight the British navy again, limiting Germany's naval power.

Affected naval strategies – The battle highlighted the dangers of large battleships and led to an increased use of submarines (U-boats) by Germany.

Boosted morale and propaganda – Both sides claimed victory, but Britain used the battle to maintain public confidence in the Royal Navy's strength.

Reasons why the Battle of Jutland was less critical:

No clear winner – The battle was indecisive; Germany inflicted more ship and sailor losses than Britain.

The naval blockade did not end. The blockade continued, but the Battle of Jutland itself did not dramatically change the war at sea.

Did not stop U-boat warfare – The German U-boat campaign against Allied shipping continued and became a bigger threat after Jutland.

No immediate strategic change – The battle did not lead to a decisive shift in naval control or bring the war to an earlier end.

Judgement:

The Battle of Jutland was vital because it confirmed British naval supremacy and limited Germany's surface fleet, thereby helping to maintain the blockade that weakened Germany.

However, it was not a decisive victory, and the German U-boat threat continued, changing the nature of the war at sea.

Overall, it was a significant event, but its impact was limited because it did not end the naval war or produce a clear victor.

Therefore, the battle was significant but not decisive in the war at sea.

3   How significant was the Enabling Act (1933) in allowing Hitler to establish a dictatorship in Germany by 1934? Explain your answer. [40]

Significance of the Enabling Act:

- Legal basis for dictatorship – The Enabling Act (March 1933) gave Hitler and his cabinet the power to make laws without the Reichstag or the President's approval for four years. This effectively dismantled parliamentary democracy and allowed Hitler to bypass any opposition.
- Suppression of political opponents – Once the Act was passed, Hitler quickly banned other

political parties (July 1933) and outlawed trade unions (May 1933). This created a one-party state and removed any organised opposition.

- Control over Länder (states) – The Act allowed Hitler to centralise power by abolishing state parliaments and bringing all regional governments under Nazi control, completing Gleichschaltung (coordination of all aspects of life under Nazi rule).
- Propaganda and censorship – With unrestricted power, Hitler and Goebbels expanded Nazi control over the media, schools, and culture, strengthening Hitler's grip on German society.

Other factors in establishing a dictatorship:

- Reichstag Fire (February 1933) – The fire gave Hitler the excuse to persuade Hindenburg to pass the Decree for the Protection of People and State, suspending civil liberties, banning Communist newspapers, and arresting 4000 communists. This weakened opposition ahead of the March elections.
- Use of terror and intimidation – The SA (Brownshirts) intimidated voters, broke up opposition meetings, and created a climate of fear that helped the Nazis secure enough support to pass the Enabling Act.

- Night of the Long Knives (June 1934) – Hitler used the SS to eliminate the SA leadership (including Röhm) and other political rivals. This reassured the army and consolidated Hitler's control over the Nazi Party itself.
- Death of Hindenburg (August 1934) – After Hindenburg's death, Hitler combined the roles of Chancellor and President, becoming Führer and head of state. The army swore an oath of loyalty to him personally, completing his dictatorship.

Conclusion:
- Very significant – The Enabling Act was the crucial turning point that legally transformed Hitler's government into a dictatorship. It allowed him to pass laws that removed rivals, centralised power, and Nazified Germany.
- But part of a wider process – The Enabling Act alone would not have worked without the suppression of opposition (Reichstag Fire Decree), the use of violence and intimidation by the SA and SS, and Hitler's careful removal of rivals during the Night of the Long Knives.
- Overall judgement – The Enabling Act was the most significant single step in creating a dictatorship because it gave Hitler the legal authority to reshape Germany without interference. However, its full impact was only realised through

later actions such as the Night of the Long Knives and the death of Hindenburg, which together secured Hitler's total control by 1934.

2022 Past papers

Chapter 12

Paper 12

HISTORY 0470/12 Cambridge IGCSE

Paper 1 - February/March 2022

Duration: 2 hours

INFORMATION

- The total mark for this paper is 60
- The number of marks for each question or part question is shown in brackets [ ]

SECTION A: CORE CONTENT

Answer any two questions from this Section.

SECTION B: DEPTH STUDIES

Answer any one question from this Section.

CHAPTER 112

Paper 12

SECTION A: CORE CONTENT

Answer any two questions from this Section.

1. The authorities were eventually able to deal with the 1848 revolutions.

    (a) What happened during the uprising in Vienna in October 1848? [4]

    (b) Why did the 'June Days' take place? [6]

    (c) 'The European revolutions of 1848–49 achieved very little.' How far do you agree with this statement? Explain your answer. [10]

2. During the 1860s, Bismarck was the key figure in Prussia.

    (a) Describe how Bismarck became Minister-President in 1862. [4]

    (b) Why was the issue of the Spanish Succession important? [6]

    (c) 'Bismarck planned the war with Austria.' How far do you agree with this statement? Explain your answer. [10]

3. Tensions between North and South continued for decades in the USA.

    (a) Describe the activities of the Ku Klux Klan. [4]

    (b) Why were carpetbaggers unpopular in the South during the Reconstruction period? [6]

(c) 'The Kansas-Nebraska Act of 1854 was the most important cause of the Civil War.' How far do you agree with this statement? Explain your answer. [10]

4. A variety of different factors helped lead to the First World War.

(a) What were dreadnoughts? [4]

(b) Why was the Bosnian Crisis of 1908–09 significant? [6]

(c) Which of the two Moroccan crises was more of a danger to international peace? Explain your answer. [10]

5. The League of Nations faced many challenges.

(a) What was the Hoare-Laval Pact of 1935? [4]

(b) Why was the Depression significant for the League of Nations? [6]

(c) 'The response of the League of Nations to Japanese actions in Manchuria was surprising.' How far do you agree with this statement? Explain your answer. [10]

6. Several factors in the 1930s made war increasingly likely.

(a) Describe the increasing militarism of Japan in the 1930s. [4]

(b) Why was the Treaty of Versailles important for Hitler's foreign policy? [6]

(c) Is it surprising that Britain and France went to war over Poland, but not over Czechoslovakia? Explain your answer. [10]

7. During the Cold War, problems for the Soviets broke out across much of Eastern Europe.

(a) Describe the events that led to the revolt in Hungary in 1956. [4]

(b) Why did many Germans dislike the Berlin Wall? [6]

(c) 'The authorities in Poland dealt effectively with Solidarity.' How far do you agree with this statement? Explain your answer. [10]

8. From 1979 to 1991, much attention was focused on Iran and Iraq.

(a) Describe the rule of Ayatollah Khomeini in Iran. [4]

(b) Why did the USA react in the way that it did to Iraq's invasion of Kuwait? [6]

(c) 'Iran and Iraq suffered equally from the Iran-Iraq War.' How far do you agree with this statement? Explain your answer. [10]

SECTION B: DEPTH STUDIES

Answer any one question from this Section.

DEPTH STUDY A: THE FIRST WORLD WAR, 1914–18

9. In the first few months, the First World War was a war of movement.

(a) Describe the actions of the British Expeditionary Force (BEF) in the first month of the war. [4]

(b) Why were the changes made to the Schlieffen Plan necessary? [6]

(c) 'The first Battle of Ypres was the most important battle on the Western Front in 1914.' How far do you agree with this statement? Explain your answer. [10]

10. Much of the fighting on the Western Front was conducted in trenches.

(a) What was 'trench foot'? [4]

(b) Why was the Battle of Verdun important to the Allies? [6]

(c) 'New types of weapons had little impact in the trench warfare of the Western Front.' How far do you agree with this statement? Explain your answer. [10]

DEPTH STUDY B: GERMANY, 1918–45

11. Many factors contributed to the Nazis' rise to power.

(a) Describe the role of Goebbels in the Nazi Party during the 1920s. [4]

(b) Why did the economy of the Weimar Republic collapse so quickly after 1929? [6]

(c) 'The Enabling Act was the most important reason why Hitler was able to consolidate his power by 1934.' How far do you agree with this statement? Explain your answer. [10]

12. The Nazi government tried to control every part of German society.

(a) Describe Nazi policies towards the churches in Germany. [4]

(b) Why did the Nazi master race theory lead to the persecution of certain groups in German society? [6]

(c) How successful was the Nazi government in controlling the German people? Explain your answer. [10]

DEPTH STUDY C: RUSSIA, 1905–41

13. Tsar Nicholas II was not a popular ruler.

(a) What were the features of the Tsar's Russification policy? [4]

(b) Why was the 1905 Revolution necessary? [6]

(c) 'By 1916, the main reason for the Tsar's unpopularity was Rasputin.' How far do you agree with this statement? Explain your answer. [10]

14. When he came to power, Stalin was determined to make essential changes.

(a) Describe what replaced the New Economic Policy (NEP) in the late 1920s. [4]

(b) Why did Stalin's policies bring about changes in the lives of Soviet women? [6]

(c) 'Stalin changed Soviet agriculture for political rather than economic reasons.' How far do you agree with this statement? Explain your answer. [10]

DEPTH STUDY D: THE UNITED STATES, 1919–41

15. Some people did well in the 1920s; others did not.

(a) What were sharecroppers? [4]

(b) Why were many American farmers in the 1920s producing more than they could sell? [6]

(c) How far was the car industry responsible for America's economic boom of the 1920s? Explain your answer. [10]

16. The New Deal was not a complete success.

(a) Who was Huey Long? [4]

(b) Why was unemployment still high at the end of the 1930s? [6]

(c) 'The first and second New Deals were very different.' How far do you agree with this statement? Explain your answer. [10]

DEPTH STUDY E: CHINA, c.1930–c.1990

17. There were reforms in China in the 1950s.

(a) What were collective farms? [4]

(b) Why did Mao introduce social reforms in the 1950s? [6]

(c) How far were the difficulties of the Great Leap Forward due to the introduction of backyard furnaces? Explain your answer. [10]

18. China experienced much change over the years.

(a) Describe what happened to the education system in China during the Cultural Revolution. [4]

(b) Why did people in China feel the way they did about the Gang of Four? [6]

(c) How different was China under Deng compared with China under Mao? Explain your answer. [10]

DEPTH STUDY F: SOUTH AFRICA, c.1940–c.1994

19. Before 1948, the lives of black South Africans were very restricted.

(a) Describe how the pass system worked in South Africa before 1948. [4]

(b) Why did many black South Africans work in the migrant labour system? [6]

(c) 'Between 1919 and 1945, the South African economy depended on gold mining.' How far do you agree with this statement? Explain your answer. [10]

20. By the mid-1980s, apartheid was coming to an end.

(a) Describe the contribution made by Oliver Tambo to the fall of apartheid. [4]

(b) Why did Mandela face opposition from some black South Africans during his discussions with de Klerk in the early 1990s? [6]

(c) How far did the State of Emergency called by Botha in 1985 help the government to stay in control? Explain your answer. [10]

DEPTH STUDY G: ISRAELIS AND PALESTINIANS SINCE 1945

21. Palestine saw much violence after the Second World War.

(a) Who was David Ben-Gurion? [4]

(b) Why was there a Jewish insurgency in Palestine between 1944 and 1948? [6]

(c) How surprising was the defeat of the Arab states in the war of 1948–49? Explain your answer. [10]

22. Israel and the Arab states found it difficult to live together peacefully.

(a) Who was Moshe Dayan? [4]

(b) Why did President Sadat decide to go to war against Israel in 1973? [6]

(c) Who benefited most from the war of 1956? Explain your answer. [10]

CHAPTER 12: Answers

SECTION A: CORE CONTENT

(Answered questions: 1, 4 and 5)

1. The authorities were eventually able to deal with the 1848 revolutions.

(a) What happened during the uprising in Vienna in October 1848? [4]

    Workers and students revolted – Workers, students, and the National Guard protested in Vienna against the government's conservative policies.

    Prime Minister resigned – The revolt forced Prince Metternich (the Austrian Chancellor) to resign and flee into exile.

    Peasants supported change – Peasants were freed from feudal obligations, which reduced support for the old order.

    Revolt crushed by army – The Austrian army later returned, attacked Vienna, defeated the rebels, and restored order by November 1848

(b) Why did the 'June Days' take place? [6]

    Closure of National Workshops – The government closed the National Workshops, which had been established to provide employment opportunities for the unemployed.

    Rising unemployment.
Thousands of workers lost their only source of income and were left jobless.

    Anger of workers.
Working-class Parisians felt betrayed by the government, which they believed had abandoned promises of social reform.

    Class tensions.
Growing division between workers (who wanted radical reforms) and the middle class (who feared socialism).

    Political repression.
The government tried to stop radical groups from influencing politics.

    Desire for social justice.
Workers sought better wages, improved working conditions, and a more equitable society, leading them to rise in revolt.

(c) 'The European revolutions of 1848–49 achieved very little.' How far do you agree with this statement? Explain your answer. [10]

Agree – Achieved very little:

- Revolts were crushed.

Most uprisings (e.g., in Austria, Italy, and the German states) were suppressed by armies, restoring conservative governments.

- Few lasting reforms.

Many of the liberal constitutions and promises of rights were cancelled once order was restored.

- National unity failed.

Germany and Italy did not achieve unification during the 1848–49 period; nationalist hopes were delayed until later decades.

- Peasant gains are limited.

In some areas, peasants gained land or were freed from feudal dues, but this was often done to weaken revolts, rather than to support liberal change.

Disagree – Some achievements:

- Metternich removed – In Austria, Prince Metternich was forced to resign, showing that the old order could be challenged.

- End of feudalism.

In parts of the Austrian Empire, peasants were permanently freed from feudal obligations.

- Inspiration for future change – The revolutions spread liberal and nationalist ideas across Europe, paving the way for later reforms and unifications.

- Some constitutions granted.

Short-lived constitutions and elected assemblies were established in several states, providing an experience of political participation.

Judgement:

- Balanced view.

The revolutions of 1848–49 achieved little in the short term because most were defeated, and conservative rule was restored.

- However, they were important in the long term as they spread new ideas about democracy, nationalism, and workers' rights, which shaped Europe in the late 19th century.

4. A variety of different factors helped lead to the First World War.

(a) What were dreadnoughts? [4]

Type of battleship.

Large, heavily armed warships were introduced by Britain in 1906.

Powerful guns.

Equipped with big guns of the same calibre, giving them greater firepower than earlier ships.

Faster and stronger – They had steam turbine engines, making them faster and harder to sink.

Naval arms race.
Sparked competition between Britain and Germany to build more dreadnoughts before World War I.

(b) Why was the Bosnian Crisis of 1908–09 significant? [6]

Austria-Hungary annexed Bosnia.
Austria-Hungary took over Bosnia-Herzegovina, angering Serbia, which had long sought the territory for itself.

Growth of Serbian nationalism.
The crisis increased Serbian determination to unite all Slavs in the Balkans under their leadership.

Support from Russia.
Russia backed Serbia but was forced to back down when Germany supported Austria-Hungary, causing humiliation for Russia.

Increased tension.
Relations between Austria-Hungary and Serbia deteriorated, increasing the likelihood of war.

Strengthened alliances.

Germany and Austria-Hungary became closer, while Russia became more determined not to back down again.

Step towards WWI.

The crisis was one of the events that destabilised the Balkans and set the stage for the assassination at Sarajevo in 1914.

(c) Which of the two Moroccan crises was more of a danger to international peace? Explain your answer. [10]

First Moroccan Crisis (1905–06)

- Kaiser's challenge.

Kaiser Wilhelm II visited Tangier and declared support for Moroccan independence, challenging France's influence.

- Conference at Algeciras.

European powers met to settle the dispute; most supported France, isolating Germany.

- Result.

Germany backed down and was humiliated, but war was avoided peacefully.

Second Moroccan Crisis (1911):

- German gunboat sent.

Germany sent the gunboat Panther to Agadir, claiming to protect German interests during a local rebellion.

- Increased tension.

Britain feared Germany would take control of the Agadir port and threaten British naval routes, so Britain supported France.

- Near-war situation.

Both Britain and Germany prepared for war, creating a real risk of conflict.

- Result.

Crisis was resolved by negotiation, but Germany was again humiliated and became more aggressive.

Which was more dangerous?

- Second crisis more dangerous – It brought Europe closer to war because both Britain and Germany prepared for military action.

- Raised stakes.

Britain, France, and Germany were now all involved, and relations between them worsened.

- Arms race intensified.

Increased mistrust led to faster naval and military buildup before 1914.

Conclusion:

- Overall judgment.

The Second Moroccan Crisis posed a greater threat to international peace, as it nearly triggered war and strengthened alliances (the Triple Entente vs. the Triple Alliance), thereby pushing Europe closer to the outbreak of World War I.

5. The League of Nations faced many challenges.
(a) What was the Hoare-Laval Pact of 1935? [4]

- Secret plan.

Agreement between British Foreign Secretary Samuel Hoare and French Prime Minister Pierre Laval.

- Aim;

Tried to end the Abyssinian Crisis by giving Italy two-thirds of Abyssinia (Ethiopia).

- Appeasement of Mussolini;

The Plan was intended to appease Mussolini and maintain him as an ally against Hitler.

- Public outrage;

When the plan became public, it caused anger in Britain and France, and the pact was dropped

(b) Why was the Depression significant for the League of Nations? [6]

- Economic problems worldwide;

Countries faced unemployment, poverty, and declining trade, causing them to focus on their own issues rather than international cooperation.

- Rise of aggressive leaders;

Economic hardship helped extremist leaders like Hitler (Germany) and Mussolini (Italy) gain power by promising intense action.

- More aggression abroad.

Countries like Japan (Manchuria, 1931) and Italy (Abyssinia, 1935) tried to solve problems by invading other nations.

- League members are reluctant to act.

Britain and France were unwilling to impose sanctions or risk war, as they sought to protect their own economies.

- Weakened collective security.

The League's ability to stop aggression was undermined as members prioritised their national interests.

- Loss of faith in the League.

Failure to act against aggressors made the League appear weak and encouraged further aggression, ultimately contributing to the outbreak of WWII.

(c) 'The response of the League of Nations to Japanese actions in Manchuria was surprising.' How far do you agree with this statement? Explain your answer. [10]

Agree – It was surprising:
- Broke League rules.

Japan invaded Manchuria (1931), which was an act of aggression clearly against the League's Covenant.
- No intense action taken;

The League did not send troops or impose economic sanctions that could halt Japan's advance.
- Very slow response.

It took the League over a year to investigate (Lytton Commission report in 1932), by which time Japan had already taken complete control of Manchuria.
- Encouraged other aggressors.

The weak response was surprising because it showed the League would not act decisively, encouraging Mussolini (Abyssinia) and Hitler (Rhineland).

Disagree – It was not surprising:
- The league had no army.

It could not enforce decisions militarily and relied on member countries to provide troops, which they were unwilling to do.
- Economic Depression.

Major powers like Britain and France were focused on their own economic problems and did not want to risk war with Japan.

- Manchuria is far away.

Many felt it was too far from Europe to be a direct threat to them.

- Japan is a significant power.

As one of the League's permanent members, punishing Japan risked weakening the League further if Japan left (which it eventually did).

Conclusion:

- Balanced view.

The League's weak response may seem surprising because it failed to uphold its key principle of collective security.

- However, given its lack of military power, economic problems, and members' unwillingness to act, the response was predictable.

SECTION B: DEPTH STUDIES

Answer any one question from this Section.

Answered Questions: 9 and 10

DEPTH STUDY A: THE FIRST WORLD WAR, 1914–18

9. In the first few months, the First World War was a war of movement.

(a) Describe the actions of the British Expeditionary Force (BEF) in the first month of the war. [4]

    Sent to France – The BEF (about 80,000 soldiers) was sent to support the French army against Germany in August 1914.

    Battle of Mons – Fought at Mons, where they slowed the German advance with accurate rifle fire.

    Great retreat – After heavy fighting, the BEF retreated southwards with the French army to avoid being surrounded.

    Battle of the Marne – Took part in the Battle of the Marne (September 1914), helping stop the German advance and saving Paris.

(b) Why were the changes made to the Schlieffen Plan important? [6]

    Fewer troops on the right wing – Germany reduced the number of troops going through Belgium, weakening the attack force.

    Strengthened the left wing – More troops were kept in Alsace-Lorraine to defend against a possible French attack.

Slowed down advance – The smaller right wing could not move as quickly or sweep around Paris as planned.

Gave Allies time to react – France and Britain had more time to mobilise and block the German advance.

Led to German failure – Germany failed to capture Paris and was stopped at the Battle of the Marne.

Resulted in stalemate – The failure of the plan led to trench warfare on the Western Front, lasting for most of WWI.

(c) 'The first Battle of Ypres was the most important battle on the Western Front in 1914.' How far do you agree with this statement? Explain your answer. [10]

Agree – It was essential:

- Secured Channel ports – The Allies kept control of ports like Calais and Dunkirk, which were vital for bringing troops and supplies from Britain.
- Stopped German advance – Prevented Germany from breaking through to the sea, protecting northern France from invasion.

- High German losses – Germany lost many trained soldiers, which weakened its army for future battles.
- Established trench line – After Ypres, both sides began digging trenches, setting the stage for trench warfare for the rest of the war.

Disagree – Other battles were also important:
- Battle of Mons – Slowed down the German advance and bought time for the French army to regroup.
- Great Retreat & Battle of the Marne – The Marne was crucial because it stopped Germany from capturing Paris and winning the war quickly.
- Race to the Sea – The series of battles before Ypres was significant because it decided where the trench lines would end.

Conclusion:
- Balanced judgment – The First Battle of Ypres was essential because it secured key ports and marked the beginning of trench warfare.
- However, the Battle of the Marne was arguably even more important because it stopped the Schlieffen Plan and saved France from defeat.

10. Much of the fighting on the Western Front was conducted in trenches.

(a) What was 'trench foot'? [4]

Infection of the feet – Caused by soldiers standing in cold, wet, muddy trenches for long periods.

Symptoms – Feet became swollen, numb, turned blue or black, and could rot.

Very painful – Made walking difficult and sometimes led to gangrene.

Treatment – Soldiers had to dry and change socks regularly; in severe cases, amputation was needed.

(b) Why was the Battle of Verdun important to the Allies? [6]

- A symbol of French resistance, Verdun became a powerful symbol of the French determination to defend their country at all costs.
- Boosted morale,
The successful defence encouraged both the French army and their Allies to keep fighting.
- Stopped the German breakthrough. Prevented Germany from capturing Verdun, which would have opened the way to Paris.
- Tied-down German forces.

The long battle forced Germany to commit a large number of troops, thereby reducing pressure on other fronts.

☐ Led to British support.

The heavy fighting encouraged Britain to launch the Somme offensive to relieve pressure on Verdun.

☐ Showed Allied strength.

Proved that the Allies could withstand a major German assault, strengthening their confidence.

(c) 'New types of weapons had little impact in the trench warfare of the Western Front.' How far do you agree with this statement? Explain your answer. [10]

Agree – Little impact:
- Machine guns maintained a stalemate – Made it easy to defend trenches and almost impossible for attackers to cross No Man's Land.
- Artillery caused heavy casualties but few breakthroughs – Most artillery bombardments warned the enemy of an attack and often failed to destroy barbed wire or trenches.
- Poison gas limited success.

Gas (chlorine, phosgene, mustard) caused fear and casualties, but gas masks reduced its effectiveness.

- Overall result.

New weapons often increased death tolls but did not end the stalemate for most of the war.

Disagree – Some impact:

- Tanks broke through trenches.

From 1916, tanks could cross trenches and crush barbed wire, aiding in battles such as Cambrai (1917).

- Aircraft improved reconnaissance.

Planes and observation balloons helped spot enemy positions and direct artillery more accurately.

- Creeping barrage tactics – Coordinated artillery fire with infantry attacks became more effective later in the war.

- By 1918 – A Combination of tanks, aircraft, and new tactics (e.g., stormtrooper units) helped break the stalemate in the final German offensives and Allied counter-attacks.

Conclusion:

- Balanced judgment.

For most of the war, new weapons had a limited impact on breaking the stalemate, mainly increasing casualties.

- However, by 1918, the development and coordination of these weapons did play a key role in ending trench warfare and bringing about victory for the Allies.

Chapter 13

Paper 13

May/June 0470/12

Paper 1 May/June 2022

INFORMATION

The total mark for this paper is 60

The number of marks for each question or part question is shown in brackets [ ]

CHAPTER 13

SECTION A: CORE CONTENT

Answer any two questions from this section.

1 Several individuals contributed to Italian unification.

(a) What was Pope Pius IX's Allocution of 1848? [4]

(b) Why was Napoleon III essential to Italian unification? [6]

(c) Who contributed more to Italian unification, Mazzini or Garibaldi? Explain your answer. [10]

2 Prussia and Austria were rivals in Germany.

(a) Describe what happened in the Frankfurt Parliament in 1848–49. [4]

(b) Why did Frederick William IV react as he did to the disturbances in Berlin in March 1848? [6]

(c) How surprising was it that Prussia emerged as the dominant power in Germany? Explain your answer. [10]

3   British imperialism affected local people in different ways.

(a) What did Lugard achieve in Nigeria? [4]

(b) Why did the Chinese try to resist the British in the Opium Wars? [6]

(c) 'The British response to the Indian Mutiny was justified.' How far do you agree with this statement? Explain your answer. [10]

4   The First World War had both long-term and short-term causes.

(a) What was the Triple Entente?

(b) Why was the launch of the first dreadnought in 1906 important? [6]

(c) 'The Austrian ultimatum to Serbia was more important than Franz Ferdinand's assassination in bringing about the First World War.' How far do you agree with this statement? Explain your answer. [10

5   Nobody got everything they wanted from the peace treaties of 1919.

(a)   What were the territorial terms of the Treaty of Sèvres?   [4]

(b)   Why did Lloyd George not want to punish Germany harshly?   [6]

(c)   Who had to compromise more during the peace negotiations in Paris, Clemenceau or Wilson? Explain your answer.   [10]

6   The League of Nations struggled to react effectively to major crises.

(a)   Describe Germany's relationship with the League of Nations during the period 1920 to 1939. [4]

(b)   Why did Haile Selassie speak to the Assembly of the League of Nations in June 1936? [6]

(c)   'The League of Nations did as much as it could in relation to the Japanese invasion of

Manchuria.' How far do you agree with this statement? Explain your answer. [10]

7   Immediately after the Second World War, relations between the Soviet Union and the United States were complicated.

(a)   What were the main disagreements at the Potsdam Conference?   [4]

(b)   Why did the blockade of Berlin fail?   [6]

(c)   'Stalin's policies in Eastern Europe in the period 1945–49 were defensive.' How far do you agree with this statement? Explain your answer. [10]

8   Iran and Iraq were not friendly neighbours.

(a)   Describe the opposition to the Shah in Iran.   [4]

(b)   Why did Iraq invade Iran in 1980? [6]

(c)   Was Saddam Hussein's invasion of Kuwait in 1990 surprising? Explain your answer. [10]

SECTION B: DEPTH STUDIES

Answer any one question from this section.

DEPTH STUDY A: THE FIRST WORLD WAR, 1914–18

9   Trench warfare dominated the Western Front for much of the war.

(a)   What was 'shell shock'?   [4]

(b)   Why did trench warfare last so long?   [6]

(c)   'Gas was the most important new weapon used in the First World War.' How far do you agree with this statement? Explain your answer.
    [10]

10   The First World War was fought on several fronts.

(a)   Describe the impact of the war on civilian populations. [4]

(b) Why was the war at sea necessary? [6]

(c) 'The Eastern Front was more important than the Western Front in the First World War.' How far do you agree with this statement? Explain your answer. [10]

DEPTH STUDY B: GERMANY, 1918–45

11 . German recovery after the First World War was initially slow.

(a) What was the Dawes Plan? [4]
(b) Why did Germany introduce a new currency in 1923? [6]
(c) 'The Revolution of 1918 was more important for Germany than the reaction of the people to the Treaty of Versailles.' How far do you agree with this statement? Explain your answer. [10]

12 The Nazis used different policies towards different groups of people.
(a) What was the League of German Maidens (BDM)? [4]
(b) Why did the Nazis make changes to the school curriculum? [6]

(c) 'Racial theories explain why minorities were persecuted in Nazi Germany.' How far do you agree with this statement? Explain your answer.
[10]

DEPTH STUDY C: RUSSIA, 1905–41

From 1917, rapid changes occurred in Russia.

(a) Describe how Trotsky contributed to the Communist victory in the Civil War. [4]

(b) Why was the New Economic Policy (NEP) critical? [6]

(c) 'The Provisional Government failed because of the Petrograd Soviet.' How far do you agree with this statement? Explain your answer. [10]

14 Stalin was ruthless in achieving and keeping power.

(a) What weaknesses of Trotsky helped Stalin become the leader of the USSR? [4]

(b) Why was Stalin's 'cult of personality' significant? [6]

(c) 'The Purges were a disaster for Stalin and the Soviet Union.' How far do you agree with this statement? Explain your answer. [10]

DEPTH STUDY D: THE UNITED STATES, 1919–41

15 The 1920s were not an easy time for many Americans.

(a) Describe ways in which the lives of many young women in cities changed during the 1920s. [

(b) Why were restrictions on immigration introduced in the 1920s? [6]

(c) 'The main problem caused by prohibition was corruption among the police and judges.' How far do you agree with this statement? Explain your answer. [10]

16 The New Deal had to address many problems.

(a) Describe how the New Deal helped farmers. [4]

(b) Why was the banking system one of the first things Roosevelt focused on during the Hundred Days? [6]

(c) 'The New Deal was opposed because it increased the power of government.' How far do you agree with this statement? Explain your answer. [10]

DEPTH STUDY E: CHINA, c.1930–c.1990

17 From the late 1920s, the Communists and Nationalists had differing views on the future of China.

(a) What happened at the Marco Polo Bridge in July 1937? [4]

(b) Why did the Communists go on the Long March? [6]

(c) 'It was the Second World War that brought about the Communist victory in the Civil War.' How far do you agree with this statement? Explain your answer. [10]

18 Different policies were introduced in China.

(a) How did the Chinese people respond to the Hundred Flowers campaign? [4]

(b) Why did Deng Xiaoping think change was necessary in China? [6]

(c) How far was the Cultural Revolution a success? Explain your answer. [10]

19 Many white South Africans benefited from the country's economic development.

(a) Describe the growth of manufacturing industries in South Africa up to 1945. [4]

(b) Why did the South African government support agriculture in the 1930s? [6]

(c) 'Land ownership was the most important issue facing black South Africans up to 1945.' How far do you agree with this statement? Explain your answer. [10]

20 South Africans had a variety of experiences in the period 1966 to 1980.

(a) What new steps did the South African government take to tighten security in the period 1966 to 1980? [4]

(b) Why did the economic improvements of 1966 to 1980 not benefit all sections of South African society? [6]

(c) 'Black consciousness was the most important part of the anti-apartheid movement in the period 1966 to 1980.' How far do you agree with this statement? Explain your answer.

[10]

DEPTH STUDY G: ISRAELIS AND PALESTINIANS SINCE 1945

21   Jews and Arabs both had claims over Palestine.

(a)   What were the Jewish objections to the United Nations' partition plan for Palestine?   [4]

(b)   Why was the future of Palestine important for Arabs at the end of the Second World War? [6]

(c)   'It was the Jewish insurgency in Palestine that persuaded Britain to withdraw.' How far do you agree with this statement? Explain your answer.

[10]

22   The issue of Palestinian refugees was affected by several different factors.

(a)   Describe the impact of the 1967 war on the issue of Palestinian refugees.   [4]

(b)   Why did the Palestine Liberation Organisation (PLO) use violent tactics?   [6]

(c)   'The Palestinian refugee crisis of 1948–49 was caused by Israel expelling Palestinians.' How far do you agree with this statement? Explain your answer.   [10]

CHAPTER 13: Answers

SECTION A: CORE CONTENT

Answer any two questions from this section

Answered Questions: 4 and 6

4   Prussia and Austria were rivals in Germany.

(a)   Describe what happened in the Frankfurt Parliament in 1848–49.   [4]

German states met to discuss unification – In 1848, representatives from across the German states gathered in Frankfurt to create a united and constitutional Germany.

A constitution was written – The Parliament drew up a liberal constitution and offered the crown of a united Germany to the King of Prussia.

The offer was rejected – King Frederick William IV of Prussia refused the crown, saying he would not accept it from "the gutter" (the people).

The Parliament failed – Without support from the kings and princes, the Frankfurt Parliament had no power, and it collapsed by 1849.

(b)   Why did Frederick William IV react as he did to the disturbances in Berlin in March 1848? [6]

Frederick William IV reacted carefully to the disturbances in Berlin in March 1848 because:

Fear of revolution spreading – The revolutions of 1848 were spreading across Europe, and Frederick William IV feared a violent uprising like the French Revolution, so he tried to calm the situation.

Wanted to avoid bloodshed – After soldiers clashed with protestors and people were killed, he tried to appear sympathetic to prevent further violence in Berlin.

Tactical move to keep control – He promised liberal reforms, a constitution, and even wore the German colours to win public support, but this was mainly a strategy to reduce tension.

No real commitment to democracy – His promises were not sincere. He still believed in absolute monarchy but used calming tactics to regain control.

Maintain his position and power – By calming the crowds, he protected his throne and later reversed many of the reforms once the situation was under control.

Influenced by military advice – He may have also been advised to avoid using the army too harshly at first, to stop things from escalating into a complete revolution.

(c) How surprising was it that Prussia emerged as the dominant power in Germany? Explain your answer. [10]

Reasons why it was NOT surprising:

    Strong military tradition – Prussia had one of the best-trained and most disciplined armies in Europe, which gave it great military strength compared to other German states.

    Efficient government and economy – Prussia had a well-organised bureaucracy and modern economy, with rapid industrial growth, especially in coal and steel.

    Leadership in the Zollverein – Prussia led the Zollverein (customs union), which united many German states economically and increased Prussia's influence.

    Weakness of Austria – Austria, Prussia's main rival, was weakened by internal problems (many different nationalities) and its defeat in wars like the Austro-Prussian War of 1866.

    Skilful leadership of Bismarck – Prussia's rise was helped by Bismarck's clever diplomacy and use of war, which strengthened its power and united the northern German states under its leadership.

Reasons why it WAS surprising:

Austria had traditionally led Germany. Before the 1860s, Austria had been the most powerful German-speaking state and dominated the German Confederation.

Prussia was once seen as a junior partner. Earlier in the 19th century, Prussia was viewed as less critical than Austria and was not expected to assume a leadership role.

Germany was made up of many states. It seemed unlikely that one state could unite them all without serious opposition from others.

Opposition from liberals and nationalists – Many people wanted a united Germany led by the people, not by a king or a militaristic state like Prussia.

Judgement:

It is not very surprising that Prussia became the dominant power in Germany. Although Austria had once been more powerful, Prussia had several advantages, including superior military strength, economic dominance, and strong leadership under Bismarck. While some people may have expected Austria to stay in charge, Prussia's rise made sense given the changes in power, economy, and war. So overall, it was expected rather than surprising.

6. The League of Nations struggled to react effectively to major crises.

a. Describe Germany's relationship with the League of Nations during the period 1920 to 1939. [4

Germany was not allowed to join in 1920. After World War I, Germany was blamed for the war in the Treaty of Versailles and was not invited to join the League of Nations.

Germany joined the League in 1926. Under the Weimar Republic, Germany was seen as becoming more peaceful, and with the support of Stresemann's foreign policy, it joined the League.

Germany was treated as an equal member. Once in the League, Germany gained a permanent seat on the League's Council, showing growing international trust.

Germany left the League in 1933. After Hitler came to power, Germany withdrew from the League because he rejected its aims and wanted to follow an aggressive foreign policy.

b. Why did Haile Selassie speak to the Assembly of the League of Nations in June 1936? [6]

To protest Italy's invasion of Abyssinia, Haile Selassie spoke out against Mussolini's invasion of his country (Abyssinia, now Ethiopia), which had begun in 1935.

To appeal for help and justice, he asked the League to take decisive action against Italy and to protect smaller nations from aggression.

To expose the League's failure, Selassie sought to demonstrate how the League had failed to prevent Italy from invading Abyssinia, despite Abyssinia being a member of the League.

To warn about future aggression – He warned that if the League did nothing, other aggressive nations might follow Italy's example, putting world peace at risk.

To defend Abyssinia's independence, Selassie sought to demonstrate that his country would not accept defeat and would continue to resist.

To garner international sympathy, his speech aimed to garner support from other countries and shame those who had failed to act, especially Britain and France.

c. 'The League of Nations did as much as it could in relation to the Japanese invasion of Manchuria.' How far do you agree with this statement? Explain your answer. [10]

Reasons to agree (The League did take some action):

The League investigated the invasion. The League sent the Lytton Commission to Manchuria to investigate the incident.

It took a clear stand – In 1933, the League published the Lytton Report, which stated that Japan was the aggressor and should withdraw from Manchuria.

Tried to act peacefully – The League followed its peaceful methods, using investigation and diplomacy rather than force.

Had limited power – The League had no army of its own and relied on member countries to enforce decisions, which limited what it could do.

Reasons to disagree (The League failed to act strongly):

The League was too slow – It took over a year to produce the Lytton Report, by which time Japan had complete control of Manchuria.

No real punishment for Japan – The League did not impose sanctions or take military action, making its decisions meaningless.

Major powers did not intervene – Britain and France were more preoccupied with their own problems, such as the Great Depression, and did not want to upset Japan.

Japan ignored the League and left. When the League criticised Japan, it left the League in 1933 with no serious consequences, showing the League's weakness.

Conclusion/judgement

While the League did take some steps, such as investigating the invasion and blaming Japan, these actions were too weak and too slow to make any meaningful difference. The League had no army, and its powerful members did not support more decisive actions. Therefore, it is not accurate to say that the League did as much as it could. It could have done much more with more decisive leadership and quicker decisions.

SECTION B: DEPTH STUDIES

Answer any one question from this section.

DEPTH STUDY A: THE FIRST WORLD WAR, 1914–18

Answered Questions: 9

9. Trench warfare dominated the Western Front for much of the war.

a) What was 'shell shock'? [4]

Shell shock was a mental illness caused by the extreme stress and trauma of warfare, especially in the trenches during World War I.

Caused by constant fear and explosions – Soldiers experienced this condition due to heavy shelling, fear of death, and the horrors of battle.

Symptoms included confusion and breakdowns – Soldiers with shell shock might suffer from trembling, nightmares, anxiety, memory loss, and even paralysis.

Often misunderstood at the time, Many officers thought it was a sign of cowardice or weakness rather than a real medical issue, and some soldiers were even punished for it.

b) Why did trench warfare last so long? [6]

Defensive advantage of trenches – Trenches provided soldiers with strong protection from enemy fire, making it very difficult to attack successfully without incurring heavy losses.

New weapons favoured defence – Machine guns, barbed wire, and artillery made it easier to defend than to advance, so attacks often failed to break through.

No effective tactics for breakthroughs – Early in the war, generals employed outdated tactics, such as charging in large numbers, which proved ineffective against modern weapons.

The land was difficult to cross. The ground between the trenches (called No Man's Land) was often muddy, cratered, and full of obstacles, slowing down any attack.

Even successful attacks gained little. When land was gained, it was often only a few metres, and the other side would quickly counterattack, leading to a stalemate.

Strong supply lines and reinforcements – Both sides had large armies and strong supply systems, so they could keep fighting for years without collapsing.

c) 'Gas was the most important new weapon used in the First World War.' How far do you agree with this statement? Explain your answer.

[10]

Arguments for gas being the most critical weapon:

- Caused fear and suffering – Gas attacks caused panic, burned lungs, blinded soldiers, and caused a slow, painful death, especially early in the war.
- Forced armies to adapt – Gas led to the development of gas masks and new safety tactics, changing the way soldiers fought.
- Psychological impact – The fear of gas made soldiers constantly alert, adding to the mental stress of trench life.

Arguments against gas being the most critical weapon:

- Limited effectiveness – Gas was unpredictable; wind could blow it back onto the attackers, and gas masks reduced its impact over time.
- Did not break the stalemate – Gas rarely led to significant victories or breakthroughs and did not end trench warfare.
- Other weapons were more deadly and decisive – Weapons like machine guns caused far more casualties and made defence much stronger than attack.
- Artillery was the biggest killer – Most deaths were caused by shellfire, not gas, and artillery had a much greater effect on the course of battles.

- Tanks had a bigger long-term impact – Though limited early on, tanks helped break through enemy lines by 1917–18 and showed how warfare would change in the future.

Judgement:
While gas was terrifying and did affect how soldiers fought, it was not the most essential weapon. It caused fear but had a limited impact on the overall course of the war. Machine guns, artillery, and later tanks played a much bigger role in shaping the fighting and breaking the stalemate. The statement is only partly true, but other weapons were more critical in determining the war's outcome.

Paper 14

Chapter 14

HISTORY   0470/13

Paper 1   May/June 2022

2 hours

DC (MB) 303421/3

© UCLES 2022

CHAPTER 14

SECTION A: CORE CONTENT

Answer any two questions from this section.

1   Several different factors contributed to Italian unification.

(a)   Describe what happened in Sicily in 1860. [4]

(b)   Why was Cavour critical to the achievement of Italian unification?   [6]

(c) 'Rome was central to the Italian struggle for unification.' How far do you agree with this statement? Explain your answer. [10]

2   The road to German unification was not always a smooth one.

(a)   What was the Convention of Gastein?   [4]

(b)   Why did Frederick William IV reject the offer by the Frankfurt Parliament of the position of Emperor of Germany?   [6]

(c) 'Bismarck's approach to foreign policy in the period 1862–71 was to react to opportunities as they arose.' How far do you agree with this statement? Explain your answer. [10]

3   The local people rarely welcomed European imperialism.

(a) What happened to the British ship 'Arrow' and its crew in October 1856? [4]

(b) Why did the French use a policy of assimilation in Senegal? [6]

(c) 'The Boxers achieved little.' How far do you agree with this statement? Explain your answer. [10]

4   Four events after 1900 gradually drew Europe closer to war.

(a) What was the result of the Algeciras Conference of 1906? [4]

(b) Why were Serbian victories in the Balkans in 1912 and 1913 important? [6]

(c) 'German colonial ambitions were more important than the naval race as a cause of the First World War.' How far do you agree with this statement? Explain your answer.

5 The victors of the war dominated the peace talks of 1919–20.

(a) What happened to Germany's colonies in the Treaty of Versailles? [4]

(b) Why was Turkey treated harshly in the Treaty of Sèvres? [6]

(c) Who did Wilson find more challenging to deal with during the peace negotiations, Clemenceau or Lloyd George? Explain your answer. [10]

6   In the 1930s, there was increasing instability.

(a) Describe the increasing militarism of Italy in the 1930s. [4]

(b) Why was the Spanish Civil War important to Hitler? [6]

(c) Which was more to blame for the war breaking out in September 1939, Germany or Britain? Explain your answer. [10]

7   The United States reacted to communism in different parts of the world.

(a) Describe how Eisenhower reacted to the Cuban revolution of 1959.

[4]

(b) Why did the American policy of 'search and destroy' in Vietnam create problems?
[6]

(c) Was the Korean War a defeat for North Korea? Explain your answer. [10]

8 Both Iran and Iraq faced difficulties during the 1970s and 1980s.

(a) Describe the consequences for Iraq of the Iran-Iraq War. [4]

(b) Why did the Kurds in Iraq resist the rule of Saddam Hussein? [6]

(c) 'The Revolution of 1979 in Iran was motivated by religion.' How far do you agree with this statement? Explain your answer. [10]

SECTION B: DEPTH STUDIES

Answer any one question from this section.

DEPTH STUDY A: THE FIRST WORLD WAR, 1914–18

9   Both conventional and new weapons were used in the First World War.

(a)   Describe the use and impact of gas on the Western Front.   [4]

(b)   Why were aircraft important on the Western Front? [6]

(c)   'The criticisms of Haig's leadership in the Battle of the Somme are justified.' How far do you agree with this statement? Explain your answer.   [10]

10   In the last years of the war, events began to go against Germany.

(a)   Describe the events in November 1918 that led to the Kaiser's abdication.   [4]

(b)   Why was the German introduction of unrestricted submarine warfare in 1917 important?   [6]

(c) 'It was the Allies' use of new tactics that led to the German failure on the battlefield in 1918.' How far do you agree with this statement? Explain your answer. [10]

DEPTH STUDY B: GERMANY, 1918–45

11   After an unsteady start, the Weimar Republic recovered.

(a)   Who was Rosa Luxemburg?   [4]

(b)   Why did Germans in the Ruhr begin passive resistance in 1923? [6]

(c)   How important was Stresemann to the recovery of the Weimar Republic? Explain your answer.
[10]

12   Despite all the efforts of the Nazis, they still faced some opposition.

(a) Describe Nazi use of censorship. [4]

(b) Why was the Gestapo important in Nazi Germany? [6]

(c) 'The most important opposition to the Nazi regime came from young people.' How far do you agree with this statement? Explain your answer. [10]

DEPTH STUDY C: RUSSIA, 1905–41

13 After the abdication of the Tsar, the future of Russia hung in the balance.

(a) Who was Kerensky? [4]

(b) Why was the mutiny at the Kronstadt Naval Base in 1921 important? [6]

(c) 'Trotsky was the main reason the Bolsheviks won the Civil War.' How far do you agree with this statement? Explain your answer. [10]

14   Stalin's ideas and policies were different from Lenin's.

(a)   What did Stalin mean by 'Socialism in one country'?   [4]

(b)   Why was Lenin's Political Testament not published in the Soviet Union at the time of his death?   [6]

(c)   'It was the Purges that gave Stalin control of the USSR.' How far do you agree with this statement? Explain your answer.   [10]

DEPTH STUDY D: THE UNITED STATES, 1919–41

15   The 1920s were a good time for many Americans.

(a)   Describe the problems faced by the coal industry in the 1920s.   [4]

(b)   Why was the motor car important in 1920s America?   [6]

(c) 'Farmers benefited from the economic boom of the 1920s.' How far do you agree with this statement? Explain your answer. [10]

16 The 1932 presidential election followed a period of crisis in America.

(a) What did Roosevelt promise the voters in the 1932 presidential election campaign? [4]

(b) Why did Wall Street crash in October 1929? [6]

(c) 'The reason why the Depression had such an impact on people's lives was Hoover's failure to deal with it.' How far do you agree with this statement? Explain your answer. [10]

DEPTH STUDY E: CHINA, c.1930–c.1990

17 The 1950s were years of change in China.

(a) What were people's courts? [4]

(b) Why was the first Five-Year Plan successful? [6]

(c) 'The social reforms of the 1950s were more important than the introduction of communes.' How far do you agree with this statement? Explain your answer. [10]

18 China's relations with other parts of the world changed frequently.

(a) What were the results of Kissinger's visit to China in July 1971? [4]

(b) Why was India important to China from the 1950s onwards? [6]

(c) 'Relations between China and the USSR were good in the period 1950 to 1976.' How far do you agree with this statement? Explain your answer. [10]

19   The introduction of apartheid led to protest movements.

(a)   Describe the part played by women in the anti-apartheid protests.   [4]

(b)   Why was Mandela put on trial for treason in 1963–64?   [6]

(c)   'Few South Africans benefited from the introduction of apartheid.' How far do you agree with this statement? Explain your answer.   [10]

20   The end of apartheid came only after a long struggle.

(a)   Describe the part played by Archbishop Tutu in the end of apartheid.   [4]

(b)   Why did de Klerk face opposition from some white South Africans during his discussions with Mandela in the early 1990s?   [6]

(c) How far was Botha's policy of 'total strategy' in the 1980s a success? Explain your answer. [10]

DEPTH STUDY G: ISRAELIS AND PALESTINIANS SINCE 1945

21 Once the Second World War had ended, the issue of Palestine had to be dealt with.

(a) What were the Arab objections to the United Nations' partition plan for Palestine? [4]

(b) Why was Palestine important for the Jews at the end of the Second World War? [6]

(c) How far were British actions to blame for the crisis in Palestine after the Second World War? Explain your answer. [10]

22 Attempts to address the issue of Palestinian refugees have not been very effective.

(a) Describe the impact on the Palestinians of Jewish West Bank settlements. [4]

(b) Why has the United Nations failed to solve the issue of Palestinian refugees? [6]

(c) How far have Arab states supported the Palestine Liberation Organisation (PLO)? Explain your answer [10]

CHAPTER 14: Answers

SECTION A: CORE CONTENT

Answer any two questions from this section.

Answered Questions: 2, 5

2. The road to German unification was not always a smooth one.

a. What was the Convention of Gastein? [4]

☐ An agreement made in 1865 – The Convention of Gastein was a deal between Austria and Prussia.
☐ About the administration of Schleswig and Holstein – These two duchies were taken from Denmark after the Second Schleswig War.
☐ Prussia controlled Schleswig. Prussia was given control of the northern duchy of Schleswig.
☐ Austria controlled Holstein – Austria took control of the southern duchy of Holstein.

☐   A temporary solution – This agreement was intended to settle the dispute over who ruled these areas, but it ultimately led to increased conflict between Austria and Prussia.

b.   Why did Frederick William IV reject the offer by the Frankfurt Parliament of the position of Emperor of Germany?   [6]

☐   Did not want to accept a crown from a popular assembly – Frederick William IV believed that the offer coming from the Frankfurt Parliament, which was made up of elected representatives, was not legitimate because it was "from the gutter" (ordinary people), not from other monarchs.

☐   He wanted the crown to come from other kings – he wanted the German Emperor title to be offered by different rulers, not by a revolutionary assembly.

☐   Believed in the divine right of kings – He thought kings ruled by the will of God, not by the approval of elected bodies or parliaments.

☐   Feared losing power or causing unrest – Accepting the crown from a revolutionary body might weaken his authority at home and upset the established order in Prussia.

☐ Concerned about the lack of support from other German states, Many German princes and states did not support the Frankfurt Parliament's offer, making the position unstable.

☐ Wanted to maintain Prussia's independence and power – He did not want to submit to a unified German state controlled by a parliament that might limit Prussia's influence.

c. 'Bismarck's approach to foreign policy in the period 1862–71 was to react to opportunities as they arose.' How far do you agree with this statement? Explain your answer. [10]

Arguments that Bismarck reacted to opportunities:
- Seized moments to provoke war – Bismarck reacted quickly to events like the Danish refusal to give up Schleswig-Holstein, which led to the Second Schleswig War (1864).

- Used diplomatic incidents to his advantage – For example, he manipulated the Ems Telegram in 1870 to provoke France into declaring the Franco-Prussian War.
- Flexible approach – He was willing to change tactics depending on what opportunities appeared, rather than strictly following a set plan.

Arguments that Bismarck was also a planner:

- Long-term goal of German unification – Bismarck had a precise aim to unify Germany under Prussian leadership and worked steadily towards this.
- Careful preparation for wars – The wars with Denmark, Austria (1866), and France (1870–71) were carefully planned to increase Prussian power and isolate enemies.
- Diplomatic skill to maintain alliances – Bismarck avoided fighting a two-front war by keeping Russia and France isolated diplomatically, showing careful strategy.
- Used wars strategically – Each war was part of a bigger plan to remove Austria from German affairs and unite the northern and southern German states.

Judgement:

Bismarck's foreign policy was a mix of reacting to events and careful planning. While he was very skilled at taking advantage of opportunities as they arose, these moves were part of a broader, straightforward strategy to unify Germany under Prussia. I partly agree with the statement, but it is essential to remember that Bismarck's approach was not merely reactionary — he had a well-defined long-term plan and utilised events to achieve his objectives.

5. The victors of the war dominated the peace talks of 1919–20.

(a) What happened to Germany's colonies in the Treaty of Versailles? [4]

Taken away from Germany – Germany lost all of its colonies in Africa and the Pacific.
Made into mandates – Colonies were put under League of Nations control as "mandates."
Given to Allies – Britain, France, Japan, and others were granted control to rule on their behalf.
Germany was not allowed to regain them. This reduced Germany's power and overseas influence permanently.

(b) Why was Turkey treated harshly in the Treaty of Sèvres? [6]

As part of the defeated Central Powers, Turkey had fought alongside Germany in World War I, so the Allies sought to punish it.

Breakup of the Ottoman Empire – Allies sought to dismantle the empire and reduce its influence in the Middle East.

Strategic interests – Britain and France wanted control of former Ottoman lands (e.g., Palestine, Syria, Iraq) for their own empires.

Control of key waterways – The Straits (Dardanelles and Bosporus) were put under international control to allow free access for Allied ships.

Support for new nations – Greece and Armenia were given land taken from Turkey as a reward for their support of the Allies.

Prevent future threats – Harsh terms (loss of territory, limited army) were meant to stop Turkey from becoming a military threat again.

(c) Who did Wilson find more challenging to deal with during the peace negotiations, Clemenceau or Lloyd George? Explain your answer. [10]

Clemenceau was more difficult:
- Wanted harsh punishment – Clemenceau wanted Germany to be severely punished: heavy reparations, a weak army, and the Rhineland demilitarised.
- Clashed with Wilson's Fourteen Points – Wilson wanted a fair peace based on self-determination and not too harsh on Germany.
- Demanded revenge – Clemenceau represented French public opinion, which wanted revenge after the enormous losses of World War I.
- Disagreed on security – Clemenceau wanted Germany permanently weakened to protect France, but Wilson worried this would cause future conflict.

Lloyd George was easier to deal with:
- More moderate aims – Lloyd George wanted Germany punished but not destroyed, because he wanted Germany to recover for trade and to stop communism spreading from Russia.

- Supported some Fourteen Points – He agreed with ideas like the League of Nations and self-determination (but with some limits).
- Still caused difficulty – He did want Germany's navy and colonies reduced, which Wilson did not fully support, but overall, he was willing to compromise.

Judgment – Wilson found Clemenceau more challenging to deal with because Clemenceau's demands for a very harsh treaty were the opposite of Wilson's idealistic vision for a just peace. However, Lloyd George could also be difficult at times, especially when protecting British interests, but he was generally more willing to compromise than Clemenceau.

SECTION B: DEPTH STUDIES

Answer any one question from this section.

Answered Questions: 9

DEPTH STUDY A: THE FIRST WORLD WAR, 1914–18

9. Both conventional and new weapons were used in the First World War.

(a) Describe the use and impact of gas on the Western Front. [4]

First use: Gas was first used by the Germans at the Second Battle of Ypres in 1915.

Types of gas: Chlorine, phosgene, and mustard gas were used, causing suffocation, blisters, and blindness.

Soldier response: Gas masks were introduced to protect soldiers and became standard equipment.

Impact: Gas caused fear and panic, but killed relatively few soldiers and did not break the trench stalemate.

(b) Why were aircraft important on the Western Front? [6]

Reconnaissance – Aircraft were used to spy on enemy troop movements and locate artillery positions.

Directing artillery – Pilots helped to correct artillery fire by reporting where shells landed.

Fighter planes – Planes were armed with machine guns and used to attack enemy aircraft (dogfights).

Bombing – Aircraft were later used to bomb enemy trenches, supply lines, and railway stations.

Communication – Aircraft improved communication between commanders and troops by providing quick updates.

Psychological impact – Aircraft boosted morale for some and created fear for those under attack

(c) 'The criticisms of Haig's leadership in the Battle of the Somme are justified.' How far do you agree with this statement? Explain your answer.
  [10]

Agree – Criticisms are justified:
- High casualties – Nearly 60,000 British soldiers were killed or wounded on the first day, showing poor planning.

- Outdated tactics – Haig continued to use mass infantry charges despite machine guns making them deadly.
- Limited gains – After months of fighting, only a few miles of ground were captured, suggesting a waste of life.
- Ignoring realities – Critics argue Haig underestimated German defences and overestimated the effect of artillery.

Disagree – Criticisms are not entirely justified:

- Heavy German losses – The Somme weakened the German army, making it harder for them to continue the war.
- Pressure off Verdun – The battle helped the French by drawing German troops away from Verdun.
- Learning curve – Tactics improved later in the battle, leading to better coordination and use of tanks.
- Difficult situation – Haig faced tough decisions and limited options due to the trench warfare stalemate.

Overall judgment – While Haig's tactics led to massive losses, some successes were achieved, and his decisions must be seen in the context of the challenges of 1916. Criticisms are partly justified but not entirely fair.

Chapter 15

Paper 14
0470/11

Paper 1   May/June 2022
2 hours

CHAPTER 15

SECTION A: CORE CONTENT

Answer any two questions from this section.

1 The struggle for Italian unification led to the declaration of the Kingdom of Italy in 1861.

(a) Describe the activities of the Young Italy movement. [4]

(b) Why was Cavour suspicious of Garibaldi? [6]

(c) 'Garibaldi's success in Sicily was the turning point in the winning of Italian unification.' How far do you agree with this statement? Explain your answer. [10]

2 Both war and diplomacy contributed to the achievement of German unification.

(a) Describe how the Zollverein worked. [4]

(b) Why did the Schleswig-Holstein question present Bismarck with opportunities? [6]

(c) 'The Franco-Prussian War was more important than the Austro-Prussian War in bringing about German unification.' How far do you agree with this statement? Explain your answer. [10]

European imperialism had a varied impact on local populations.

(a) Describe the work of missionaries in nineteenth-century Africa. [4]

(b) Why was the Boxer Rising important for China? [6]

(c) Which was more beneficial for the local population, indirect rule in Nigeria or assimilation in Senegal? Explain your answer. [10]

4 Before the First World War, Austria-Hungary and Germany were two of the great European powers.

(a) What was 'Weltpolitik'? [4]

(b) Why was Austria-Hungary interested in events in the Balkans? [6]

(c) Which was more to blame for the arms race, Britain or Germany? Explain your answer. [10]

5   The peace treaties of 1919 had to deal with many different issues.

(a) What territorial demands did Clemenceau make during the Paris Peace Conference? [4]

(b) Why was the break-up of the Austro-Hungarian Empire confirmed in the Treaty of Sèvres? [6]

(c) Who had to compromise more during the peace negotiations in Paris, Clemenceau or Lloyd George? Explain your answer. [10]

6   Hitler's policies brought war closer.

(a) Describe the events in February and March of 1938 that led to Anschluss. [4]

(b) Why was involvement in the Spanish Civil War of benefit to Hitler? [6]

(c) 'Hitler agreed to the Nazi-Soviet Pact to avoid war against the Soviet Union.' How far do you agree with this statement? Explain your answer. [10]

7 After the Second World War, the United States was concerned about the threat of communism in Europe.

(a) What was the Truman Doctrine? [4]

(b) Why was the failure of the Berlin Blockade important? [6]

(c) Was it surprising that Britain and the United States agreed at Yalta that Eastern Europe should be a Soviet sphere of influence? Explain your answer. [10]

8   The United States was faced with challenges in various parts of the world.

(a)   Describe MacArthur's role in the Korean War. [4]

(b)   Why did Kennedy go ahead with the Bay of Pigs invasion in 1961? [6]

(c)   'It was the United States' strategy and tactics that led to its failure in Vietnam.' How far do you agree with this statement? Explain your answer. [10]

SECTION B: DEPTH STUDIES

Answer any one question from this section.

DEPTH STUDY A: THE FIRST WORLD WAR, 1914–18

9   The first few months of the war saw nine significant events, indicating that it would not be over by Christmas.

(a)   Describe the conduct of the German army as it advanced through Belgium. [4]

(b)   Why did the introduction of trenches by both sides ensure the war would not be over quickly? [6]

(c)   How far did the British Expeditionary Force (BEF) succeed in achieving its aims? Explain your answer.   [10]

10   The tide of the war began to turn against Germany in 1917.

(a)   What was the Hindenburg Line? [4]
(b)   Why was a republic declared in Germany in November 1918?   [6]
(c)   How decisive was the American entry into the war in 1917? Explain your answer.   [10]

DEPTH STUDY B: GERMANY, 1918–45

11   It took some time for the Nazi Party to win popular support.

(a)   Describe the role of the SA in the Nazi Party during the 1920s. [4]

(b)   Why was the Nazi Party able to attract increasing support in the early 1930s? [6]

(c)   'Hitler showed little leadership quality during the Munich Putsch.' How far do you agree with this statement? Explain your answer. [10]

12   The Nazi regime used a range of different methods to control Germany.

(a)   Describe how the SS controlled German society. [4]

(b)   Why was there some opposition to Nazi rule? [6]

(c)   'The Nazis' economic policies were more effective than their use of the mass media in winning the support of the German people.' How far do you agree with this statement? Explain your answer. [10]

DEPTH STUDY C: RUSSIA, 1905–41

13   The years after 1905 were crucial ones for the Tsar and for Russia.

(a)   What was Bloody Sunday? [4]

(b)   Why was the Tsar's decision in 1915 to take personal command of the Russian army important? [6]

(c)   'The 1905 Revolution led to a period of significant reform.' How far do you agree with this statement? Explain your answer. [10]

Stalin was determined to achieve power and then maintain it.

(a) What were the 'gulags'? [4]

(b) Why did Stalin introduce the Great Purges in the mid-1930s? [6]

(c) 'Stalin's policy ideas explain why he, and not Trotsky, emerged as leader of the USSR in the mid-1920s.' How far do you agree with this statement? Explain your answer. [10]

DEPTH STUDY D: THE UNITED STATES, 1919–41

15 During the 1920s, there were many examples of intolerance.

(a) Who were Sacco and Vanzetti? [4]

(b) Why did many Americans disapprove of the 'Roaring Twenties'? [6]

(c) 'Prohibition was introduced because some people believed drinking alcohol caused poverty and neglect of families.' How far do you agree with this statement? Explain your answer. [10]

16 The Depression changed everything in the United States.

(a) What were the 'Okies'? [4]

(b) Why was Roosevelt able to win over many voters during his 1932 election campaign? [6]

(c) How far were speculators on the stock market responsible for the Depression? Explain your answer. [10]

DEPTH STUDY E: CHINA, c.1930–c.1990

Between 1930 and 1949, the Nationalists' strength gradually declined.

(a) What actions by the Nationalists lost them support during the Second World War? [4]

(b) Why were the Communists able to survive the five extermination campaigns by the Nationalists? [6]

(c) 'The Communists won the Civil War because of their tactics.' How far do you agree with this statement? Explain your answer. [10]

18 As China's power grew, its relations with other countries became more important.

(a) Describe the improvement in relations between China and the United States in the early 1970s. [4]

(b) Why did China sign the Panchsheel Agreement of 1954? [6]

(c) Which has been more critical to China, Taiwan or Vietnam? Explain your answer. [10]

19 Apartheid was introduced and consolidated during the 1950s and 1960s.

(a) What was the Sabotage Act of 1962? [4]

(b) Why did the South African government introduce the Group Areas Act of 1950? [6]

(c) 'The Sharpeville Massacre was a turning point for South Africa.' How far do you agree with this statement? Explain your answer. [10]

20 In the period 1966 to 1980, the South African government used a range of methods to support apartheid.

(a) What was the Bureau of State Security (BOSS)? [4]

(b) Why, from 1976, did the South African government claim to be giving independence to the Bantustans? [6]

(c) How effective were the government's methods of suppression in the period 1966 to 1980? Explain your answer. [10]

DEPTH STUDY G: ISRAELIS AND PALESTINIANS SINCE 1945

21 War broke out between Arab states and Israel in 1967 and 1973.

(a) Describe the USA's role in the Yom Kippur War. [4]

(b) Why was the Yom Kippur War important to the Arabs? [6]

(c) 'The Arab states were to blame for the Six-Day War.' How far do you agree with this statement? Explain your answer. [10]

22 It has been impossible to resolve the issue of Palestine and the Palestinians.

(a) What is the West Bank? [4]
(b) Why did the emergence of Hamas make a peace settlement with Israel less likely? [6]

(c) How far have the Likud and Labour parties agreed over Palestine? Explain your answer.
[10]

CHAPTER 15 ANSWER 15

SECTION A: CORE CONTENT

Answer any two questions from this section.

Answered Questions: 4 and 6

4. Before the First World War, Austria-Hungary and Germany were two of the great European powers.

(a) What was 'Weltpolitik'? [4 marks]

    Meaning – 'Weltpolitik' means 'world policy' in German.
    German aim – Kaiser Wilhelm II's foreign policy was to make Germany a world power.
    Actions – Included building a strong navy, gaining overseas colonies, and competing with Britain and France.
    Impact – Increased tensions in Europe contributed to the causes of the First World War.

(b) Why was Austria-Hungary interested in events in the Balkans? [6 marks]

A multi-ethnic empire, Austria-Hungary had many different nationalities, including Slavs, and feared that Slav nationalism would inspire revolts.

Serbian threat – Serbia wanted to unite all Slavs in the Balkans, which threatened Austria-Hungary's control over its own Slavic population.

Desire for influence – Austria-Hungary wanted to expand its power and influence in the Balkans as the Ottoman Empire weakened.

Prevent Russian dominance – Austria-Hungary sought to prevent Russia from gaining excessive influence in the Balkans, which would threaten its own security.

Strategic importance – The Balkans provided access to the Mediterranean Sea and trade routes, which Austria-Hungary wanted to control.

Maintain the 6empire's strength – Intervening in the Balkans was seen as a way to show power and maintain Austria-Hungary's position as a great power.

(c) Which was more to blame for the arms race, Britain or Germany? Explain your answer. [10 marks]

Germany is more to blame:
- Naval expansion – Germany built a powerful navy, including Dreadnought-class battleships, to challenge Britain's naval dominance.
- Weltpolitik policy – Germany's foreign policy aimed at becoming a world power, which alarmed Britain and pushed it to expand its own forces.
- Military spending – Germany significantly increased spending on its army, which encouraged other nations to do the same.
- Aggressive image – The Kaiser's actions and speeches made Germany appear threatening, forcing Britain to respond.

Britain is more to blame:
- Naval supremacy – Britain had the world's largest navy and was determined to keep a 'two-power standard', forcing others to catch up.
- Dreadnought race – Britain's launch of the Dreadnought in 1906 made all previous battleships obsolete and forced Germany to build more.
- Colonial defence – Britain's focus on protecting its vast empire meant it expanded its navy, which escalated tensions with Germany.

Conclusion– Germany is more to blame because its naval build-up and aggressive foreign policy created fear and competition. Britain's actions were primarily defensive in nature to maintain its maritime supremacy.

6. Hitler's policies brought war closer.

(a) Describe the events in February and March of 1938 that led to Anschluss. [4]

Berchtesgaden meeting – In February 1938, Austrian Chancellor Schuschnigg met Hitler, who demanded that Nazis be given key government positions in Austria.

Austrian concessions – Schuschnigg agreed, giving Seyss-Inquart (a leading Austrian Nazi) control of the police and other positions.

Plebiscite planned – Schuschnigg announced a referendum (plebiscite) to let Austrians vote on independence.

German invasion – Hitler sent troops into Austria in March 1938; Seyss-Inquart invited them in, and Austria was united with Germany (Anschluss).

(b) Why was involvement in the Spanish Civil War of benefit to Hitler? [6]

Tested weapons – Germany utilised the war to test new weapons, including tanks, aircraft, and bombs, which were later employed in WWII.

Military experience – The Luftwaffe (air force) gained valuable combat experience, primarily through the bombing of Guernica.

Strengthened alliances – Cooperation with Mussolini in Spain improved relations with Italy, paving the way for the Rome–Berlin Axis.

Weakened communism – Hitler helped Franco defeat left-wing (communist-supported) forces, reducing the spread of communism in Europe.

Distracted Britain and France – The war diverted Britain and France's attention from Hitler's plans in central Europe.

Boosted confidence – Germany's success in Spain made Hitler more confident in pursuing an aggressive foreign policy.

(c) 'Hitler agreed to the Nazi-Soviet Pact to avoid war against the Soviet Union.' How far do you agree with this statement? Explain your answer. [10]

Agree – To avoid war with the USSR:

- Avoid a two-front war – Hitler wanted to prevent fighting the USSR while planning to invade Poland and later France.
- Short-term peace – The pact gave Germany temporary security from Soviet attack, allowing Hitler to focus on the West.
- Bought time – Hitler knew he would eventually invade the USSR (Operation Barbarossa), but needed time to prepare.

Disagree – Other reasons were more important:

- Divide Poland – The pact secretly agreed to split Poland between Germany and the USSR, making invasion easier.
- Prevent British/French-Soviet alliance – The pact stopped Stalin from joining Britain and France against Germany.
- Confidence to act – The pact gave Hitler the confidence to invade Poland, knowing the USSR would not interfere.
- Strategic advantage – The deal secured raw materials from the USSR (oil, grain) to support Germany's war effort.

Conclusion: Avoiding war with the USSR was a key reason, but the main benefit was freedom to invade

Poland without fear of Soviet intervention. The pact was as much about enabling aggression as it was about avoiding war.

SECTION B: DEPTH STUDIES

Answer any one question from this section.

DEPTH STUDY B: GERMANY, 1918–45

Answered Questions: 12

12. The Nazi regime used a range of different methods to control Germany.

(a) Describe how the SS controlled German society. [4]

- Terror and intimidation – The SS arrested, imprisoned, and executed anyone who opposed Nazi rule.
- Concentration camps – They ran camps where political prisoners, Jews, and other groups were sent.

- Police state – The SS controlled the Gestapo (secret police), spying on citizens and crushing dissent.
- Ideological control – They promoted Nazi ideas and racial policies, enforcing loyalty to Hitler.

(b) Why was there some opposition to Nazi rule? [6]

- Political opponents – Communists and Social Democrats opposed Nazi policies and wanted democracy restored.
- Religious groups – Some Christians objected to Nazi interference in church affairs and persecution of minorities.
- Youth resistance – Groups like the Edelweiss Pirates and White Rose opposed strict Nazi control and propaganda.
- Military officers – Some army leaders disliked Hitler's aggressive foreign policy and planned assassinations (e.g., the July Plot of 1944).
- Persecution of minorities – Many Germans disapproved of the treatment of Jews, Roma, and others.

- Loss of freedoms – Censorship, fear, and lack of free speech angered some citizens who wanted more personal freedom.

(c) 'The Nazis' economic policies were more effective than their use of the mass media in winning the support of the German people.' How far do you agree with this statement? Explain your answer. [10]

Agree – Economic policies were more effective:
- Reduced unemployment – Public works (Autobahns), rearmament, and conscription created jobs and gave people security.
- Strengthened economy – The Nazis improved industry, farming, and trade to prepare Germany for war (Four-Year Plan).
- Volkswagen and leisure schemes – Programs like Strength Through Joy (KdF) promised affordable cars and holidays, boosting morale.
- Restored pride – Many Germans supported the Nazis because they brought stability and prosperity after the Depression.

Disagree – Mass media was equally or more effective:

- Propaganda everywhere – Radios, newspapers, posters, and films constantly praised Hitler and the Nazis.
- Control of culture – Books, art, music, and education were censored to promote Nazi ideology and shape opinions.
- Mass rallies – Events like the Nuremberg rallies created excitement and made people feel part of something powerful.
- Limited opposition – Propaganda hid Nazi failures and presented Hitler as Germany's saviour, ensuring continued loyalty.

Conclusion – Economic success provided people with practical reasons to support the Nazis, but propaganda ensured that this support remained strong. Both were important, but without economic improvement, propaganda alone might not have worked.

Chapter 16

Page 16

DC (JP/CT) 304185/2
© UCLES 2022
HISTORY   0470/21

Paper 2   May/June 2022

2 hours

INFORMATION

The total mark for this paper is 50.

The number of marks for each question or part question is shown in brackets [ ].

CHAPTER 16

Option A: Nineteenth-century topic

WAS THE KU KLUX Klan's MAIN PURPOSE TO DEFEAT THE REPUBLICAN PARTY?

Study the Background Information and the sources carefully, and then answer all the questions.

Background Information

There has been considerable discussion about the primary objectives of the Ku Klux Klan. Some contemporaries and historians have emphasised that it wanted to intimidate voters who supported the Republican Party. It tried to defeat the Republicans in elections and achieve conservative Democratic control of the southern states. However, few Democrats were willing to admit the Klan's political character and purpose. Others have argued that its main aim was to oppose Reconstruction and that it was a reaction to the poor government, crime, and chaos that prevailed during that period. Some have suggested that the emergence of the Klan was based on a deep fear of black people and their newly gained rights. They have pointed to a desire to destroy the cultural, economic and social independence that ex-slaves had gained with emancipation.

How far was the Ku Klux Klan's primary purpose a party political one – to defeat Republicans?

SOURCE A

In 1866, General Nathan Bedford Forrest founded the Ku Klux Klan in Tennessee as a 'social club'. By 1868, it had evolved into a hooded terrorist organisation that its members called 'The Invisible Empire of the South'. Forrest was its first leader or 'Grand Wizard'. White Southerners from all classes joined the Klan's ranks. In the name of preserving law and order in a white-dominated society, Klansmen punished newly freed ex-slaves for a variety of reasons, including behaving in an 'impudent' manner towards white people. They whipped the teachers of freedmen's schools and burnt their schoolhouses. However, first and foremost, the Klan sought to do away with Republican influence in the South by terrorising and murdering its party leaders and all those who voted for it. In the time leading up to the 1868 presidential election, the Klan's activities picked up in speed and brutality. In 1871, Congress passed the Ku Klux Klan Act, which allowed the government to act against terrorist organisations. However, with the overwhelming support for the Klan in the South, convictions were difficult to obtain.

From a recent history book.

SOURCE B

The Klan, a white supremacist group, was founded by Confederate army veterans in Pulaski, Tennessee, in December 1865. Dressed up in scary costumes with hoods, they rode about at night, threatening and frightening black people. They demanded that black people either vote Democrat or not at all. The Klan loved weird titles, and a former Confederate general, Nathan Bedford Forrest, is said to have been the Klan's leader for a time as Grand Wizard. The Klan's main aim was to keep black people down and white supremacy intact, and it committed dreadful crimes against them. It also worked to restrict the black labouring class by attacking their attempts to be economically independent. Any white people who purchased cotton from black farmers were threatened, beaten and killed. Black churches, as well as schools established by the Freedmen's Bureau, were also attacked. The Klan faded away in the 1870s after the federal government had taken action.

SOURCE C

A cartoon that appeared in the Independent Monitor newspaper of Tuscaloosa, Alabama, 1 September 1868. The caption read, 'Hang dogs! Hang! Stand fast, to their hanging! The above represents the fate in store for those great pests of Southern society – the carpet-bagger and the scalawag – if found in Dixie's land after the break of day on 4th of March.' 4 March 1869 was the day Democrats
hoped Horatio Seymour would become President. Dixie was a nickname for the Southern United States.

SOURCE D

The leading cause of the Ku Klux Klan's existence is the Union League. These were composed of black men, with a sprinkling of white people. They had political and criminal aims. They were organised for the purpose of committing crimes against white people. During the Reconstruction era, Alabama had no courts. Everything was chaotic. The Ku Klux Klan was organised to counteract the aims and acts of the Union Leagues, and to punish crime where the laws failed to provide justice. Under the Reconstruction measures, many men were not capable of serving as judges or prosecutors. They were unfit to administer the laws.

R B Lindsay, Governor of Alabama, giving evidence to a Congressional Committee investigating the Ku Klux Klan, 1871. Lindsay was a Democrat. Union Leagues were men's clubs set up to promote loyalty to the Union and support the Republican Party.

SOURCE E

There were numerous organisations of the Democratic Party known as the Ku Klux Klan, whose aims were to intimidate Republicans and prevent them from voting. These organisations were armed and patrolled night and day, committing murders and outrages on Republicans. They produced such terror among freedmen and others belonging to the Republican Party that it was unsafe to hold meetings. A great many freedmen who desired to vote Republican were forced to vote Democrat by violence, fraud and intimidation.

A Republican supporter giving evidence to a Congressional Committee
Investigating the Ku Klux Klan, 1871.

SOURCE F

A cartoon was published in an American magazine in October 1874.

SOURCE G

CHARACTER AND AIMS OF THE ORDER

This is an institution of Chivalry, Humanity, Mercy and Patriotism.

To protect the weak, the innocent and the defenceless from the wrongs and outrages of the lawless, the violent and the brutal.
Questions to ask candidates interested in joining the Ku Klux Klan. Did you belong to the Federal Army during the late war?
Are you opposed to black equality?
Are you in favour of a white man's government in this country?
Are you in favour of Constitutional liberty and a government of fair laws instead of violence and oppression?
Are you in favour of the return of the Southern people to all their rights, civil and political?

From the 'Organisation and Principles of the Ku Klux Klan', 1868.

SOURCE H

The Klan came to my brother's door and spoke in an outlandish tone, which I had heard they generally used at a black man's house. They said, 'Where is Elias?' My brother's wife said, 'He lives across the yard.' They carried me into the yard and said, 'Who burned our houses?' I told them it was not me. I could not burn houses. They said, 'Haven't you been preaching against the Ku Klux? Doesn't a Republican Party newspaper come to your house?' One had a horsewhip, and he struck me eight times on my hip bone. One of them took a strap and buckled it around my neck and said, 'Let us take him to the river and drown him.' One of them told my sister-in-law to pick me up. As she stooped down, one of them struck her with a strap. Then they said, 'Will you put a card in the paper to renounce all republicanism?' They said if I did not, they would come back the next week and kill me.

Evidence given by Elias Hill to a committee of the Senate that was investigating the situation in North Carolina, 1871. Hill was an ex-slave and was crippled in both legs and arms. He taught black children to read and write, and was a leading figure in the local black community.

Now answer all the following questions. You may use any of the sources to help you answer the questions, in addition to those sources which you are told to use. When answering the questions, use your knowledge of the topic to help you interpret and evaluate the sources.

1   Study Sources A and B.

How far do these two sources agree? Explain your answer using details of the sources.   [7]

2   Study Source C.

Why was this cartoon published in 1868? Explain your answer using details of the source and your knowledge.   [8]

3   Study Sources D and E.

Does Source D mean that Source E cannot be believed? Explain your answer using details of the sources and your knowledge.   [8]

4   Study Source F.

What is the cartoonist's message? Explain your answer using details of the source and your knowledge. [8]

5   Study Sources G and H.

Does Source G make Source H surprising? Explain your answer using details of the sources and your knowledge. [7]

6   Study all the sources.

How far do these sources provide convincing evidence that the Ku Klux Klan's primary purpose was to ensure the defeat of the Republicans? Use the sources to explain your answer.   [12]

Option B: Twentieth-century topic

COULD THE SOVIET UNION RELY ON THE POLISH AUTHORITIES TO DEAL WITH THE PROTESTS AND STRIKES IN 1980-81?

Study the Background Information and the sources carefully, and then answer all the questions.

Background Information

When the Solidarity movement emerged in Poland following the strikes and protests of 1980, the Soviet Union had to decide whether to intervene. On previous occasions, such as the Hungarian Revolution of 1956 and the Prague Spring in 1968, the Soviet Union had used armed forces. The Soviet Union clearly wanted Solidarity to be suppressed, but could it depend on the Polish leadership to do this? In September 1980, Edward Gierek was replaced as leader of Poland by Stanislaw Kania. However, under pressure from the Soviet Union, Kania was replaced by General Jaruzelski in October 1981. All three leaders promised to address Poland's problems and suppress the protests.

Could the Soviet Union rely on the Polish leadership to deal with the situation?

SOURCE A

The Soviet Union is postponing as long as possible the agonising decision of whether or not to invade Poland. To disguise their dilemma, however, the Soviets are stepping up the psychological pressure on Poland. Brezhnev drew parallels between Poland in 1981 and Czechoslovakia in 1968 this week. The military preparations have included the mobilisation of Warsaw Pact forces on the Polish borders and three-week-long Warsaw Pact manoeuvres in and around Poland.

Meanwhile, Soviet diplomatic moves toward the West include the first indication of an interest in reductions in medium-range weapons. This can be interpreted in different ways. The Soviets may be hiding their true intent of invading Poland behind a false arms-control smoke screen. The Kremlin failed to stem democratisation in Poland last September. Since then, Solidarity has become a mass patriotic movement. The hard-line Polish Communists, whom Moscow might have used, have become demoralised. The Soviet Union cannot now depend on the Polish security forces and Army to suppress a Polish strike, but would have to do the job itself.

From an article by an American journalist, 8 April 1981.

SOURCE B

We asked Kania whether the Party had a plan for an emergency in which an open threat would arise to the people's rule. He said that such a plan exists, and that they know who should be arrested and how to utilise the army. We gained a comprehensive understanding of the causes of the crisis and the severity of the counter-revolutionary threat. Kania carefully took down everything we said. As far as Kania is concerned, he made a good impression on other comrades who took part in the negotiations and on me. He is a serious and thoughtful person. It is clear that he is a good political leader; we will judge him only by his deeds.

Brezhnev reporting to the Soviet Politburo about a meeting with the Polish leadership, 31 October 1980. The Politburo was the main policy-making body in the

Soviet Union.

SOURCE C

For a long time, developments in Poland have caused anxiety and concern. Kania has failed to take measures. When he took office, we emphasised that it was necessary to launch a decisive attack on counter-revolution. He agreed, but then followed a policy of compromise. Kania has been a significant hindrance to the struggle for socialism. The question arose of restoring the leadership to a sound position. The Poles put forward Jaruzelski. Change in leadership is a positive fact.

The Party approved the actions of the Politburo relating to the crisis in Poland.

An evaluation of the situation in Poland by Brezhnev, given to the Congress of the Soviet Communist Party, October 1981.

SOURCE D

Citizens of the People's Republic of Poland! Today, I address myself to you as a soldier and as the head of the Polish government. I address you concerning fundamental questions. Our homeland is on the verge of collapse. The state structures no longer work. Our struggling economy is given more shocks every day. Strikes and protests have become normal. It cannot be said that we did not show moderation and patience – sometimes too much. We created an opportunity to deepen the system of democracy and widen the reforms, but there was no leadership from Solidarity. Party members, you must oppose propaganda that states martial law was imposed from outside. This offends us. We made this decision, we accomplished it, and we are responsible for it.

Jaruzelski speaking on state radio and TV in the morning of 13 December 1981.

SOURCE E

'LIFE IN POLAND IS SPEEDILY RETURNING TO NORMAL...' (Polish Radio)

A cartoon published in Britain, 14 December 1981. It shows Walesa, the leader of Solidarity

SOURCE F

Martial law in Poland has been in effect for a month. As Jaruzelski says, the counter-revolution is now crushed. Relative stability has been introduced into the country. Jaruzelski can now take advantage of martial law to carry out a sweeping purge of the Polish Communist Party. This might yield good results. One gets the impression that Jaruzelski is very strong and is able, on most occasions, to find proper solutions. It is good that he is studying the Hungarian experience in struggling against counter-revolution.

Brezhnev speaking at a meeting of the Soviet Politburo on January 14, 1982.

SOURCE G

A cartoon was published in the USA in 1982. The figure in the cartoon is Jaruzelski.

Now answer all the following questions. You may use any of the sources to help you answer the questions, in addition to those sources which you are told to use. When answering the questions, use your knowledge of the topic to help you interpret and evaluate the sources.

1   Study Source A.

What impressions does this source give of the Soviets? Explain your answer using details of the source.   [7]

2   Study Sources B and C.

Does Source B make Source C surprising? Explain your answer using details of the sources and your knowledge.   [8]

3   Study Source D.

Why did Jaruzelski make this speech in December 1981? Explain your answer using details of the source and your knowledge.   [8]

4   Study Source E.

What is the cartoonist's message? Explain your answer using details of the source and your knowledge.   [8]

5   Study Sources F and G.

How far does Source G prove that Brezhnev (Source F) was right? Explain your answer using details of the sources and your knowledge.   [7]

6   Study all the sources.

How far do these sources provide convincing evidence that the Polish leadership was able to deal with the problems in Poland? Use the sources to explain your answer.   [12]

Chapter 17

Paper 17

0470/22

Paper 2   February/March 2022

2 hours

INFORMATION

- The total mark for this paper is 50.
- The number of marks for each question or part question is shown in brackets [ ].

CHAPTER 17

Option A: Nineteenth-century topic

HOW IMPORTANT WAS VICTOR EMMANUEL II?

Study the Background Information and the sources carefully, and then answer all the questions.

Background Information

Victor Emmanuel II became King of Piedmont-Sardinia in 1849 when his father, Charles Albert, abdicated. By 1861, he had become the first King of a united Italy.

How much of this achievement was due to Victor Emmanuel is a matter of debate. Some historians who question his significance argue that Cavour, his Prime Minister, led him. They claim that it was Cavour who drew Piedmont into the Crimean War to secure France's support for Italian independence, and that the fall of the Kingdom of the Two Sicilies was primarily due to Garibaldi's actions.

How far was Victor Emmanuel a leading figure in the unification of Italy?

SOURCE A

It was Victor Emmanuel who was most enthusiastic about Piedmont taking part in the Crimean War. This was not because he hoped it would lead to a future war with Austria and to Italian unification. Instead, he wanted to go to war to gain a glorious reputation as a military power for his country and recognition as a great general for himself. He attempted to lead his forces personally and even offered his services to the British and French as commander-in-chief of all their forces. They turned him down.

So, while Cavour was in careful negotiations with the French and British over territorial gains from Austria, Victor Emmanuel was telling the French that Piedmont would be joining the war. If that meant sacking Cavour, it would be even better – this would be the excuse he needed to do it. Cavour was therefore forced to support entry into the war or lose his job. His careful attempts to gain more for Piedmont out of the war had been destroyed by the King's hasty promises to the French of Piedmont's participation.

From a book published in 2015.

SOURCE B

Victor Emmanuel, though he sometimes criticised Garibaldi's military abilities and was jealous of Garibaldi's huge military success and popularity, had many more ideas than Cavour of how to deal with this challenging but indispensable guerrilla general. The King swore on his word of honour that he had nothing to do with the Thousand. Nevertheless, on the other hand, he let it be known that he had given a large sum of money to help reinforcements reach Garibaldi in Sicily. It is safe to assume that he was ready either to gain from Garibaldi's success or to disown him if he failed. Unlike Cavour, he was prepared to keep friendly with revolutionaries in case they should win.

Contrary to Cavour's expectation, Garibaldi turned out to be a loyal monarchist whose chief aim was to make Victor Emmanuel King of a united Italy. The King was thus reinforced in his resistance to

Cavour. He established means of communication with Garibaldi which were entirely outside Cavour's control. Written messages were marked for return to the King only. Garibaldi was instructed to trust the King and no one else, and to inform the King of any new plans.

Some people have suggested that Victor Emmanuel had personally guided the main stages of Garibaldi's revolution. He certainly showed courage and good judgment, but his passion for war, his incompetence as a military commander, and his opposition to his prime minister were unfortunate aspects. However, he probably did as much as Cavour to shape a united Italy.

From a book published in 1971.

SOURCE C

THE GIANT AND THE DWARF.
"BRAVO, MY LITTLE FELLOW! YOU SHALL DO ALL THE FIGHTING, AND WE'LL DIVIDE THE GLORY!"

A British cartoon published in June 1859. It shows Napoleon III and Victor Emmanuel during the Battle of Magenta

SOURCE D

Cavour rejected the idea of peace except under the condition of the liberation of northern Italy, as agreed with Napoleon III. He said the peace contradicted the principle of Italian unity, which guided his whole policy. He said promises were promises and should be kept. Cavour, as a last resort, wanted us to carry on the war alone. As military men, we declined. It would have been madness. Victor Emmanuel refused to risk our certain gains of Lombardy and the Duchies. He said they increased the chances of ultimately liberating Venice and uniting Tuscany with parts of the Papal States. However, Cavour would not listen and resigned.

From an account written at the time by the head of the Piedmontese army about events immediately after Austria and France signed an armistice at Villafranca in July 1859.

SOURCE E

His Majesty said, 'The advantage of an armistice was all on our side. Had the fighting gone on, we should have had to fight another battle with our diminished forces, while a month's delay would enable me to strengthen our army.'

His Majesty talked of Count Cavour's resignation. I think he was much disturbed by it, although he claimed it was of no importance. He said, 'Cavour is a muddle-head who is always pushing me into trouble. He is mad. However, he is finished now.' To my statement that Count Cavour would soon be back in office, the King gave a serious denial.

An Englishman's account of a conversation he had with Victor Emmanuel shortly
after the signing of the armistice of Villafranca.

SOURCE F

Having already written officially as King to you, I suggest that you reply to me in these terms. Say that you are full of devotion for the King and that you would wish to follow his advice. However, your duties towards Italy will not allow you to refuse to help the people of Naples when they call you to free them from a government which no loyal Italian can trust. Say that you cannot follow the King's wishes as you want to keep your freedom of action.

A secret letter from Victor Emmanuel to Garibaldi, 23 July 1860. It was delivered to Garibaldi at the same time as another letter from the King that asked Garibaldi not to
Sail from Sicily to the mainland.

SOURCE G

Garibaldi is planning the wildest schemes. He is putting off the day when Sicily will demand annexation to Piedmont, for he wants to retain his dictatorial powers, which will enable him to raise an army to conquer Naples, then Rome, and ultimately Venice. The government here does not influence him.

From a letter by Cavour to a leading Piedmontese diplomat, 12 July 1860.

SOURCE H

The shining helmets had attracted all the peasants of the area, who welcomed Garibaldi with their usual enthusiasm. Garibaldi desperately tried to divert attention from himself to the King. Keeping his horse a few paces behind, he cried, 'This is Victor Emmanuel, your King, the King of Italy.' The peasants stared and listened, and then, not understanding again, shouted, 'Long live Garibaldi!'

A description by one of Garibaldi's soldiers of the meeting between Garibaldi and
Victor Emmanuel on 26 October 1860.

Now answer all the following questions. You may use any of the sources to help you answer the questions, in addition to those sources which you are told to use. When answering the questions, use your knowledge of the topic to help you interpret and evaluate the sources.

1   Study Sources A and B.

How far do these two sources agree about Victor Emmanuel? Explain your answer using details of the sources. [7]

2   Study Source C.

What is the cartoonist's message? Explain your answer using details of the source and your knowledge. [8]

3   Study Sources D and E.

How far does Source D prove that what Source E claims about the armistice of Villafranca is wrong? Explain your answer using details of the sources and your knowledge. [7]

4   Study Sources F and G.

Why did Victor Emmanuel send the secret letter (Source F)? Explain your answer using details of the sources and your knowledge. [8]

5   Study Source H.

How surprised are you by this source? Explain your answer using details of the source and your knowledge. [8]

6   Study all the sources.

How far do these sources provide convincing evidence that Victor Emmanuel was the central figure in the achievement of Italian unification? Use the sources to explain your answer.   [12]

Option B: Twentieth-century topic

DID WILSON FAIL IN THE PARIS PEACE TALKS?

Study the Background Information and the sources carefully, and then answer all the questions.

Background Information

Textbooks often describe President Wilson as an idealist, very unlike Clemenceau and Lloyd George. It is usually stated that they were primarily interested in benefiting their own countries, whereas Wilson sought to achieve something beneficial for the entire world.

At the Paris Peace Talks, how far was Wilson able to achieve his aims?

SOURCE A

US President Woodrow Wilson, in a speech in January 1918, explained his vision for the postwar world. His Fourteen Points were the basis of his plan for a comprehensive overhaul of international relations. He called for, amongst other things, an immediate end to the war, the establishment of an international peacekeeping organisation and international disarmament. Wilson's Fourteen Points were hugely influential in shaping the postwar world and in spreading the language of peace and democracy worldwide. He was also responsible for establishing the League of Nations, an international peacekeeping organisation tasked with resolving international disputes without resorting to military force. He was also able to fulfil his promise of self-government through the creation of Poland, Yugoslavia and Czechoslovakia.

One of the most contentious provisions of the Treaty of Versailles was the War Guilt Clause, which held Germany responsible for the war. Germany was also forced to disarm, to make territorial concessions, and to pay reparations to the Allied powers. Although US President Woodrow Wilson was opposed to such harsh terms, he was outmanoeuvred by French Prime Minister Georges Clemenceau. Germany was appalled by these terms. Although the treaty reflected Wilson's vision for the postwar world, isolationists in the US

Congress made sure that it was not ratified and that the United States never became a member of the League of Nations. However, Wilson's vision shaped much of the postwar world, and for his peacemaking efforts, he was awarded the 1919 Nobel Peace Prize.

From a website about American history.

SOURCE B

Wilson had called for a 'peace without victory' and had set out his Fourteen Points as a basis for a treaty. Unfortunately, these Points were largely forgotten in the peace negotiations. However, a key point was to establish a League of Nations as the foundation for a new international order, aimed at preventing future wars. The Treaty did create the League of Nations, but Wilson did not achieve 'peace without victory' as many of the Treaty's terms punished Germany harshly.

Aside from the establishment of the League of Nations, a primary aim of Wilson's was to establish a lasting peace; however, he conceded many controversial points to the other powers present at the conference. Germany was required to pay war reparations and was subjected to military occupation in the Rhineland. Additionally, the treaty specifically named Germany as responsible for the war. Germany hated these terms, which contributed little to the chance of lasting peace in Europe.

Wilson's other main aim at the Paris Peace Conference was to use self-determination as the primary basis of international borders. Despite this, he agreed to the creation of mandates in former German and Ottoman territories, allowing the European powers and Japan to establish colonies in the Middle East, Africa, and Asia, undermining his promise of self-government. The conference finished negotiations in May 1919, at which point German leaders viewed the treaty for the first time. They were shocked by its terms and immediately rejected it.

From a recent history book.

SOURCE C

I am leaving Paris, after eight fateful months, with conflicting emotions. Looking back on the conference, there is much to commend and yet much to regret. It is easy to say what should have been done, but it is more difficult to find a way of doing it. To those who argue that the treaty is flawed and should never have been made, and that it will lead to difficulties in its enforcement, I am inclined to agree. However, I would also say in reply that empires cannot be shattered and new states raised upon their ruins without disturbance. To create new boundaries is to create new troubles. The one follows the other. While I should have preferred a different peace, I doubt very much whether it could have been made, for the ingredients required for such a peace were lacking at Paris.

From the diary of Edward House, June 1919. House was Wilson's chief advisor at the peace negotiations. In March 1919, the two men argued, with Wilson unhappy with the
The compromises the House was ready to make in the negotiations.

SOURCE D

This nation entered this war with the intention of seeing it through to the end, and the end has not yet arrived. This marks the beginning of the processes that will make another war like this impossible. The peace treaty is excellent; it is a treaty of justice. The USA was formed to bring liberty and justice to the world. Now we are called upon to deliver that promise.

From a speech by Wilson in Missouri, USA, 5 September 1919

SOURCE E

A cartoon published in a British newspaper, 13 May 1919

SOURCE F

A cartoon published in a British newspaper, July 1920. Lloyd George is saying to Germany, 'Off with the spiked hat! What do you think we fought for if not to abolish militarism?'

SOURCE G

An American cartoon published in 1919. The writing in the bottom right of the cartoon says 'WAR'

SOURCE H

It is with hesitation that I agree to give my views on Woodrow Wilson, because my relationship with him may persuade some to say that I am not an impartial observer.

I do not agree with those who hastily judge the President's work at the Peace Conference a failure. Whatever the imperfections of the Treaty from a political or economic standpoint, he did not fail. The outstanding thing for which he fought was the permanent peace of the world. Wilson laid the foundations of world peace and a new order in the Treaty. This is his most excellent work. The fact that the crowning structure has not yet reached completion, halted by the selfishness of politicians and the greed of national interests, has not destroyed these foundations. America will lead humanity and civilisation to brotherhood and world order. This will not come immediately, but it will come inevitably in the slow process of time.

From a statement to the press by a leading member of Wilson's government.
It was issued as Wilson left office on 4 March 1921.

Now answer all the following questions. You may use any of the sources to help you answer the questions, in addition to those sources which you are told to use. When answering the questions, use your knowledge of the topic to help you interpret and evaluate the sources.

1   Study Sources A and B.

How far do these two sources agree? Explain your answer using details of the sources.   [7]

2   Study Sources C and D.

How far does Source C prove that Wilson was lying in Source D? Explain your answer using details of the sources and your knowledge. [8]

3   Study Sources E and F.

How similar are these two cartoons? Explain your answer using details of the sources and your knowledge.   [8]

4   Study Source G.

What is the cartoonist's message? Explain your answer using details of the source and your knowledge. [7]

5   Study Source H.

Do you find this source surprising? Explain your answer using details of the source and your knowledge. [8]

6   Study all the sources.

How far do these sources provide convincing evidence that Wilson achieved his aims in the Treaty of Versailles? Use the sources to explain your answer. [12]

CHAPTER 17: Answers

Answered Question: Option B: Twentieth-century topic

DID WILSON FAIL IN THE PARIS PEACE TALKS?

1. How far do Sources A and B agree? [7 marks]

Areas of Agreement

- Both sources acknowledge that Wilson established the League of Nations as a key achievement
- Both agree that Wilson was opposed to harsh terms against Germany but was outmanoeuvred by other leaders (particularly Clemenceau)
- Both recognise that the Treaty included punitive measures against Germany, including reparations and the War Guilt Clause
- Both sources agree that Wilson had idealistic aims but faced practical limitations

Areas of Disagreement

- Wilson's overall success: Source A presents a more positive view, stating "the treaty reflected

Wilson's vision for the postwar world" and emphasising his achievements, such as creating Poland, Yugoslavia, and Czechoslovakia. Source B is more critical, saying his "Fourteen Points were largely forgotten"

- Self-determination: Source A suggests Wilson fulfilled his promise of self-government through the creation of a new nation. Source B argues he "undermined his promise of self-government" by agreeing to mandates in former German and Ottoman territories
- Overall assessment: Source A emphasises Wilson's Nobel Peace Prize and lasting influence, while Source B focuses more on his failures and compromises

Conclusion - The sources partially agree on the basic facts but differ significantly in their assessment of Wilson's success and the extent to which he achieved his objectives.

2. How far does Source C prove that Wilson was lying in Source D? [8 marks]

Evidence suggesting that Wilson was being dishonest

- Source C shows Wilson's advisor House expressing "conflicting emotions" and admitting the treaty was problematic: "the treaty is bad and should never have been made"

- House acknowledges "much to regret" about the conference outcomes
- The context notes that Wilson and House had argued in March 1919, with Wilson "unhappy with the compromises House was ready to make" Evidence that Wilson was not necessarily lying
- Source D was delivered in September 1919, several months after House's June diary entry, giving Wilson time to rationalise or genuinely believe in the treaty's value
- Wilson's statement reflects his characteristic idealism and belief in long-term goals rather than immediate perfection
- Politicians often present public optimism while privately acknowledging difficulties
- Wilson's reference to this being "the beginning of the processes" suggests he recognised it was not perfect but believed it was a foundation for future progress

Historical Context

Wilson was on a speaking tour, attempting to garner American support for the League of Nations. His health was declining, and he may have genuinely believed his rhetoric or felt compelled to defend the treaty publicly despite private doubts.

Conclusion

Source C does not definitively prove Wilson was lying, but it does suggest he was presenting a more optimistic public face than the private reality warranted.

3. How similar are Sources E and F? [8 marks]

Similarities

- Both are British newspaper cartoons critical of Germany
- Both depict Germany's military defeat and subjugation
- Both show satisfaction with Germany's reduced status
- Both use symbolic imagery to represent Germany's humiliation
- Both reflect British public opinion, celebrating victory over Germany

Differences

- Timing: Source E (May 1919) was published during treaty negotiations, while Source F (July 1920) came after ratification and implementation
- Focus: Source E appears to focus on Germany's general defeat, while Source F specifically targets German militarism (the "spiked hat" representing Prussian military culture)

- Tone: Source F includes Lloyd George's direct statement about abolishing militarism, making the anti-militarist message more explicit
- Specific imagery: Source F's focus on the spiked helmet specifically targets German military symbols

Both cartoons reflect British satisfaction with victory, but Source F's focus on militarism aligns with the specific goal of demilitarising Germany through the treaty terms.

The cartoons are pretty similar in their anti-German sentiment and celebration of Germany's defeat, but differ in their specific focus and timing.

4. What is the cartoonist's message in Source G? [7 marks]

Visual Analysis

- Shows a figure (likely representing America/Wilson) walking away from a building
- The word "WAR" appears at the bottom correctly, suggesting ongoing conflict or threat
- The figure appears to be leaving or abandoning something important

The Message

The cartoonist appears to be criticising America's isolationist stance and failure to join the League of

Nations. The message suggests that by America walking away from international commitments (likely the League), the threat of future war remains.

Context:
- This cartoon was published in 1919, the same year the U.S. Senate rejected the Treaty of Versailles
- Wilson's health collapsed during his speaking tour promoting the League
- American isolationists successfully prevented U.S. membership in the League of Nations
- Without American participation, the League was significantly weakened

Criticism: The cartoon implies that America's withdrawal from international responsibilities leaves the world vulnerable to future conflicts, undermining Wilson's goal of preventing another war.

Conclusion: The cartoonist's message is that American isolationism threatens world peace and undermines the very foundations Wilson tried to establish for preventing future wars.

5. Do you find Source H surprising? [8 marks]

Potentially Surprising Elements

- The overwhelmingly positive assessment of Wilson's work, calling it successful rather than a failure
- The claim that Wilson "did not fail" despite acknowledging treaty imperfections
- The prophetic tone about America leading "humanity and civilisation to brotherhood"
- The timing - issued as Wilson left office in defeat in March 1921

Reasons Why It Might Not Be Surprising

- Loyalty factor: The author admits potential bias due to his "relationship with him"
- Political context: As a "leading member of Wilson's government," loyalty and support would be expected
- Historical perspective: Writing with some distance from the immediate negotiations
- Idealistic tradition: Reflects the Wilsonian idealistic approach to international relations

Context

- Wilson left office having failed to get Senate approval for the League of Nations
- His health had collapsed, and his presidency ended in relative political failure
- Republicans had gained control, signalling rejection of Wilson's internationalist approach

Assessment

The source is somewhat surprising in its unqualified optimism, given the apparent failures, but not entirely unexpected given the author's position and loyalty to Wilson.

Conclusion

While the overwhelmingly positive tone might seem surprising given Wilson's apparent defeats, it is less surprising when considering the source's bias and the tendency of political allies to defend their leader's legacy.

6. How far do these sources provide convincing evidence that Wilson achieved his aims? [12 marks]

Evidence Supporting Wilson's Success

From the Sources

- Source A: Emphasises significant achievements - League of Nations establishment, creation of new nations (Poland, Yugoslavia, Czechoslovakia), Nobel Peace Prize, lasting influence on international relations
- Source H: Strong defence of Wilson's work, arguing he laid "foundations of world peace and a new order"
- Source D: Wilson's own confident assertion that the treaty was "a treaty of justice" and the beginning of lasting peace

Historical Context

Wilson's Fourteen Points did influence the post-war settlement, and the principle of self-determination did reshape the map of Europe.

Evidence Against Wilson's Success:

From the Sources

- Source B: "Fourteen Points were largely forgotten," failed to achieve "peace without victory," and undermined self-determination through mandates
- Source C: Wilson's own advisor expressing serious doubts and "conflicting emotions," admitting "much to regret"
- Source G: American cartoon suggesting Wilson's failure through U.S. non-participation in the League
- Sources E & F: British cartoons showing the harsh, punitive nature of the treaty that Wilson opposed

Failures

- Failed to prevent harsh terms against Germany
- The U.S. never joined the League of Nations, undermining its most outstanding achievement
- The treaty arguably contributed to future instability rather than lasting peace

Balanced Assessment:

Partial Successes
- League of Nations was established (though weakened without U.S. participation)
- Some new nations were created based on self-determination
- International law and peacekeeping concepts were advanced

Significant Failures
- Treaty was more punitive than Wilson wanted
- Failed to gain American support for his own treaty
- Long-term peace was not achieved (World War II occurred 20 years later)

Source Reliability Issues:
- Source A (website) may oversimplify Wilson's achievements
- Source H shows clear bias from a Wilson ally
- Sources E & F reflect British rather than American/international perspectives

Conclusion:
The sources provide mixed evidence about Wilson's success. While he achieved some aims (establishing the League, achieving some self-determination), he failed in crucial areas (preventing harsh terms, securing American

participation, and achieving lasting peace). The sources suggest Wilson was more successful in establishing frameworks and principles than in achieving immediate practical results. His vision influenced the future, but his specific aims at Paris were only partially fulfilled, making his overall success limited rather than complete.

Chapter 18

Paper 18

HISTORY   0470/22

Paper 2   May/June 2022

2 hours

INFORMATION

- The total mark for this paper is 50.
- The number of marks for each question or part question is shown in brackets [ ].

DC (NF/CT) 304186/2

© UCLES 2022

CHAPTER 18

Option A: Nineteenth-century topic

HOW FAR WAS THE KU KLUX KLAN SUPPORTED?

Study the Background Information and the sources carefully, and then answer all the questions.

Background Information

The first Ku Klux Klan emerged at the end of 1865 and, by the early 1870s, had been suppressed after the US government passed laws against it. It aimed to restore white supremacy and oppose what it saw as the corruption and incompetence of the Republican governments that appeared in the South during Reconstruction. However, it actually conducted a reign of terror against black people and Republicans, committing thousands of murders and beatings.

For some people in the South, it stood for something important. However, did it really have much support?

SOURCE A

In 1866, the Ku Klux Klan (Klan) was a topic of much discussion in the South. Its mysteriousness created much interest. Every issue of the local paper contained some reference to it. These notices were copied into other papers, and in this manner, the way was prepared for its rapid growth, which was helped by the common belief that the Klan had some significant mission.

One significant concern of the time was the transition of ex-slaves to citizenship. They not only had no self-control, but many of them regarded themselves as free, not only from bondage to former masters, but from the laws of the state. The enforcement of the law had been only partially re-established, and there was much disorder. However, the Klan had organisation – through Grand Wizards, written constitutions, and coordinated actions. Those familiar with the facts will know that the Klan provided immense service during this period of Southern history. Without it, life would have been intolerable for decent people in many sections of the South. For a while, the robberies ceased, and the lawless behaved well.

From a book published in 1884. The author was a member of the Ku Klux Klan.

SOURCE B

Although the Klan's membership was often exaggerated, it was large, and it exerted a vast, terrifying power.

Pain, injury and death.

It inflicted real

SOURCE C

A cartoon was published in an American magazine in October 1874.

SOURCE D

There is plenty of evidence of a secret organisation in many parts of this State, of men who, under the cover of masks, armed with knives and other deadly weapons, do appear at night to commit violence on peaceable citizens, robbing and murdering them, inflicting on them the most cruel treatment. This organisation has become a widespread and alarming evil in this State, defying all law.

Any person away from his home, wearing a mask, or disguised in costume, shall be held guilty of a high crime.

A law outlawing the Ku Klux Klan was passed by the Alabama legislature in 1868.

SOURCE E

Movements of the Mystic Klan

A reliable correspondent writes that about a week ago, the Ku Klux came into town to regulate matters. They were here from eleven p.m. to three o'clock a.m. — five hundred in all. They shot one evil black man. They also hanged three or four black men nearly dead, and whipped others severely to make them tell them about their nightly meetings. The strongest thing about them was that they did not hesitate to unmask themselves when asked to do so. Everyone who saw them says their horses were more beautiful than any in the surrounding countryside. They spoke little but always to a purpose. They did not disturb anyone else, nor did they take anything except a few Enfield rifles, which were found in possession of some evil black men. They called on the tax officer. What was said is unknown, but it has made a significant improvement in his behaviour. The visitors' arrival has been beneficial to the community.

From a Tennessee newspaper, December 1868.

SOURCE F

In 1868, six bloody and terrible massacres occurred. Over two thousand persons were killed or wounded within a few weeks of the presidential election. Half of Louisiana was overrun by violence, raids, murder and riot to keep the people in constant terror until the Republicans surrendered all claims and the Democratic Party won the election. One of the bloodiest riots on record occurred in the parish of Saint Landry, Louisiana. The Ku Klux Klan killed and wounded over two hundred Republicans, hunting and chasing them for two days and nights, through fields and swamps. Thirteen captives were taken from the jail and shot. A pile of twenty-five dead bodies was found half-buried in the woods. Having conquered the Republicans, killed and driven off their white leaders, the Ku Klux Klan captured the masses, led them to the polls and made them vote Democrat.

From a report by a committee of the US House of Representatives, 1875.

SOURCE G

I have never recognised the present government in Tennessee. If the militia is called out and does not interfere with anyone, I do not think there will be any fight. If they commit outrages upon the people, they and the Governor, Mr Brownlow, and his government will be swept out of existence; not a radical will be left alive. If the militia is called out, we will see it as a declaration of war because Mr Brownlow has already issued his order directing them to shoot down the Ku Klux Klan, and he calls all southern men Ku Klux Klan. There is such an organisation all over the South with approximately 550,000 men. I intend to kill radicals, and if trouble should break out, not one of them will be left alive.

From an interview between General Forrest and a journalist, August 1868. Twice, Forrest denied saying most of what is in this interview – when it was published, and in 1871 during his testimony to the Ku Klux Klan hearings in Washington. Forrest was the first 'Grand Wizard' of the Ku Klux Klan.

Now answer all the following questions. You may use any of the sources to help you answer the questions, in addition to those sources which you are told to use. When answering the questions, use your knowledge of the topic to help you interpret and evaluate the sources.

1   Study Sources A and B.

How far do these two sources agree? Explain your answer using details of the sources. [7]

2   Study Source C.

How valuable is this source to a historian studying this period? Explain your answer using details of the source and your knowledge. [7]

3   Study Source D.

Are you surprised by Source D? Explain your answer using details of the source and your knowledge. [8]

4   Study Sources E and F.

How far does Source F make you doubt the account in Source E? Explain your answer using details of the sources and your knowledge. [8]

5   Study Source G.

Why do you think Forrest denied saying what was reported in Source G? Explain your answer using details of the source and your knowledge. [8]

6   Study all the sources.

How far do these sources provide convincing evidence that people supported the Ku Klux Klan? Use the sources to explain your answer. [12]

Option B: Twentieth-century topic

WAS THE SOVIET UNION WILLING TO INTERVENE MILITARILY IN POLAND IN 1980–81?

Study the Background Information and the sources carefully, and then answer all the questions.

Background Information

In the summer of 1980, Poland was facing an economic crisis. Basic goods were rationed, prices were high, and widespread poverty was prevalent. Unrest grew, and Solidarity, a trade union led by

Lech Wałęsa, organised strikes and demonstrations. By 1981, ten million people had joined the trade union. The Soviet Union was worried about communist rule in Poland being overthrown and had to decide whether to intervene militarily. In 1981, General Jaruzelski was appointed to lead Poland, aiming to deal more firmly with Solidarity and the protests. On 13 December 1981, he introduced martial law, Solidarity was suppressed, and thousands of people were imprisoned. At the time, Jaruzelski stated that he introduced martial law to address the Solidarity movement. However, later he claimed he was trying to prevent an invasion by the Soviet Union, although the Soviet Union denied it had plans to invade.

Was the Soviet Union willing to intervene militarily in Poland?

SOURCE A

Contrary to reports by U.S. intelligence, no preparations were underway for Soviet military intervention. The Soviet Union was reluctant to intervene because of its economic problems, the war in Afghanistan and fears that it would lead to a national uprising in Poland. Kania, the Polish leader, was overheard criticising the Soviet leadership, and Jaruzelski was appointed to replace him. He was under pressure from the Soviets to deal with the protests more decisively, but he demanded military intervention by them if he ran into trouble while imposing martial law. As late as December 1981, Jaruzelski was begging for Soviet intervention, but it was not forthcoming. After a meeting of Warsaw Pact defence ministers on 4 December 1981, he complained, 'Our allies left us on our own. They do not want to shoulder any of the responsibility.' Despite this, martial law was introduced on 13 December. Ever since, Jaruzelski has denied that he invited Soviet troops in and insisted that martial law was aimed at preventing a Soviet military intervention. The Soviets have insisted that an invasion was never seriously considered.

From a recent history book.

SOURCE B

As early as December 1980, Soviet leaders ordered a Warsaw Pact military exercise as a cover for a potential Warsaw Pact intervention. Still, Kania, leader of the Polish Workers' Party, managed to persuade them to call off the intervention. Jaruzelski replaced Kania to deal with the protests more forcefully. He claimed in his memoirs, written ten years later, that in December 1981, he requested only Soviet moral backing for martial law, which he introduced to prevent a Soviet intervention. On 4 December 1981, a meeting of Warsaw Pact defence ministers drafted statements referring to 'the fulfilment of alliance obligations by the armed forces of the Warsaw Pact member states' and declaring that 'the Polish nation can rely completely on the support of the socialist states'. In his speech on December 13, 1981, announcing the imposition of martial law, Jaruzelski blamed Solidarity for refusing to cooperate with the government. He has since defended martial law as a 'tragic necessity' to prevent a Soviet-led Warsaw Pact invasion.

From a recent history book

SOURCE C

"Excuse me sir — is this lady bothering you?"

A cartoon published in Britain, 5 December 1980. The figure on the right represents Brezhnev.

SOURCE D

Published in the Netherlands on 12 December 1980. Brezhnev is saying to Walesa, 'I would never interfere in Poland's domestic affairs!'

SOURCE E

That is our primary concern.

Andropov speaking at a Politburo meeting, 10 December 1981. Andropov was a leading member of the Soviet government and succeeded Brezhnev as leader in 1982. The Politburo was the highest policy-making body in the USSR.

SOURCE F

VERY URGENT!

At a meeting of the top officers of the USSR's armed forces, plans were agreed upon to send the Soviet Army, the National People's Army of East Germany, and the Czechoslovak People's Army into Poland. Currently, representatives from these armies, dressed in civilian clothing, are conducting reconnaissance on potential invasion routes. The plans include the intervening armies to move to all major Polish Army bases to perform manoeuvres with live ammunition. Then, depending on how things develop, all major cities, especially industrial cities, are to be sealed off.

Finally, I regret to say that everyone in the Polish Army who has seen the plans is depressed, and no one is contemplating active resistance to the Warsaw Pact action. There are even those who say the presence of such enormous military forces may calm the nation.

JACK STRONG

A report from Jack Strong to the American Intelligence Service (CIA), early December 1981. Jack Strong was the codename for Ryszard Kuklinski, an officer in the Polish Army. He started spying for the USA after the brutal repression of Polish protests in 1970. The Americans got him out of Poland and to the USA just before
Martial law was imposed on 13 December 1981

SOURCE G

A cartoon published in the Netherlands in 1981.
Brezhnev, leader of the Soviet Union,
is saying, 'Whatever you do, do not look at him!'

SOURCE H

At first, the Soviets gave us an ultimatum: either bring the situation under control, or we will cut off supplies of oil, gas and other raw materials. I was summoned to the Soviet Union three times. On the last occasion, in September 1981, I was shown army manoeuvres all along the Polish border. The Soviet army leader, Marshal Ustinov, informed me that what was happening in Poland was intolerable. We had to convince our allies that we would not undermine the Warsaw Pact or allow the state to be undermined. The introduction of martial law allowed us to avoid military intervention.

General Jaruzelski speaking in 1995 in an interview with a Western author.

Now answer all the following questions. You may use any of the sources to help you answer the questions, in addition to those sources which you are told to use. When answering the questions, use your knowledge of the topic to help you interpret and evaluate the sources.

1 Study Sources A and B.

How far do these two sources agree? Explain your answer using details of the sources. [7]

2   Study Sources C and D.

How far would these two cartoonists have agreed? Explain your answer using details of the sources and your knowledge. [8]

3   Study Sources E and F.

Does Source F prove that Andropov was lying in Source E? Explain your answer using details of the sources and your knowledge. [8]

4   Study Source G.

What is the cartoonist's message? Explain your answer using details of the source and your knowledge. [7]

5   Study Source H.

Are you surprised by this source? Explain your answer using details of the source and your knowledge. [8]

6   Study all the sources.

How far do these sources provide convincing evidence that the Soviet Union was willing to send armed forces into Poland? Use the sources to explain your answer.   [12]

CHAPTER 18 Answers

Option A: Nineteenth-century topic

HOW FAR WAS THE KU KLUX KLAN SUPPORTED?

1. Study Sources A and B.

How far do these two sources agree? Explain your answer using details of the sources. [7]

Sources A and B agree on several key points but differ significantly in their interpretation and emphasis.

Areas of Agreement:

Both sources acknowledge the Klan's significant size and influence. Source A describes its "rapid growth" and widespread presence, while Source B confirms "it was large and it exerted a vast, terrifying power." This suggests both authors recognise the Klan as a substantial organisation.

Both sources agree on the Ku Klux Klan's organisational structure. Source A mentions "Grand Wizards, written constitutions and coordinated actions," while Source B implies organised activity through its reference to coordinated violence across regions.

Both acknowledge the Klan's impact on society - Source A admits it created "much interest" and had influence, while Source B recognises its "vast, terrifying power."

Disagreements:

The sources fundamentally disagree on the nature and justification of Klan activities. Source A presents a sympathetic view, claiming the Klan was "of immense service" and that "without it, in many sections of the South, life would have been intolerable for decent people." It portrays the Klan as restoring order where "robberies ceased and the lawless behaved well."

Source B takes a completely opposing moral stance, describing the Klan's activities as inflicting "real pain, injury and death" - clearly condemning rather than justifying their actions.

Different perspectives on legitimacy: Source A frames Klan activity as necessary law enforcement during a period when "enforcement of the law had been only partially re-established." Source B implies the Klan's power was inherently illegitimate and terroristic.

The disagreement reflects the authors' different positions - Source A is written by a Klan member seeking to justify their actions, while Source B represents modern historical condemnation of Klan violence.

2. Study Source C.

How valuable is this source to a historian studying this period? Explain your answer using details of the source and your knowledge. [7]

Source C is beneficial to historians, though with significant limitations that must be considered.

Strengths and Usefulness:

Contemporary perspective: Published in October 1874, this cartoon provides an immediate contemporary reaction to the Klan during the height of Reconstruction conflicts. It shows how the issue was perceived and debated at the time.

Political context: The cartoon reveals Northern Republican attitudes toward the Klan and Southern Democrats. The imagery suggests the cartoonist viewed the Klan as a tool of Democratic Party intimidation, which aligns with historical evidence about the 1874 elections.

Visual evidence of public awareness: The cartoon demonstrates that Klan activities were widely known and discussed in national media, contradicting any claims that their activities were successfully secret or limited in scope.

Symbolic representation: The imagery provides insight into how contemporaries understood the relationship between the Democratic Party, the Klan, and intimidation of voters, particularly African American voters.

Limitations:

Partisan bias: Published in a Republican-leaning publication during a highly polarised political period, the cartoon represents one side's propaganda rather than objective reporting.

Limited geographical scope: Represents Northern perspective rather than Southern views, potentially missing significant regional variations in opinion.

Artistic interpretation: As a political cartoon rather than documentary evidence, it may exaggerate or distort actual events for dramatic effect.

Lack of specific detail: Provides general impressions rather than specific factual information about particular incidents or locations.

Historical Context: The 1874 date is significant because it marked a time when Republican control was weakening across the South, and the cartoon reflects Republican concerns about Democratic/Klan electoral intimidation that would ultimately culminate in the end of Reconstruction by 1877.

Overall Assessment: Beneficial for understanding contemporary political discourse and Northern perceptions, but must be used alongside other sources for a complete picture.

3. Study Source D.

Are you surprised by Source D? Explain your answer using details of the source and your knowledge. [8]

Source D is not surprising when considered in the context of Reconstruction politics and federal-state tensions, though it does reveal the severity of the crisis.

Why it might seem surprising:

The strong language used - describing the Klan as "a widespread and alarming evil" and their activities as "defying all law" - suggests the Alabama legislature recognised the severity of the threat. For a Southern state government to condemn an organisation that claimed to defend white supremacy might seem unexpected.

The decisive action taken - making wearing masks or disguises "a high crime" - appears to challenge an organisation that many whites might have supported directly.

Why it's not actually surprising:

Political necessity: By 1868, Alabama had a Republican government installed under Congressional Reconstruction, including many African American legislators and white Republicans ("scalawags"). This government had every reason to oppose the Klan, which directly threatened their political survival and constitutional authority.

Federal pressure: The federal government was demanding that Southern states restore law and order. States that failed to control violence risked continued military occupation and loss of readmission to the Union. Alabama's leaders faced pressure from Washington to act.

Constitutional legitimacy: A legitimate government must maintain a monopoly on the use of force and law enforcement. The Klan's actions directly challenged state authority, forcing even sympathetic officials to respond or risk governmental collapse.

Historical knowledge context: This law was part of a broader pattern across the South in 1868-1870, as Republican governments tried to establish control. However, the effectiveness of such laws was often limited due to local sympathy for the Klan and difficulty obtaining convictions from white juries.

Economic concerns: Continued violence and lawlessness threatened economic recovery that even white Southerners needed, creating pressure for stability regardless of political preferences.

Timing significance: 1868 was a presidential election year, and Republicans needed to demonstrate they could maintain order to retain federal support.

The source actually demonstrates the complex political pressures of Reconstruction rather than surprising moral opposition to white supremacy.

4. Study Sources E and F.

How far does Source F make you doubt the account in Source E? Explain your answer using details of the sources and your knowledge. [8]

Source F significantly undermines the credibility of Source E's account, though both sources confirm that Klan activity occurred.

Major contradictions that create doubt:

Scale and nature of violence: Source E describes relatively limited, targeted action - "shot one evil black man" and "hanged three or four black men nearly dead" with specific purposes. Source F describes massive, systematic violence - "over two thousand persons were killed or wounded" and "over two hundred Republicans" killed in one incident alone. The scale difference is enormous.

Tone and justification: Source E presents a sympathetic, almost admiring tone, describing "beautiful horses," purposeful action, and the benefits to the community. Source F describes systematic terrorism - "hunting and chasing them for two days and nights" and "a pile of twenty-five dead bodies." These represent completely different interpretations of the same organisation's activities.

Community response: Source E claims the Klan visit was "to the benefit of the community" and improved local behaviour. Source F describes deliberate political terrorism designed to "keep the people in constant terror" and force electoral outcomes.

Reasons to doubt Source E specifically:

Source bias: Source E originates from a Tennessee newspaper in December 1868, likely a Democratic paper sympathetic to the Klan, whereas Source F represents an official US House investigation with access to multiple testimonies and evidence.

Euphemistic language: Source E uses euphemisms like "regulate matters" and describes near-fatal hangings as merely making people "tell them about their nightly meetings," suggesting deliberate minimisation of violence.

Selective reporting: Source E focuses on a single incident that may be exceptional, while Source F provides systematic evidence across multiple locations and timeframes.

Historical context supporting Source F: Congressional investigations of 1870-1871 documented extensive Klan violence with thousands of testimonies. Federal intervention under the Force Acts was based on documented evidence of systematic terrorism, not isolated incidents.

Electoral context: Source F's connection between violence and Democratic electoral victories aligns with historical evidence that Klan activity intensified around elections to suppress Republican voting.

Pattern consistency: Source F's account of systematic violence is consistent with documented Klan activities in other states during the same period.

Conclusion: While Source E may describe an actual incident, Source F's broader context and official nature make it far more credible regarding the Klan's overall impact and methods.

5. Study Source G.

Why do you think Forrest denied saying what was reported in Source G? Explain your answer using details of the source and your knowledge. [8]

Forrest likely denied these statements for multiple strategic and legal reasons, as the interview was highly damaging to both him personally and the Klan organisation.

Legal self-protection:

The interview contains explicit threats of violence - "I intend to kill radicals" and "not one of them will be left alive." By 1871, when Forrest testified to Congressional hearings, the federal government was actively prosecuting Klan members under the Force Acts. These statements could have been used as evidence of conspiracy and incitement to violence.

Revealing organisational secrets: Forrest provides specific information about Klan membership ("about 550,000 men") and admits his leadership role. This intelligence would be valuable to federal investigators trying to understand and prosecute the organisation.

Political embarrassment: The statements reveal open defiance of legitimate government - "I have never recognised the present government in Tennessee" - which undermines any claims that the Klan was maintaining law and order rather than engaging in rebellion.

Strategic timing considerations:

Changing political climate: By 1871, federal pressure had intensified significantly. President Grant was actively using military force against the Klan, making open defiance more dangerous than it had been in 1868.

Klan dissolution: Forrest had actually ordered the Klan to disband in early 1869, partly due to the violence getting out of control. Admitting to these 1868 statements would contradict his later position that the organisation should cease operations.

Reputation management: As a former Confederate general trying to rebuild his post-war reputation, being associated with ongoing terrorist activities was increasingly damaging to his business and social standing.

Interview context problems:

Journalistic reliability: The informal interview setting in 1868 may have involved alcohol or casual conversation that Forrest later regretted.

Journalists sometimes embellished or misquoted subjects.

Political manipulation: The timing of the interview's publication may have been calculated to embarrass Forrest or the Democratic Party, providing him with a reason to claim misrepresentation.

Historical knowledge context:

Forrest was known for violent rhetoric but also for political calculation. By denying the statements, he could maintain plausible deniability while the Klan continued operating through local leadership.

The Congressional hearings of 1871 were attempting to build legal cases against Klan leaders, making any admission of leadership or violent intent legally dangerous.

Conclusion: Forrest's denials represent typical behaviour of someone trying to avoid legal consequences while maintaining political influence - denying the most damaging statements while not necessarily ending his involvement in Klan activities.

6. Study all the sources.

How far do these sources provide convincing evidence that people supported the Ku Klux Klan? Use the sources to explain your answer.

The sources provide strong evidence of significant support for the Ku Klux Klan among specific segments of the white Southern population, but also reveal the contested and problematic nature of this support.

Evidence of Strong Support:

Organisational scale and effectiveness: Source A describes the Klan's "rapid growth" facilitated by "common belief that the Klan had some great and important mission," suggesting widespread enthusiasm for its goals. Source G claims "550,000 men" membership across the South, indicating massive organisational support if accurate.

Media attention and mystique: Source A notes that "every issue of the local paper contained some reference to it" and these notices were "copied into other papers," suggesting considerable public interest and sympathy. The "mysteriousness created much interest" indicates the Klan positively captured public imagination.

Community approval: Source E's Tennessee newspaper account describes the Klan visit as "to the benefit of the community" and notes they "did not hesitate to unmask themselves when asked," suggesting local acceptance and recognition. The description of their "beautiful horses" and purposeful behaviour indicates admiration rather than fear among supporters.

Operational success: According to Source A, after Klan activity, "robberies ceased and the lawless behaved well," while Source E reports a "great improvement" in local behaviour. This suggests a community appreciation for their self-appointed role as law enforcement.

Political effectiveness: Source F demonstrates that Klan violence successfully influenced elections, "captured the masses, led them to the polls and made them vote Democrat." This political success would have reinforced support among white Democrats who benefited from it.

Evidence of Limited or Problematic Support:

Geographic and demographic limitations: The support was clearly concentrated among white Southerners, particularly those who identified as Democrats. Source D shows that Republican state governments actively opposed the Klan, indicating significant opposition existed even within Southern society.

Coercion versus genuine support: Source F reveals that Klan activities involved "hunting and chasing" people through "fields and swamps" and creating "constant terror." This suggests their political success came through intimidation rather than genuine popular support.

Official condemnation: Source D's Alabama law demonstrates that legitimate governmental authority opposed the Klan, even in the South. The strong language, referring to it as "a widespread and alarming evil," indicates official recognition that it poses a threat to social order.

Media criticism: Source C's 1874 cartoon represents national criticism of the Klan, showing that beyond the South, the organisation was viewed negatively as a tool of political intimidation.

Leadership denials: Source G shows that even Klan leaders like Forrest found it necessary to deny their involvement when questioned officially, suggesting awareness that their activities were controversial and potentially criminal.

Quality and reliability of support evidence:

Source bias considerations: Source A is written by a Klan member seeking to justify their activities, making it an unreliable source of objective evidence of support. Source E comes from a sympathetic Tennessee newspaper, likely reflecting editorial bias rather than balanced reporting.

Contemporary versus retrospective accounts: Sources A and E represent contemporary accounts that may reflect immediate community reactions, while sources such as B and F represent later investigations with access to broader evidence and testimony.

Regional variations: The sources suggest that support was geographically concentrated in rural areas and small towns, where the Klan could operate effectively, rather than representing a universal opinion throughout the South.

Economic and social context: Historical knowledge indicates that Klan support correlated with financial anxiety, racial fears, and resentment over

Republican Reconstruction policies. This suggests that support was conditional and context-dependent, rather than reflecting a deep ideological commitment.

Conclusion:

The sources provide convincing evidence that the Ku Klux Klan enjoyed substantial support among specific segments of the white Southern population, particularly rural Democrats who felt threatened by Reconstruction changes. The evidence of organisational success, media attention, community approval, and political effectiveness all point to significant grassroots support.

However, this support was geographically and demographically limited, based partly on intimidation and coercion, and opposed by legitimate governmental authority. The support appears to have been tactical and conditional - based on the Klan's utility in resisting Reconstruction rather than broad ideological agreement with terrorist methods.

The sources suggest that while the Klan had enough support to operate effectively and achieve political goals, this support was problematic, contested, and ultimately unsustainable when faced with determined federal opposition. The evidence suggests significant but narrow support, rather than broad-based widespread approval.

[12]

Chapter 19

Paper 19

A: Nineteenth-century topic Option B: Twentieth-century topic

- Follow the instructions on the front cover of the answer booklet. If you need additional answer paper, ask the invigilator for a continuation booklet.

0470/23

Paper 2   May/June 2022

2 hours

INFORMATION

The total mark for this paper is 50.

The number of marks for each question or part question is shown in brackets [ ].

CHAPTER 19

Option A: Nineteenth-century topic

HOW FAR WAS LINCOLN RESPONSIBLE FOR CAUSING THE SPLIT BETWEEN NORTH AND SOUTH IN 1860–61?

Study the Background Information and the sources carefully, and then answer all the questions.

Background Information

Between December 1860 and June 1861, eleven states, starting with South Carolina, seceded from the USA. These secessions were an essential factor in bringing about the Civil War, which began in April 1861, shortly after Lincoln took office as President.

Some historians argue that it was Lincoln himself who was responsible for the decision of some Southern states to secede – he was hated and feared by many people in the South. However, relations between North and South had worsened long before Lincoln became President, especially over the issue of slavery.

How far did Lincoln cause the split with the South?

SOURCE A

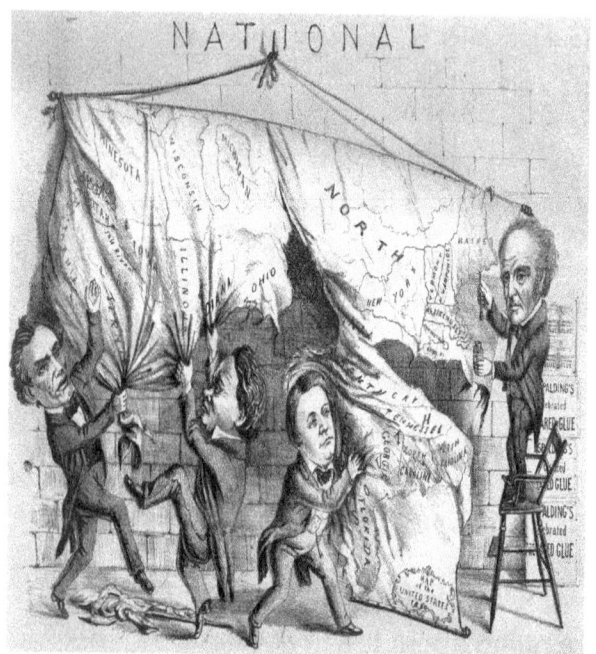

A cartoon published during the 1860 presidential election campaign. The candidates are (left to right) Lincoln, Douglas, Breckinridge and Bell. Bell is applying glue from a tiny pot.

SOURCE B

THE DIS-UNITED STATES—A BLACK BUSINESS.

A cartoon published in a British magazine, November 1856

SOURCE C

What will be the consequences of acceptance by the Southern States of the rule of Abolitionism at Washington, in the person of Lincoln?

The first consequence must be a powerful consolidation of the strength of the Abolition party of the North. If, after all the threats of resistance and disunion, the Southern States submit, the demoralisation of the South will be complete. Immediate danger will be brought to slavery in all Frontier States, and the underground railroad will become an overground railroad.

Before Lincoln can be installed in Washington, the Southern States can dissolve their union with the North peacefully. If we do not dissolve our union with the North, we make the triumph of our Abolition enemies complete. If the South accepts the rule of the Abolitionists, there will be an end to all peaceful separation of the Union. We can then only escape by war. The ruin of the South will be the loss of liberty, property, home, country – everything that makes life worth having.

From the 'Charleston Mercury' newspaper, 16 October 1860. Charleston is in South Carolina.

SOURCE D

I think that it would be unwise for the Southern states to secede if Lincoln were to be elected. I believe that in the Union, we would still be able to resist aggression against the equal rights of the people of the Southern states. We would still have a majority in the US Senate opposed to the abolitionists. Without the consent of that body, no law could be passed. We also have the US Supreme Court, whose opinions are favourable to equality, both of persons and of property. We also have a majority of the United States opposed to the faction led by Lincoln.

From a published letter by a Breckinridge supporter, Kentucky, October 1860.

SOURCE E

Do not consider any compromise regarding the extension of slavery. The instant you do, they have us beaten; all our labour is lost, and sooner or later will have to be done all over again. Douglas is sure to be trying again to bring in his 'Popular Sovereignty'. Have none of it. The conflict has to come, and better now than later. You know, I think the fugitive slave clause of the Constitution ought to be enforced
– or at least it ought not to be resisted.

A letter from Lincoln to William Kellogg, 11 December 1860. Kellogg, a Republican congressman, had proposed a compromise including an extension to the Missouri Compromise line.

SOURCE F

The people of Georgia have dissolved their political connection with the Government of the United States of America. For the last ten years, we have had numerous causes of complaint against non-slave-holding States. They have endeavoured to weaken our security, to disturb our domestic peace and tranquillity. The Federal Government has tried to deprive us of an equal enjoyment of the common Territories of the Republic. This hostile policy has placed the two sections of the Union in a state of virtual civil war for many years. Recent events have fully demonstrated the necessity of separation.

Northern States have, by a large majority, committed the Government of the United States into the hands of the party of Lincoln, called the Republican party, which, under its present name and organisation, is openly an anti-slavery party. While it supports waste and corruption in the administration of Government, anti-slavery is its mission and its purpose.

From Georgia's declaration of secession, 29 January 1861.

Now answer all the following questions. You may use any of the sources to help you answer the questions, in addition to those sources which you are told to use. When answering the questions, use your knowledge of the topic to help you interpret and evaluate the sources.

1   Study Source A.

What impressions does this cartoon give of the presidential candidates? Explain your answer using details of the source. [6]

2   Study Source B.

What is the cartoonist's message? Explain your answer using details of the source and your knowledge. [8]

3   Study Sources C and D.

How far does Source D prove that the author of Source C was wrong? Explain your answer using details of the sources and your knowledge. [8]

4   Study Source E.

Are you surprised that this was Lincoln's position in December 1860? Explain your answer using details of the source and your knowledge. [8]

5   Study Source F.

Why was this source issued in January 1861? Explain your answer using details of the source and your knowledge. [8]

6   Study all the sources.

How far do these sources provide convincing evidence that it was Lincoln who split the South from the North in 1860-61? Use the sources to explain your answer. [12]

Option B: Twentieth-century topic

HOW FAR WAS JARUZELSKI IN CONTROL IN POLAND IN 1981?

Study the Background Information and the sources carefully, and then answer all the questions.

Background Information

Jaruzelski became the leader of Poland on 18 October 1981, as the Soviet Union had become dissatisfied with Kania's handling of Solidarity and the strikes and protests occurring across Poland. However, under Jaruzelski, these conditions continued and even worsened. On 13 December, Jaruzelski announced to the Polish people that he was imposing martial law. Some historians claim he was pressured into doing this by the Soviet Union, while others argue that he was trying to avoid a Soviet military invasion.

How strong a leader was Jaruzelski? Was he being told what to do by the Soviet Union, or was he in control?

SOURCE A

Content removed due to copyright restrictions.

The front cover of the American 'Time' magazine, 28 December 1981.

SOURCE B

I wanted to congratulate you on your election to the post of First Secretary of the Polish Communist Party. There is no other individual in the Polish

Workers' Party whose authority is equal to yours. We are confident that you will successfully tackle the challenging tasks ahead and take all necessary steps to address the severe problems facing your country. It is essential, without wasting time, to take the decisive measures you intend against the counter-revolution. We hope everyone will sense that things in Poland will move along differently.

Brezhnev speaking on the telephone to Jaruzelski, 19 October 1981.

SOURCE C

We greeted your election as First Secretary of the Polish Communist Party with great hopes. We were aware that earlier in the struggle against anti-socialist forces, you were hindered by the party leadership's indecisiveness in politics. Now this obstacle has been eliminated. We had hoped that people in Poland would sense that things in Poland were finally on a different course. We spoke on the phone about the need for a turnabout in the situation. However, one gets the impression that this has not been achieved. The anti-socialist forces are continuing to spread their influence among ever-wider segments of the population. It seems to me that you must mobilise the entire party in the struggle to win the hearts and minds of people.

I want to mention another matter. A lot has been written about your meeting with Walesa and the agreement to set up a 'Front of National Accord'. How far can you go with such agreements without losing control over the situation? Agreements must not make concessions to the enemies of socialism. We are aware that there are still individuals in your party's leadership who wish to continue the bankrupt course of Kania.

A message from Brezhnev to Jaruzelski, 21 November 1981.

SOURCE D

Published in the Netherlands on 12 December 1980. Brezhnev is saying to Walesa, 'I would never interfere in Poland's domestic affairs.

SOURCE E

A cartoon published in the Netherlands, 16 December 1981. The two men shown are Jaruzelski and Brezhnev.

SOURCE F

A cartoon published in Poland. It was published immediately after the imposition of martial law in December 1981

SOURCE G

The rigours of martial law have complicated everyday life. However, these restrictions are a lesser evil than the invasion that has long threatened us. The introduction of martial law has saved Poland from a danger whose true character and seriousness are still not fully comprehended everywhere. On 13 December, there was no alternative to the state's disintegration. Where was Poland going? How long could the country, torn by strikes, aflame with tensions and sinking into a climate of artificially created hatred, have continued to survive? There is still room in Poland for responsible, independent unions and the democratisation begun last year will continue. I state that the reports of alleged tens or hundreds of fatal casualties, of thousands arrested, held in the freezing conditions, beaten up and tortured, are a lie. One cannot hide the truth about Poland in Poland. Sooner or later, it will be known to the whole world.

Jaruzelski speaking to the Polish people on the radio, 25 December 1981.

Now answer all the following questions. You may use any of the sources to help you answer the questions, in addition to those sources which you are told to use. When answering the questions, use your knowledge of the topic to help you interpret and evaluate the sources.

1   Study Source A.

What impressions does this source give of Jaruzelski? Explain your answer using details of the source.   [7]

2   Study Sources B and C.

How far does Source B make Source C surprising? Explain your answer using details of the sources and your knowledge.   [8]

3   Study Sources D and E.

These two cartoons are by the same cartoonist. Had he changed his opinion between drawing the two cartoons? Explain your answer using details of the sources and your knowledge. [8]

4   Study Source F.

What is the cartoonist's message? Explain your answer using details of the source and your knowledge. [7]

5   Study Source G.

Why did Jaruzelski make this announcement to the Polish people on 25 December 1981? Explain your answer using details of the source and your knowledge. [8]

6   Study all the sources.

How far do these sources provide convincing evidence that Jaruzelski was in control of Poland? Use the sources to explain your answer. [12]

CHAPTER 19: Answers

Question

Option A: Nineteenth-century topic

HOW FAR WAS LINCOLN RESPONSIBLE FOR CAUSING THE SPLIT BETWEEN NORTH AND SOUTH IN 1860–61?

Now answer all the following questions. You may use any of the sources to help you answer the questions, in addition to those sources which you are told to use. When answering the questions, use your knowledge of the topic to help you interpret and evaluate the sources.

1. Study Source A.

What impressions does this cartoon give of the presidential candidates? Explain your answer using details of the source. [6]

The cartoon presents contrasting impressions of the four 1860 presidential candidates, with clear editorial bias.

Lincoln (leftmost figure): Appears strong and determined, actively pulling on the map of America. His posture suggests he has a clear vision and the strength to implement it. The cartoonist portrays him as the most dynamic and decisive candidate, capable of taking firm action.

Douglas (second from left): Also appears to be actively engaged in pulling the map, suggesting he, too, has definite policies and the energy to pursue them. However, he seems slightly less dominant than Lincoln, positioned as a strong but secondary figure.

Breckinridge (third from left): Shown as actively pulling in opposition to Lincoln and Douglas, representing the Southern Democratic position. His stance suggests determination to resist Northern policies, portraying him as a defender of Southern interests.

Bell (rightmost figure): Presented as weak and ineffective, holding only "a tiny pot" of glue while the others engage in the main struggle. This suggests the cartoonist viewed Bell's Constitutional Union Party's compromise approach as inadequate to address the nation's crisis. His small glue pot implies his solutions are insufficient for the magnitude of the problem.

Overall impression: The cartoon suggests the nation is being pulled apart by conflicting forces, with Bell's moderate attempts at unity being pathetically inadequate. The cartoonist appears to favour active leadership (Lincoln/Douglas) over weak compromise (Bell), while acknowledging the determination of Southern resistance (Breckinridge).

Editorial perspective: The cartoon reflects Northern Republican sympathies, portraying Lincoln as the strongest leader while mocking Bell's ineffective moderation.

2. Study Source B.

What is the cartoonist's message? Explain your answer using details of the source and your knowledge. [8]

The British cartoonist's message is that American slavery is fundamentally incompatible with the nation's founding principles of freedom and equality, creating an unsustainable contradiction.
Central symbolic message: The cartoon shows the Statue of Liberty (representing American ideals) literally breaking under the weight of slavery. The chains and shackles at the base represent the burden of slavery that is destroying the very foundation of American liberty and democracy.
Timing significance: Published in November 1856, this work follows the violent "Bleeding Kansas" conflicts and the caning of Senator Charles Sumner, during which British observers were increasingly critical of the contradictions between American democratic ideals and the institution of slavery.
British perspective: As an external observer, the British cartoonist can critique American hypocrisy without the domestic political constraints that limit their criticism in the United States. Britain had abolished slavery in its empire in 1833, thereby gaining moral authority to criticise American practices.
Structural critique: The image suggests that slavery is not just morally wrong but structurally incompatible with American constitutional

principles. The statue's breaking implies that the nation cannot indefinitely maintain both liberty and bondage without destroying itself.

Historical context: 1856 was a pivotal year marked by the formation of the Republican Party, the violence in Kansas, and escalating sectional tensions. The British, having recently fought the Crimean War partly over principles of freedom, were particularly sensitive to contradictions between stated ideals and actual practices.

Prophetic element: The cartoon essentially predicts the coming crisis - suggesting that America must choose between its founding principles and slavery, as both cannot coexist permanently.

International implications: The image also reflects British diplomatic and economic concerns about American instability affecting international relations and trade.

The cartoonist's message is that America's internal contradiction between slavery and freedom is unsustainable and will ultimately destroy the nation's moral authority and political stability.

3. Study Sources C and D.

How far does Source D prove that the author of Source C was wrong? Explain your answer using details of the sources and your knowledge. [8]

Source D provides a strong counterargument to Source C's panic, but does not entirely prove the Charleston Mercury author was wrong about the fundamental threat Lincoln represented.

Where Source D challenges Source C:

Constitutional protections: Source D argues that institutional safeguards would protect Southern interests even under Lincoln - "We would still have a majority in the US Senate opposed to the abolitionists" and "We have also the US Supreme Court, whose opinions are favourable to the equality, both of persons and of property." This directly contradicts Source C's claim that Lincoln's election would mean immediate "rule of Abolitionism."

Political mathematics: Source D points out that Republicans lacked total control - "We have a majority of the United States opposed to the faction of which Lincoln is the head." This suggests Source C's fears of complete Northern domination were premature.

Tactical reasoning: Source D argues that working within the Union would be more effective than secession for protecting Southern rights, directly opposing Source C's call for immediate separation.

Where Source D may be inadequate:

Long-term trajectory: Source C focuses on future threats - "Immediate danger will be brought to slavery in all Frontier States" and the growth of abolitionist strength. Source D addresses only immediate constitutional protections, not long-term political trends.

Republican Party growth: Historical knowledge shows that Republican strength was indeed growing rapidly in the North. Source C correctly identified that Lincoln's election would encourage further Republican organising and recruitment.

Symbolic importance: Source C understood that Lincoln's election would symbolically legitimise the Republican anti-slavery position nationally, potentially encouraging resistance to fugitive slave laws and supporting Underground Railroad activities.

Historical vindication: Events proved Source C partially correct about Republican intentions. While Lincoln initially promised not to interfere with existing slavery, the Republican Party did eventually support the 13th Amendment, abolishing slavery entirely.

Context of authorship: Source D comes from Kentucky, a border state with more moderate views than South Carolina. The Charleston Mercury represented the most radical Southern position, while the Breckinridge supporter represented more conservative Southern opinion.

Conclusion: Source D successfully challenges Source C's immediate panic and calls for secession, but doesn't prove wrong the underlying assessment that Lincoln's election represented a long-term existential threat to slavery. Source C was incorrect regarding timing but arguably correct in its assessment of the ultimate Republican intentions.

4. Study Source E.

Are you surprised that this was Lincoln's position in December 1860? Explain your answer using details of the source and your knowledge. [8]

Lincoln's position is not surprising given his consistent political stance, but the timing makes it particularly significant and somewhat more rigid than might be expected.

Why this position is not surprising:

Consistent Republican doctrine: Lincoln's rejection of compromise on the extension of slavery was a fundamental Republican Party policy since 1854. The party was explicitly founded to oppose slavery's expansion into new territories, making this position entirely predictable.

Historical precedent: Lincoln had articulated this position clearly in the Lincoln-Douglas debates of 1858 and throughout his political career. His "House Divided" speech explicitly rejected the idea that slavery could be permanently contained through compromise.

Strategic calculation: Lincoln understood that any compromise on slavery extension would split the Republican Party and undermine its core purpose. As he states, "all our labour is lost, and sooner or later will have to be done all over again."

Constitutional interpretation: His support for enforcing the fugitive slave clause shows he distinguished between constitutional obligations and political compromises, maintaining that existing constitutional protections for slavery should be honoured.

Why the timing makes it somewhat surprising:

Political pressure: By December 1860, South Carolina had already seceded (December 20), making Lincoln's inflexibility potentially costly. Many expected the president-elect to demonstrate a greater willingness to compromise to preserve the Union.

Crittenden Compromise context: Historical knowledge reveals that serious compromise proposals were being debated in Congress, including the Crittenden Compromise, which extended the Missouri Compromise line to the Pacific. Lincoln's flat rejection seems rigid given the crisis.

Presidential responsibility: As president-elect facing imminent national breakup, some flexibility might have been expected to prevent war, even if it meant temporary political setbacks.

Moderate Republican pressure: Many Republicans, including William Kellogg (the letter's recipient), were urging compromise to prevent secession, making Lincoln's adamant refusal potentially divisive within his own party.

Historical knowledge context: This letter was written just nine days before South Carolina seceded, when the crisis was escalating rapidly. Lincoln's unwillingness to compromise suggests he believed that it would only delay, rather than resolve, the fundamental conflict.

Conclusion: While Lincoln's position was consistent with his political principles, the crisis context makes his inflexibility somewhat surprising, as it demonstrates his conviction that the slavery issue had to be resolved definitively rather than postponed through compromise.

5. Study Source F.

Why was this source issued in January 1861? Explain your answer using details of the source and your knowledge. [8]

Georgia issued this declaration to justify its decision to secede and rally support both within the state and among other Southern states.

Legal and constitutional justification:

Georgia needed to legitimise its secession from the Union by presenting it as a constitutional right rather than a rebellion. The declaration argues that "recent events have fully demonstrated the necessity of separation," framing secession as a reluctant but necessary response to Northern aggression.

Political timing context:

January 1861 was a critical time - South Carolina had seceded in December 1860, and other states were debating their response. Georgia needed to justify its decision to join the secession movement and encourage other states to follow suit.

Historical knowledge shows that by January 1861, Mississippi, Florida, and Alabama had also seceded, making Georgia's declaration part of a coordinated effort to create a critical mass for Southern independence.

Response to Lincoln's election:

The declaration directly addresses Lincoln's victory, stating that "Northern States have by a large majority committed the Government of the United States into the hands of the party of Lincoln." This timing suggests the declaration was triggered explicitly by Republican electoral success.

Internal Georgia politics:

Georgia faced significant internal division on secession - many Georgians, including Alexander Stephens, opposed immediate secession. The declaration needed to convince wavering Georgians that secession was both necessary and justified.

Building Southern unity:

The declaration uses collective Southern identity - referring to "non-slave-holding States" as the enemy and emphasising shared Southern grievances over "the last ten years." This timing helped build momentum for the Confederacy, which would be formed in February 1861.

International legitimacy:
By formally articulating grievances, Georgia sought to present secession as a justified resistance to oppression rather than an illegal rebellion, potentially gaining international recognition and support.

Economic and practical considerations:
Historical knowledge indicates that Georgia's economy was deeply tied to slavery and cotton production. The declaration's timing enabled coordination with other cotton-producing states for economic cooperation and mutual defence.

Federal response:
January 1861 represented the last opportunity to secede before Lincoln's inauguration in March. The declaration's timing allowed Georgia to present its case while Buchanan's weak federal government was still in office.

Conclusion: The January 1861 timing was strategically chosen to justify Georgia's decision, build Southern momentum, and establish legal precedent before Lincoln took office and potentially used federal power to prevent further secessions.

6. Study all the sources.
How far do these sources provide convincing evidence that it was Lincoln who split the South from the North in 1860-61? Use the sources to explain your answer. [8]

The sources provide mixed evidence about Lincoln's responsibility, showing he was both a catalyst and a symbol of deeper divisions, rather than the fundamental cause of the North-South split.

Evidence supporting Lincoln's responsibility:
Direct Southern fears of Lincoln: Source C demonstrates intense Southern anxiety specifically about Lincoln's election, warning that "acceptance by the Southern States of the rule of Abolitionism at Washington, in the person of Lincoln" would lead to complete Southern "demoralisation." This suggests

that Lincoln was personally seen as the immediate threat.

Republican Party identification with Lincoln: Source F directly blames "the party of Lincoln, called the Republican party" for forcing secession, making Lincoln personally responsible as the party's leader and symbol. The timing of secessions immediately after his election supports this interpretation.

Lincoln's inflexibility: Source E illustrates Lincoln's refusal to compromise on the extension of slavery in December 1860, even as the Union was dissolving. His adamant position - "Do not consider any compromise" - suggests he prioritised Republican principles over preserving the Union.

Symbolic significance: Source A portrays the 1860 election as fundamentally divisive, with candidates pulling the nation in different directions. Lincoln's victory represented a definitive Northern triumph that Southern states couldn't accept.

Evidence limiting Lincoln's responsibility:
Pre-existing tensions: Source B from 1856 reveals that fundamental contradictions between slavery and American principles existed four years before Lincoln's election. The British cartoonist recognised that the conflict was structural rather than personal to any individual politician.

Long-term grievances: Source F lists complaints going back "ten years" (to 1851), indicating that Southern grievances predated Lincoln's national prominence. The declaration mentions "numerous causes of complaint" that developed over a decade, not specifically Lincoln's policies.

Constitutional protections argument: Source D suggests that Lincoln's election didn't necessarily threaten immediate Southern interests, arguing that institutional safeguards would prevent abolitionist dominance. This implies that secession was premature and not necessarily caused by Lincoln's specific threat.

Alternative Southern perspectives: Source D shows that not all Southerners viewed Lincoln's election as requiring immediate secession, suggesting that the split wasn't inevitable based solely on Lincoln's victory.

Analysis of causation versus correlation:

Lincoln as catalyst rather than cause: The sources suggest that Lincoln's election was the trigger, rather than the underlying cause, of secession. Source B indicates fundamental contradictions existed independently of Lincoln, while Source F's list of decade-long grievances suggests accumulated tensions rather than Lincoln-specific problems.

Structural versus personal factors: Historical knowledge reveals that issues such as the Missouri Compromise, the Kansas-Nebraska Act, the Dred Scott decision, and John Brown's raid created the conditions for conflict before Lincoln became a prominent national figure. Lincoln represented these broader trends rather than making them.

Regional economic and social divisions: The sources suggest more profound economic and social disparities. Source F mentions concerns about "property" and "domestic tranquillity," which reflect fundamental differences between enslaved persons and free labour systems.

Republican Party growth: Sources suggest that Lincoln was part of a broader Republican movement rather than its sole cause. The party's growth reflected Northern antislavery sentiment that would have existed regardless of Lincoln's specific leadership.

Assessment of source reliability:

Contemporary bias: Sources C and F represent Southern propaganda designed to justify secession, potentially exaggerating Lincoln's personal responsibility. Source E shows Lincoln's private correspondence, providing more reliable evidence of his actual positions.

British perspective: Source B offers external validation that American contradictions over slavery were fundamental structural problems rather than personality-driven conflicts.

Political context: Sources A and D reflect different political perspectives within the American debate, showing that Lincoln's election was contested but not universally seen as catastrophic.

Conclusion:

The sources provide limited convincing evidence that Lincoln personally split the South from the North. While they clearly show that Lincoln's election was the immediate trigger for secession, they also demonstrate that fundamental conflicts over slavery existed long before Lincoln's prominence.

Lincoln appears to have been both a catalyst and a symbol - his election crystallised existing tensions rather than creating them. His refusal to compromise (Source E) may have accelerated the crisis. Still, Sources B and F indicate that more profound structural contradictions made conflict almost inevitable regardless of Lincoln's specific actions.

The most convincing evidence suggests Lincoln was responsible for the timing of the split rather than its underlying causes. His election forced the

South to choose between accepting Republican antislavery principles or leaving the Union, but these contradictions had been building for decades before Lincoln became president.

Chapter 20

Paper 20

HISTORY

Paper 4: Alternative to Coursework

You will need: Answer booklet (enclosed)

0470/41

May/June 2022

1 hour

INFORMATION

- The total mark for this paper is 40.
- The number of marks for each question or part question is shown in brackets [ ].

06_0470_41_2022_1.7

© UCLES 2022

CHAPTER 20

Answer one question from your chosen Depth Study.

DEPTH STUDY A: THE FIRST WORLD WAR, 1914–18

1 How important was the British Expeditionary Force (BEF) in the early stages of the war on the Western Front? Explain your answer. [40]

2 How significant were British naval operations to the outcome of the war? Explain your answer.
[40]

DEPTH STUDY B: GERMANY, 1918–45

3 How important was the Kapp Putsch in the development of Weimar Germany to 1923? Explain your answer. [40]

4 How significant was the use of concentration camps in dealing with opposition to Nazi rule after 1933? Explain your answer. [40]

DEPTH STUDY C: RUSSIA, 1905–41

5   How important was Russification as an aspect of Tsarist rule in Russia up to 1914? Explain your answer. [40]

6   How significant were factions in the Communist Party as a reason for Stalin's purges in the 1930s? Explain your answer. [40]

DEPTH STUDY D: THE UNITED STATES, 1919–41

7   How important was overproduction as a reason for the problems faced by agriculture and older industries in the USA in the 1920s? Explain your answer. [40]

8   How significant were bribery and corruption as reasons why Prohibition failed by 1933? Explain your answer. [40]

DEPTH STUDY E: CHINA, c.1930–c.1990

9   How important was Mao's leadership as a reason for the Communist victory in 1949? Explain your answer. [40]

10 How significant was propaganda in enabling Mao to establish Communist rule in China after 1949? Explain your answer. [40]

DEPTH STUDY F: SOUTH AFRICA, c.1940–c.1994

11 How important were government limitations on travel in maintaining segregation between the races in South Africa before 1948? Explain your answer. [40]

12 How significant was the growth in Black Consciousness in weakening the system of apartheid in South Africa? Explain your answer. [40]

DEPTH STUDY G: ISRAELIS AND PALESTINIANS SINCE 1945

13 How important was the British mandate as a factor that shaped events in Palestine, 1945-49? Explain your answer. [40]

14   How significant was Hamas in increasing tensions between Israelis and Palestinians? Explain your answer.   [40]

CHAPTER 20: Answer

Answer one question from your chosen Depth Study.

Answered Questions:

DEPTH STUDY D: THE UNITED STATES, 1919–41 (No. 7)

DEPTH STUDY B: GERMANY, 1918–45 (No. 3)

7. How important was overproduction as a reason for the problems faced by agriculture and older industries in the USA in the 1920s? Explain your answer. [40]

Overproduction – Fundamental reason:

- Agricultural surplus – Farmers produced too much wheat, corn, and cotton, leading to falling prices and lower profits.
- New technology – Tractors and mechanised farming increased yields, but demand did not keep up.
- Impact of WWI ending – During WWI, Europe bought US food, but after the war, demand dropped, leaving farmers with excess crops.
- Falling incomes – Farmers could not pay back loans taken during the war years, leading to debt and bankruptcies.

Other reasons – Equally or more important:

- Foreign competition – Countries like Canada and Argentina exported cheaper grain, worsening the price collapse.
- Decline in older industries – Coal, textiles, and shipbuilding faced competition from oil, electricity, and new synthetic fabrics, leading to job losses.
- Unequal prosperity – Many rural Americans could not afford consumer goods, so demand for manufactured goods stayed low.
- Technological change – Older industries struggled to modernise and were left behind by faster-growing sectors like cars and chemicals.
- Government policies – High tariffs (Fordney-McCumber Tariff) meant less international trade, reducing export markets for farm produce.

Conclusion:
- Overall importance – Overproduction was a significant cause of agricultural problems and triggered falling prices, but it was not the only factor.
- Relative weight – Problems in older industries were also linked to changing technology, foreign competition, and falling demand.
- Balanced view – Overproduction was crucial for farming difficulties, but economic change and

lack of markets played an equally significant role in causing widespread problems.

3. How important was the Kapp Putsch in the development of Weimar Germany to 1923? Explain your answer. [40]

Importance of the Kapp Putsch:
- Showed weakness of the Weimar government – The government had to flee Berlin and relied on a general strike rather than its army to stop the putsch, showing limited control.
- Army's disloyalty – The Reichswehr refused to act against the Freikorps, proving the army could not be fully trusted to defend the Republic.
- Strengthened right-wing forces – The light punishments given to putsch leaders encouraged future right-wing uprisings and undermined confidence in democracy.
- Increased political instability – The putsch deepened divisions between left and right, making government cooperation more difficult.

Other events to 1923 – Equally or more important:
- Spartacist Uprising (1919) – Left-wing revolt crushed by the Freikorps, showing danger from communists and forcing the government to rely on anti-republican forces.

- Treaty of Versailles (1919) – Created resentment (war guilt, reparations, territorial losses) which weakened the Republic's popularity from the start.
- Ruhr Crisis (1923) – French and Belgian occupation of the Ruhr and passive resistance worsened hyperinflation, causing economic chaos and social hardship.
- Hyperinflation (1923) – Destroyed savings and pensions, leading many Germans to lose faith in the Republic and turning them towards extremist parties.
- Munich Putsch (1923) – Though it failed, it gave Hitler publicity and a platform to spread his ideas, laying the groundwork for future Nazi growth.

Conclusion:
- Overall importance – The Kapp Putsch was significant as it exposed the government's dependence on others and its inability to control the army.
- Relative weight – However, other events such as Versailles, the Ruhr Crisis, and hyperinflation had a bigger impact on everyday life and did more to weaken Weimar democracy.
- Balanced view – The Kapp Putsch was an important early test of Weimar stability, but

economic crises and widespread discontent posed a greater challenge by 1923.

Chapter 21

Paper 21

HISTORY

Paper 4: Alternative to Coursework

You must answer in the enclosed answer booklet.

You will need: Answer booklet (enclosed)

0470/42

February/March 2022

1 hour

Answer one question from your chosen Depth Study.

- Follow the instructions on the front cover of the answer booklet. If you need additional answer paper,

Ask the invigilator for a continuation booklet.

INFORMATION

- The total mark for this paper is 40.
- The number of marks for each question or part question is shown in brackets [ ].

03_0470_42_2022_1.7

© UCLES 2022

CHAPTER 21

Answer one question from your chosen Depth Study.

DEPTH STUDY A: THE FIRST WORLD WAR, 1914–18

1   How vital was the machine gun in the development of trench warfare during the First World War? Explain your answer. [40]

2   How significant were women in carrying out the roles as an aspect of the Allied war effort? Explain your answer.   [40]

DEPTH STUDY B: GERMANY, 1918–45

3   How important was economic recovery after 1923 as a reason for the lack of Nazi electoral success by 1928? Explain your answer. [40]

4   How significant was the Hitler Youth in the development of Nazi rule after 1933? Explain your answer.   [40]

DEPTH STUDY C: RUSSIA, 1905–41

5   How important was the First World War as a cause of the March Revolution in 1917? Explain your answer. [40]

6   How significant was the introduction of the New Economic Policy (NEP) to the survival of the Bolshevik dictatorship, 1917-24? Explain your answer. [40]

DEPTH STUDY D: THE UNITED STATES, 1919–41

7   How important was the First World War as a reason why Prohibition was introduced in the USA? Explain your answer. [40]

8   How significant were the 'Hundred Days' in dealing with the economic problems in the USA during the Depression? Explain your answer. [40]

DEPTH STUDY E: CHINA, c.1930–c.1990

9   How vital was industry to the social and economic development of Communist China by 1960? Explain your answer. [40]

10   How significant were relations with foreign countries to the economic progress of Communist China up to 1976? Explain your answer. [40]

DEPTH STUDY F: SOUTH AFRICA, c.1940–c.1994

11   How important was Afrikaner nationalism as a reason for the defeat of the United Party in 1948? Explain your answer.   [40]

12   How significant was P.W. Botha in weakening white minority rule in South Africa after 1978? Explain your answer.   [40]

DEPTH STUDY G: ISRAELIS AND PALESTINIANS SINCE 1945

13   How vital was superpower involvement in shaping Arab-Israeli relations after 1948? Explain your answer. [40]

14　　How significant were the Camp David meetings in the development of the peace process after 1973? Explain your answer. [40]

CHAPTER 21: Answers

Answer one question from your chosen Depth Study.

Answered Questions:

DEPTH STUDY A: THE FIRST WORLD WAR, 1914–18 (No. 1)

DEPTH STUDY D: THE UNITED STATES, 1919–41 (No 7)

1   How vital was the machine gun in the development of trench warfare during the First World War? Explain your answer. [40]

Importance of the Machine Gun

- Deadly defensive weapon – Machine guns could fire 400–600 rounds per minute, mowing down attackers crossing No Man's Land.
- Stopped early offensives – At battles like Mons, the Marne, and First Ypres (1914), machine guns caused massive casualties and prevented rapid movement.
- Encouraged digging trenches – Soldiers dug deep trenches for protection from the devastating firepower of machine guns.

- Maintained stalemate – Whenever an army attacked, defenders with machine guns inflicted heavy losses, meaning neither side could advance far.
- Shaped tactics – Attacks had to be carefully planned, using artillery bombardments and creeping barrages to silence enemy machine guns before infantry could advance.

Other Important Factors in Trench Warfare

- Artillery – The biggest killer of the war; artillery bombardments forced soldiers underground and turned battlefields into craters, making trench systems necessary.
- Barbed wire – Slowed down attacking troops, leaving them exposed to machine gun fire, further encouraging trench defence.
- Defensive mindset – Both sides expected a quick victory but soon realised that staying put and defending was safer and more effective.
- Failure of the Schlieffen Plan – When Germany was stopped at the Marne, both sides "dug in" to protect their positions, leading to the Race to the Sea and the creation of continuous trench lines.
- Technological stalemate – Weapons like rifles, grenades, and later poison gas made open

fighting too deadly, reinforcing the need for trenches.

Evaluation

- Very important factor – The machine gun was the main reason why open warfare became too costly and why attackers could not break through easily.
- However, it was not the only factor: artillery, barbed wire, and strategic decisions were equally significant in creating and sustaining trench warfare.
- Combined effect – It was the combination of machine guns with other defensive weapons that truly made trench warfare dominant.

Overall judgment –

The machine gun was crucial in the development of trench warfare, as it rendered attacking troops highly vulnerable and compelled armies to adopt defensive positions. However, it should be viewed as part of a broader set of technological and strategic factors that collectively made trench warfare the primary feature of the Western Front.

7. How important was the First World War as a reason why Prohibition was introduced in the USA? Explain your answer.

Introduction– Prohibition (the ban on alcohol from 1920) had many causes. The First World War played a significant role, but it was not the sole reason.

Importance of the First World War

- Anti-German feeling – Many big breweries were owned by German-Americans (e.g., Anheuser-Busch). During the war, drinking beer was seen as "unpatriotic," which helped the Prohibition movement.
- Saving grain for soldiers – Supporters argued that grain used to make alcohol should instead be used to feed troops and the population during wartime.
- Boost to temperance movement – War gave extra momentum to temperance campaigners who claimed alcohol made workers less productive in wartime industries.
- Moral pressure – Wartime propaganda encouraged sacrifice and discipline; banning alcohol fitted this message.

Other Important Reasons

- Religious and moral arguments – Groups like the Anti-Saloon League and the Women's Christian Temperance Union campaigned for years, claiming alcohol led to crime, poverty, and broken families.

- Social problems – Alcohol was blamed for domestic violence, poor health, and disorder in society.
- Rural support – Many rural communities supported Prohibition as part of a broader campaign for traditional, "clean" American values.
- Political influence – Temperance groups lobbied politicians successfully, persuading them to support a constitutional amendment banning alcohol.
- Progressive reforms – Early 20th-century reformers wanted to improve society; Prohibition was seen as one way to achieve this.

Evaluation
- WWI made Prohibition more likely – It accelerated its introduction by creating anti-German feeling, encouraging grain conservation, and strengthening moral campaigns.
- However, the movement for Prohibition existed long before WWI, and religious, moral, and social pressures also shaped the decision.
- Overall view – WWI was a critical "final push," but Prohibition would probably have happened eventually due to strong pre-war campaigns and social attitudes.

Chapter 22

Paper 22

Paper 4: Alternative to Coursework

You must answer in the enclosed answer booklet.

You will need: Answer booklet (enclosed) 0470/42

May/June 2022

1 hour

INFORMATION

- The total mark for this paper is 40.
- The number of marks for each question or part question is shown in brackets [ ].

06_0470_42_2022_1.6
© UCLES 2022

CHAPTER 22

Answer one question from your chosen Depth Study.

DEPTH STUDY A: THE FIRST WORLD WAR, 1914–18

1   How important were new and improved weapons in the development of a war of attrition on the Western Front? Explain your answer. [40]

2   How significant was Turkish resistance as a reason for Allied failure in the Gallipoli campaign? Explain your answer.   [40]

DEPTH STUDY B: GERMANY, 1918–45

3   How important were Stresemann's economic policies to the stability of the Weimar Republic, 1923-29? Explain your answer. [40]

4   How significant were resistance groups in the opposition to Nazi rule? Explain your answer. [40]

DEPTH STUDY C: RUSSIA, 1905–41

5   How important was Russia's continued involvement in the First World War as a reason for increased support for the Bolsheviks between March and November 1917? Explain your answer. [40]

6   How significant were gulags to Stalin's system of control in the Soviet Union after 1928? Explain your answer. [40]

DEPTH STUDY D: THE UNITED STATES, 1919–41

7   How important was government economic policy as a cause of prosperity in the USA in the 1920s? Explain your answer. [40]

8   How significant were problems in agriculture as an aspect of the Great Depression in the USA? Explain your answer. [40]

DEPTH STUDY E: CHINA, c.1930–c.1990

9   How vital was the Japanese invasion of China as a reason for increased support for the

Chinese Communist Party before 1949? Explain your answer. [40]

10 How significant was the treatment of landlords as an aspect of Mao's land reforms in the 1950s? Explain your answer. [40]

DEPTH STUDY F: SOUTH AFRICA, c.1940–c.1994

11 How important was the PAC in determining the nature of resistance to apartheid in the 1950s and 1960s? Explain your answer. [40]

12 How significant was Desmond Tutu in ending white minority rule in South Africa? Explain your answer. [40]

DEPTH STUDY G: ISRAELIS AND PALESTINIANS SINCE 1945

13 How vital was Jewish immigration as a cause of tension in the Middle East by 1948? Explain your answer. [40]

14 How significant were Israeli military tactics in determining the outcome of the Yom Kippur War, 1973? Explain your answer. [40]

CHAPTER 22: Answers

Answer one question from your chosen Depth Study.

Answered Questions:

DEPTH STUDY A: THE FIRST WORLD WAR, 1914–18 (No. 1)

DEPTH STUDY D: THE UNITED STATES, 1919–41 (No. 8)

1   How important were new and improved weapons in the development of a war of attrition on the Western Front? Explain your answer.[40]

New and improved weapons – very important:
•   Machine guns – Fired hundreds of rounds per minute, making it almost impossible for infantry to cross no man's land, forcing both sides into defensive trenches.
•   Heavy artillery – Long-range guns caused massive casualties and destroyed trenches, but rarely led to breakthroughs, prolonging the stalemate.

- Poison gas – Caused fear, injuries, and deaths, but often depended on the wind; it killed relatively few but added to the misery of trench warfare.
- Tanks – First used in 1916; helped cross trenches and crush barbed wire, but were slow and unreliable early on, so they did not end the stalemate quickly.
- Barbed wire – Simple but deadly, it slowed attacks and made defenders much stronger, increasing the difficulty of rapid advances.

Other factors – equally or more important:

- Trench systems – Deep, fortified trenches meant defenders had the advantage, making battles lengthy and costly.
- Poor tactics – Generals often relied on mass infantry attacks ('over the top'), which failed against modern weapons, leading to high casualties and stalemate.
- Railways and supply lines – Allowed armies to reinforce and resupply quickly, preventing decisive victories and prolonging the war.
- Communication issues – Slow or broken communications during battles meant attacks could not adapt quickly, wasting lives and preventing breakthroughs.

- War aims and determination – Both sides were willing to fight a protracted war, hoping to wear the other down, which naturally created a war of attrition.

Judgement
- Overall importance – New weapons were crucial in making attacks so costly that neither side could win quickly, leading to stalemate and attrition.
- Relative weight – However, trench systems, defensive tactics, and the determination to fight to the end were also key in creating a war of attrition.
- Balanced view – Weapons were an important cause, but the combination of technology, strategy, and leadership decisions together made the Western Front a war of attrition.

8. How significant were problems in agriculture as an aspect of the Great Depression in the USA? Explain your answer.   [40]

Agricultural problems – highly significant:
- Falling crop prices – Overproduction and falling demand caused prices of wheat, corn, and cotton to collapse, leaving farmers unable to make a profit.

- Debt crisis – Many farmers had borrowed heavily in the 1920s and could not repay loans, leading to foreclosures and bankruptcies.
- Dust Bowl – Severe drought and over-farming led to soil erosion in the Great Plains, driving thousands of families (e.g., "Okies") to migrate in search of work.
- Impact on rural communities – Farm closures caused widespread poverty, hunger, and loss of land, deepening the Depression in rural areas.
- Reduced demand – Struggling farmers could not buy manufactured goods, worsening the economic downturn in other industries.

Other aspects of the Great Depression – equally or more significant:

- Bank failures – Thousands of banks collapsed, wiping out savings and reducing confidence in the economy.
- Collapse of industry – Factories closed as consumer demand fell, leading to mass unemployment in cities.
- Stock market crash – The Wall Street Crash of 1929 triggered panic, wiped out investments, and caused further economic decline.

- International trade slump – High tariffs (e.g., Smoot-Hawley Tariff) reduced global trade, hurting US exports.
- Unemployment crisis – By 1933, a quarter of the workforce was jobless, causing homelessness and urban poverty (e.g., "Hoovervilles").

Judgement

- Overall significance – Agricultural problems were a significant part of the Depression, especially in rural America, and contributed to reduced demand for goods.
- Relative weight – However, the collapse of banking, industry, and employment had a more widespread effect on the entire economy.
- Balanced view – Agricultural problems were significant, but were just one aspect of a much larger economic collapse that affected both rural and urban areas.

Chapter 23

Paper 23

Paper 4: Alternative to Coursework

You must answer in the enclosed answer booklet.

You will need: Answer booklet (enclosed)

0470/42

May/June 2022

1 hour

- Answer one question from your chosen Depth Study.
- Follow the instructions on the front cover of the answer booklet. If you need additional answer paper,

Ask the invigilator for a continuation booklet.

INFORMATION

- The total mark for this paper is 40.
- The number of marks for each question or part question is shown in brackets [ ].

06_0470_42_2022_1.6

© UCLES 2022

CHAPTER 23

Answer one question from your chosen Depth Study.

DEPTH STUDY A: THE FIRST WORLD WAR, 1914–18

1   How important were new and improved weapons in the development of a war of attrition on the Western Front? Explain your answer. [40]

2   How significant was Turkish resistance as a reason for Allied failure in the Gallipoli campaign? Explain your answer.   [40]

DEPTH STUDY B: GERMANY, 1918–45

3   How important were Stresemann's economic policies to the stability of the Weimar Republic, 1923-29? Explain your answer.   [40]

4   How significant were resistance groups in the opposition to Nazi rule? Explain your answer.   [40]

DEPTH STUDY C: RUSSIA, 1905–41

5 How important was Russia's continued involvement in the First World War as a reason for increased support for the Bolsheviks between March and November 1917? Explain your answer. [40]

6 How significant were gulags to Stalin's system of control in the Soviet Union after 1928? Explain your answer. [40]

DEPTH STUDY D: THE UNITED STATES, 1919–41

7 How important was government economic policy as a cause of prosperity in the USA in the 1920s? Explain your answer. [40]

8 How significant were problems in agriculture as an aspect of the Great Depression in the USA? Explain your answer. [40]

DEPTH STUDY E: CHINA, c.1930–c.1990

9 How vital was the Japanese invasion of China as a reason for increased support for the

Chinese Communist Party before 1949? Explain your answer. [40]

10   How significant was the treatment of landlords as an aspect of Mao's land reforms in the 1950s? Explain your answer. [40]

DEPTH STUDY F: SOUTH AFRICA, c.1940–c.1994

11   How important was the PAC in determining the nature of resistance to apartheid in the 1950s and 1960s? Explain your answer. [40]

12   How significant was Desmond Tutu in ending white minority rule in South Africa? Explain your answer. [40]

DEPTH STUDY G: ISRAELIS AND PALESTINIANS SINCE 1945

13   How vital was Jewish immigration as a cause of tension in the Middle East by 1948? Explain your answer. [40]

14 How significant were Israeli military tactics in determining the outcome of the Yom Kippur War, 1973? Explain your answer. [40]

CHAPTER 23: Answers

Answer one question from your chosen Depth Study.

Answered Questions:

DEPTH STUDY A: THE FIRST WORLD WAR, 1914–18 (No 1)
DEPTH STUDY D: THE UNITED STATES, 1919–41 (No 8)

1 How important were new and improved weapons in the development of a war of attrition on the Western Front? Explain your answer.[40]

New and improved weapons – very important:

• Machine guns – Fired hundreds of rounds per minute, making it almost impossible for infantry to cross no man's land, forcing both sides into defensive trenches.

• Heavy artillery – Long-range guns caused massive casualties and destroyed trenches, but rarely led to breakthroughs, prolonging the stalemate.

- Poison gas – Caused fear, injuries, and deaths, but often depended on the wind; it killed relatively few but added to the misery of trench warfare.
- Tanks – First used in 1916; helped cross trenches and crush barbed wire, but were slow and unreliable early on, so they did not end the stalemate quickly.
- Barbed wire – Simple but deadly, it slowed attacks and made defenders much stronger, increasing the difficulty of rapid advances.

Other factors – equally or more important:
- Trench systems – Deep, fortified trenches meant defenders had the advantage, making battles lengthy and costly.
- Poor tactics – Generals often relied on mass infantry attacks ('over the top'), which failed against modern weapons, leading to high casualties and stalemate.
- Railways and supply lines – Allowed armies to reinforce and resupply quickly, preventing decisive victories and prolonging the war.
- Communication issues – Slow or broken communications during battles meant attacks could not adapt quickly, wasting lives and preventing breakthroughs.

- War aims and determination – Both sides were willing to fight a protracted war, hoping to wear the other down, which naturally created a war of attrition.

Judgement

- Overall importance – New weapons were crucial in making attacks so costly that neither side could win quickly, leading to stalemate and attrition.
- Relative weight – However, trench systems, defensive tactics, and the determination to fight to the end were also key in creating a war of attrition.
- Balanced view – Weapons were an important cause, but the combination of technology, strategy, and leadership decisions together made the Western Front a war of attrition.

8. How significant were problems in agriculture as an aspect of the Great Depression in the USA? Explain your answer. [40]

Agricultural problems – highly significant:

- Falling crop prices – Overproduction and falling demand caused prices of wheat, corn, and cotton to collapse, leaving farmers unable to make a profit.

- Debt crisis – Many farmers had borrowed heavily in the 1920s and could not repay loans, leading to foreclosures and bankruptcies.
- Dust Bowl – Severe drought and over-farming led to soil erosion in the Great Plains, driving thousands of families (e.g., "Okies") to migrate in search of work.
- Impact on rural communities – Farm closures caused widespread poverty, hunger, and loss of land, deepening the Depression in rural areas.
- Reduced demand – Struggling farmers could not buy manufactured goods, worsening the economic downturn in other industries.

Other aspects of the Great Depression – equally or more significant:

- Bank failures – Thousands of banks collapsed, wiping out savings and reducing confidence in the economy.
- Collapse of industry – Factories closed as consumer demand fell, leading to mass unemployment in cities.
- Stock market crash – The Wall Street Crash of 1929 triggered panic, wiped out investments, and caused further economic decline.

- International trade slump – High tariffs (e.g., Smoot-Hawley Tariff) reduced global trade, hurting US exports.
- Unemployment crisis – By 1933, a quarter of the workforce was jobless, causing homelessness and urban poverty (e.g., "Hoovervilles").

Judgement

- Overall significance – Agricultural problems were a significant part of the Depression, especially in rural America, and contributed to reduced demand for goods.
- Relative weight – However, the collapse of banking, industry, and employment had a more widespread effect on the entire economy.
- Balanced view – Agricultural problems were significant, but were just one aspect of a much larger economic collapse that affected both rural and urban areas.

Chapter 24

Paper 24

Paper 4: Alternative to Coursework

0470/43

May/June 2022

1 hour

INSTRUCTIONS

- Answer one question from your chosen Depth Study.
- Follow the instructions on the front cover of the answer booklet. If you need additional answer paper,
Ask the invigilator for a continuation booklet.

INFORMATION

- The total mark for this paper is 40.
- The number of marks for each question or part question is shown in brackets [ ].

06_0470_43_2022_1.7
© UCLES 2022

CHAPTER 23

Answer one question from your chosen Depth Study.

DEPTH STUDY A: THE FIRST WORLD WAR, 1914–18

1   How important was the Battle of the Marne to the nature of the fighting on the Western Front by the end of 1914? Explain your answer.
    [40]

2   How significant were the military campaigns on the Eastern Front to the outcome of the war? Explain your answer.   [40]

DEPTH STUDY B: GERMANY, 1918–45

3   How important was the Munich Putsch to Nazi Party support and membership by 1930? Explain your answer.   [40]

4   How significant was racial policy in bringing about the kind of society the Nazis wanted after 1933? Explain your answer.   [40]

DEPTH STUDY C: RUSSIA, 1905–41

5   How important was the secret police (Okhrana) in the maintenance of Tsarist rule up to 1914? Explain your answer.   [40]

6   How significant was Stalin's control of religion and culture in creating a totalitarian state in the Soviet Union after 1928? Explain your answer.   [40]

DEPTH STUDY D: THE UNITED STATES, 1919–41

7   How important was the entertainment industry as an aspect of the 'Roaring Twenties'? Explain your answer.   [40]

8   How significant a part of the New Deal were the Alphabet Agencies? Explain your answer.   [40]

DEPTH STUDY E: CHINA, c.1930–c.1990

9   How important were improved relations with the USA in China's foreign policy after 1970? Explain your answer.   [40]

10   How significant were changes in education to the development of China after 1949? Explain your answer. [40]

DEPTH STUDY F: SOUTH AFRICA, c.1940–c.1994

11   How vital was gold mining in shaping the economic development of South Africa by 1948? Explain your answer.   [40]

12   How significant was international opposition in challenging apartheid? Explain your answer.   [40]

DEPTH STUDY G: ISRAELIS AND PALESTINIANS SINCE 1945

13   How important was pressure from the USA as a reason for the British withdrawal from Palestine in 1948? Explain your answer. [40]

14   How significant was Jordan in Arab-Israeli relations after 1948? Explain your answer. [40]

CHAPTER 24: Answers

Answer one question from your chosen Depth Study.

Answered Questions:

DEPTH STUDY A: THE FIRST WORLD WAR, 1914–18 (No 1)

DEPTH STUDY D: THE UNITED STATES, 1919–41 (No. 7)

1   How important was the Battle of the Marne to the nature of the fighting on the Western Front by the end of 1914? Explain your answer.

[40]

Importance of the Battle of the Marne:

• Stopped the Schlieffen Plan – The German advance was halted just 40 km from Paris. This prevented a quick German victory and saved France from defeat.

• Led to the "Race to the Sea" – Both sides tried to outflank each other, but this resulted in a continuous line of trenches from the Swiss frontier to the English Channel.

• Set the pattern for stalemate – The failure to break through meant neither side could win a decisive victory quickly. This turned the war into a war of attrition.

- Boosted Allied morale – The French and British armies proved that the Germans could be stopped, raising morale and strengthening the Allied war effort.

Other factors that shaped the nature of fighting by late 1914:

- Technological developments – Machine guns, artillery, and barbed wire favoured defence over attack, making breakthroughs costly and complex.
- Failure of early offensives – Battles like Mons and the First Battle of Ypres also showed that quick victory was impossible and contributed to the stalemate.
- Logistical realities – Both sides dug in to protect supply lines and secure positions, which created the trench system regardless of the Marne.
- Sheer scale of forces – The vast number of troops on both sides meant neither could outflank the other, reinforcing a static front.

Conclusion:

- Crucial role – The Battle of the Marne was vital as it prevented German victory and forced

both sides into defensive positions, making trench warfare inevitable.
- But not the only cause – The development of modern weaponry, failed offensives elsewhere, and the scale of mobilisation also contributed to the stalemate.
- Overall judgement – The Marne was a turning point because it ensured the war would not be short and decisive. Still, other military and technological factors were equally important in shaping the trench-dominated fighting on the Western Front by the end of 1914.

7. How important was the entertainment industry as an aspect of the 'Roaring Twenties'? Explain your answer. [40]

Importance of the entertainment industry:
- Growth of cinema – The 1920s saw the rise of Hollywood as the centre of the film industry. Silent movies became extremely popular, and by 1927, "talkies" were introduced (e.g., The Jazz Singer). This created mass entertainment that reached millions and became a key part of popular culture.

- Jazz music and dance – Jazz spread from African American communities to mainstream culture, influencing nightlife, dance halls, and youth culture. It symbolised freedom and rebellion, especially among young people and women (the 'flapper' generation).
- Radio and mass media – Radios became affordable, allowing millions to listen to music, news, and sports broadcasts. This created a shared national culture and helped to spread consumer advertising.
- Impact on society – Entertainment helped challenge traditional values, encouraged consumer spending (e.g., fashion, cosmetics, cars to attend leisure events), and gave Americans a sense of prosperity and modernity.

Other essential aspects of the 'Roaring Twenties':

- Economic boom – The boom was driven by mass production, technological innovation (Ford's assembly line), and consumer credit. This had a direct impact on living standards and employment, shaping the "roaring" economy.
- Social change – The position of women improved: more entered the workforce, gained political rights (vote in 1920), and adopted new fashions and lifestyles that challenged conservative norms.

- Prohibition and crime – The ban on alcohol (1920–1933) encouraged illegal speakeasies and gangster culture. This was a defining feature of the decade and often overshadows entertainment in shaping the era's image.
- Harlem Renaissance – Growth of African American culture (literature, art, music) created pride and identity, influencing American culture far beyond Harlem.
- Rural vs. urban divide – Tensions remained between traditional rural America (religion, conservatism) and modern urban America (science, evolution, nightlife), showing that the "Roaring Twenties" was not universally shared.

Conclusion:
- Very important – The entertainment industry symbolised the excitement and dynamism of the 1920s, making it one of the most visible aspects of the decade. It shaped fashions, music, and leisure, and created a shared culture across the USA.
- But not the whole story – The economic boom, women's liberation, and prohibition had just as much impact on how the 1920s were experienced. Many Americans in rural areas did not fully share in the new entertainment culture.
- Overall judgement – The entertainment industry was highly significant as it represented the

modern, urban, and youthful spirit of the "Roaring Twenties," but its importance must be considered alongside economic, political, and social change to get a complete picture of the decade.

Author Qualifications and Honours

D.D., Doctor of Divinity

Certificate in Bible Studies

Theology

Laws

(LLM)Master of Laws.

Postgraduate Laws

legal research,

Business, CSR, Corporate social responsibility and human rights law."

Institutional development and management,

International Law.

BA (Hons), Laws

Law: includes Criminal, Tort, damages, Contract, Property, Equity and Trust, European Law, Public, Constitutional, Judicial Review, and Agency.

Advance Dip. Business Law, Level 4: Employment, Agency, Damages, Tort, Contract, employment tribunal, etc.

Dip. Criminology

Accounting

BA (Hons)op.

Financial Accountant

Management Accountant

Cert. Acct. (Certified accountant)

(PCA)Professional Certificate in Financial and Management Accounting

Dip. Book-keeping, Level 3

Nursing

Nursing: RMN Registered Mental Nurse)

GN (General Trained Nurse)

Lecturer qualifications

DD Doctor of Divinity

LLM Master of Laws

BA (Hons)

BSc Hons o/g) Psychology with counselling

Cert. in Education (Lecturer)

Business Certificate in Advanced Management

Cert. Business Enterprise

Advanced Food Hygiene

Intermediate Health and Safety

Dip. Safety Management

International Entrepreneur for over 25 years

(NVQ); Internal Verifier, (V1)

Trainer and Assessor A1 (NVQ)

Computers

Diploma: Cisco Level 2 Technician (build, repair, networking)

Microsoft Specialist

Dip. Claire Plus (in all software)

New Clait Dip. Level 2

ECDL Level 2

Scrip writer

Diploma in script writing.

TV, radio, stage, and film

Diploma in writing.

Autobiography

Biography

Family History

Certificate in Poetry

Psychology and Counselling

BSc(Hons o/g) psychology with counselling

Diploma in Counselling and Psychology

Cert. in Counselling and Psychology

Certificate in Social Science

Photography

Cert. (PGFP).

Portrait, Glamour and Figure

Plumbing

Level 3 City and Guild

Hypnotherapy

Dip. Hypnotherapy

Other Books by the Author James Safo

162 book Titles.

Academic, Faith and non-faith books

Faith books- in 5 different languages :

Arabic, Chinese, English, French, Spanish

ALL FAITHS

Theology

Love All Faiths

Faith Unity

Religion and Law: Religion influences National and international laws.

CHRISTIANITY

BIBLE New Testament; 1,111 QUESTIONS AND ANSWERS: Plus, synopsis and Test yourself

Bible Old Testament 1,064 Questions and Answers and Synopsis

Jesus Christ is Coming Soon

God Loves Christianity

God's/Allah's Messengers

Islam v. Christianity

Jesus Christ is coming soon

Psychology of religion, politics and marriage

Faith unity.
Faith Unity Simplified Version.
Islamism versus Christianity.
Love all faith.

ISLAM (In English)
QUR'AN; 1,044 Questions & Answers.
Allah Loves Islam
Islam v. Christianity

BUDDHISM (In English)
God Enlighten Buddhism

HINDUISM (In English)
Parama Nandra Loves Hindus

FREEMASON (In English)
In Search of Wisdom in Freemasonry

FRENCH BOOKS (Religious)
Allah Aimel'islam (Allah loves Islam)

Aimetouteslesfois (Love All Faiths)
Islamism. V. christianisme (Islam v Christianity)
Dieu Aime Le Christianisme (God loves Christianity)

Les Messagers De Dieu/ Allah (God/Allah Messengers)

A LA Recherche De La Sagesse Dans La Franc - Maconnerie (In Search of wisdom)

SPANISH BOOKS (Religious)

En Busca De La Sabiduria Masoneri (In search of wisdom in freemasonry)

Ametodas las creencias (Love All Faith)

Mensajeros de Dios (God Messengers)

4Dios Ama El Christianismo (God Loves Christianity)

Islam vs Christianity (Islam vs Christianity)

Allah am el Islam (Allah Loves Islam)

ARABIC (Religious)

(Allah loves Islam) الله يحب الاسلام. .

حب جميع الأديان . Love All Faith

CHINESE BOOKS (Religious)

Books in Chinese

伊斯蘭教訴基督教 (Islam vs. Christianity)

上帝爱伊斯兰教 (Allah Loves Islam) - Traditional Chinese Edition

NON-FAITH BOOKS- IN ENGLISH LANGUAGE

LAW:
Global Injustice
The Journey to Law Graduation
THE JOURNEY TO MASTER OF LAWS
International Laws plus 30 dissertation
Laws - United Kingdom +30 dissertation
The Law (Over 1,160 Questions and Answers)
Business Law volume 1; over 800 Q&A (contract, employment, types of Human Rights
Business Law Volume 2 over 600 Q&A (Tort, CSR, Equity, Trust
Criminology: (Over 1,300 Questions and Answers)
Religion And Law

POEMS
102 Poems on North America
70 Poems on South American Countries and Cities
80 POEMS ON THE ARCTIC AND ANTARCTICA
102 POEMS ON AUSTRALIA, OCEANIA, NEW ZEALAND

101 Poems on Asia countries and cities
118 USA POEMS: 50 States, Cities and Maps
114 Poems on 54 African countries
Over 200 Love Poems plus over 100 love icebreakers
Over 100 Poems on Faith & Victory
107 Poems on Discrimination, Racism & Suffering
Jesus Christ, Prophet, Arch Angels, Saint (Over 150 poems and Biography
The One - Over 130 Poems "DCF"
105 Poems on 54 European Countries & Cities

BUSINESS
Developing and Managing Institutions and Organisations Volume 1
Developing and Managing Institutions and Organisations Volume 2
Set up and manage a business
How to set up a care home and care agency
How to manage a care home and a care agency
Care Home: Staff training

COMPUTER
Computing for beginners + 310 questions and answers.
How to Build and Upgrade a Computer and Network

The Path of Information to the Computer Screen
Computer Programming, Coding & Science
Dissertation

ACCOUNT

Financial Accounting (Over 1,241 Questions and Answers)

Management Accounting (1015 Questions & Answers Plus 100 Self-Assessment Questions)

PSYCHOLOGY

Journey to Psychology Graduation Volume 1

Journey to Psychology Graduation Volume 2

Psychology of Religion, Politics & Marriage

COUNSELLING

Journey to Counselling Graduation Volume 1

Journey to Counselling Graduation Volume 2

Counselling: Journey to Graduation Volume 3

Mood Disorder & Therapy

HISTORY

History: Journey to Graduation: 38 Essays

ENEMIES Within the Earth

Slavery And Suffering

Slavery to Mastership

GEOGRAPHY

Geography: The Road to Graduation: 30 Essays

Medical/Nursing/ Health & Social

Drugs for Diseases: 1,007 Questions and Answers

Health and Social Care

Journey to Nursing Graduation: 51 Essays

Mental and Physical Diseases - Plus Nursing and 53 Dissertations

Health and Social Care - Plus 50 Dissertations

SOCIAL SCIENCE

Understanding Sociology Science - Plus 56 Dissertations

WOMEN

Women are superior to men

Sweet and Sour Women (plus over 500 love letters from women)

MANAGEMENT

Project management

RESEARCH

Research

Midwifery

A modern approach to Agriculture, Introduction level,

Added Value to Agriculture: Advanced Level.

The Roadmap to Sustainable Agriculture in Rural Development.

The beekeeper's blueprint: growing your apiary from the ground up

Addictive Manufacturing

Quantity Survey

Building and Construction

Drug and Substance Abuse Rehabilitation

Education Volume 1 and 2

Radiology

Mental health V1,2, and 3

Geography Physical

Geography of Africa

Geography Techniques

History Glossary

A

ab urbe condita (AUC)

absolute monarchy

A system of government headed by a monarch as the only source of power, controlling all functions of the state.

abstract

A summary of a textual source.

access rights

Information about who can access the resource or an indication of its security status.

accrual method

The method by which items are added to a collection.

accrual periodicity

The frequency with which items are added to a collection.

accrual policy

The policy governing the addition of items to a collection.

administrative history

A subdiscipline of historiography that studies the history of state administrations and bureaucracies, focusing primarily on changes in administrative ideology and legal codes over time, as well as the roles of civil servants and the relationships between government and society.

Aeon/Age of Exploration.

The time period between approximately the late 15th century and the 17th century, during which seafarers from various European polities travelled to, explored, and charted regions across the globe which had previously been unknown or unfamiliar to Europeans and, more broadly, during which previously isolated human populations became socially, politically, and/or economically aware of and connected. These explorations, often commissioned and funded by state governments, were spurred by advances in cartography and maritime technology at the beginning of the early modern period, particularly the introduction of sailing vessels capable of enduring extremely long transoceanic voyages. Consequently, the Age of Discovery largely overlaps with the Age of Sail. The period is also associated with the emergence of colonialism and imperialism as practiced by European monarchies, particularly the colonization of the Americas and the establishment of oceanic trade routes to India and Southeast Asia, which are sometimes identified with the origins of the global economy and of globalization, as well as the exchange, intentional and unintentional, of plants, animals, diseases, technologies, and ideas between previously isolated parts of the world.

Age of Enlightenment/ agent provocateur

A person who goes undercover in the ranks of the enemy during a social or political conflict with the intention of damaging or compromising the enemy from within by provoking actions that might not otherwise have taken place. Agents provocateurs have sometimes been employed by governments or businesses to provoke armed clashes between groups, create disorder, or incite controversies that might be used as an excuse for war or foreign intervention.[1]

alternate modernity

In postcolonialism and development studies, the theory posits that different parts of the world experienced the onset of modernity at varying times and in their own unique fashion, such that to people living in certain places, "modernity" means something quite specific and distinct from that experienced elsewhere.[2]

anachronism

A chronological inconsistency, in particular, is the introduction of an object, linguistic term, technology, idea, or anything else into a period in time to which it does not belong.

Ancient history/ antiquity.

Annales school

A style of historiography linked to the French scholarly journal Annales d'histoire économique et sociale and broadly associated with the social history of cultural practices.

annals

Historical accounts of facts and events are arranged in chronological order, year by year. The term is also used more loosely to describe any historical record.

Anno Domini (AD)/anthropology

The study of humanity, culturally and physically, in all times and places.

Antiquarian/ antiquary.

A historian who studies antiquities or things of the past, often with particular attention to artefacts, archives, manuscripts, or archaeological sites from ancient history, as opposed to more recent history. In a broader sense, an antiquarian may also be a person who is simply a collector or aficionado of such artefacts and not necessarily a professional historian.

antiquarianism

Historical study that focuses on the empirical evidence of the past, including manuscripts and archives, as well as archaeological and historic sites and artefacts. The term is now often used in a pejorative sense to refer to an excessively narrow interest in historical trivia, excluding a sense of historical context or process.

antiquities

Objects or artefacts from ancient history, particularly from the Classical civilisations and cultures of the Mediterranean region and the ancient Near East.

antiquity

See ancient history and Classical antiquity.

archaeology

The study of human history and prehistory through the excavation of sites and the analysis of physical remains.

architectural history

The study of buildings in their historical and stylistic contexts.

archival bond

The relationship that each archival record has with other documents produced as part of the same transaction or activity and located within the same group.

archival research/ science

The study and theory of building and curating archives.

archive

An accumulation of historical documents and records, or the physical repository in which they are located.

archontology

The study of historical offices and important positions in state, international, political, religious, and other organisations and societies, including chronologies, succession of officeholders, their biographies, and related records.

armiger

A person entitled to bear a coat of arms; more broadly, a gentleman or an esquire.[3]

armory

The study of coats of arms, also known as heraldry.[3]

arrested decay

A state or condition in which specific historic sites are preserved, where little or no significant restoration or renovation work is performed in modern times, except that which is necessary to maintain fundamental structural integrity and prevent total deterioration of historical objects. The concept is often contrasted with conservation efforts, which attempt to preserve or improve buildings or artefacts by deliberately applying techniques which may dramatically alter their appearance or material properties, particularly when these efforts are perceived as damaging their intrinsic historical value. The term is used primarily when referring to immovable cultural property such as historic buildings and places such as ghost towns which have remained essentially unchanged since they were last occupied, with neither demolition nor re-development having significantly altered them in the intervening time, as well as places which have been extensively damaged but which for various reasons it is undesirable or impossible to restore, such as the ruins of ancient civilizations or of battlefields intended to serve as war memorials.

art history

The study of objects of art in their historical and stylistic contexts.

Artefact/artefact.

Any material object associated with a culture, such as a tool, an article of clothing, or a prepared food item.

audience

A class of entity, often a specific demographic, for whom a given resource is intended or useful./**authorised biography**

autobiography

An individual's account of their own life.

Auxiliary sciences of history/Also ancillary sciences of history.

The set of specialist scholarly disciplines that help evaluate and utilise historical sources, often used to support historical research. These disciplines may include but are not limited to archaeology, archival science, philology, genealogy, numismatics, philately, and heraldry.

Avalonia

A separate plate in the Early Palaeozoic consisted of much of what is now Northern Europe, Newfoundland, Nova Scotia, and some coastal parts of New England.

B

Baltica

A separate continental plate of the Early Palaeozoic composed of what is now the United Kingdom, Scandinavia, European Russia and Central Europe. It is named for the Baltic Sea.

barbarian

A Greek word adopted by the Romans to refer to any people who did not adopt the Roman way of life. It is said to have come originally from the sound "bar-bar", which, according to the Greeks, was supposed to be the noise that people made when speaking foreign languages.

Before Christ (BC)

Before the Common Era (BCE)

Bering Land Bridge/Also Beringia.

The vast tundra plain that was exposed as a land bridge between the continents of Asia and North America during the Last Glacial Maximum, about 21,000 years ago. It is theorised to have served as a migration route for people, animals, and plants for several thousand years before being once again submerged beneath rising sea levels.

bibliography

A list of written works, including books, journals, and essays, about or detailing a particular subject.

Big History

big lie

biography

An account of an individual's life, especially one written by someone other than the individual featured in the account.

black legend

Blitzkrieg

German for "lightning war". A military strategy employed by the German Army at the beginning of World War II aimed to achieve victory through a series of rapid offensives, particularly in Belgium, the Netherlands, and France. The strategy involved a heavy initial bombardment, followed by the rapid mobilisation of armour and motorised infantry to break the weakest parts of the enemy line.

Bolsheviks

A small, tightly organised, revolutionary Marxist group in early 20th-century Russia, which split from the Russian Socialist movement in 1903 and was led by Vladimir Lenin. In November 1917, during the so-called October Revolution, the Bolsheviks ("Majority") took control of a chaotic Russia, becoming the de facto rulers after the subsequent civil war. They then renamed themselves the Communist Party of the Soviet Union (CPSU).

book review

A critical examination of a text, usually including a summary of the work and opposing views.

bottom-up approach

An approach to historical scholarship that attempts to explain the experiences or perspectives of ordinary people, as opposed to elites or leaders.[4] Contrast the top-down approach.

bourgeoisie

The capitalist class, which came to be known as the middle class, fell between the aristocracy and the working class. A new middle class of merchants and businessmen prospered throughout Europe from the 16th century, and especially in Britain, which Napoleon described as a "nation of shopkeepers". In modern times, the term "bourgeois" is often used derogatorily to describe anything considered humdrum, unimaginative, and/or selfishly materialistic.

Bronze Age

In Britain, a period from approximately 2300 to 700 BCE, when metal first began to be widely used, possibly as a result of increased contact with mainland Europe. However, various types of stone, particularly flint, remained very important long after metal became available. The Bronze Age saw the introduction of cremation of the dead and burials in round barrows—the latter (and best-known) phases of construction at Stonehenge also date from this period.

Buranji

Written chronicles of the Ahoms, a medieval kingdom of Assam, India.

C

Caesar

A Roman family name best known for being used by several rulers of Ancient Rome. Contrary to popular opinion, the name "Caesar" did not originally mean "emperor", although in modern times it has come to be defined as a synonym for autocrat. When the Roman leader Gaius Julius Caesar was assassinated in 44 BCE, his nephew and successor, Augustus, had himself formally adopted by the deceased and thus adopted the family name Caesar. Tiberius and Caligula also inherited it by adoption. Later Roman emperors acquired the name upon their succession or when they were formally adopted as heirs to the throne.

calendar

A descriptive list of archival documents, sometimes compiled in sufficient detail that it can be used as a substitute for the originals.

cartulary

A register of lands and privileges granted by charter, occasionally recorded on a roll of paper but more often in book form.

Cathaysian Terranes

A set of small landmasses that developed in tropical to subtropical latitudes on the eastern side of Pangaea during the Permian and Triassic, comprising what is now North China (Sino-Korea), South China (Yangtze), Eastern Qiangtang, Tarim, and Indochina.

century

A period of 100 years. Centuries are numbered ordinally (e.g. 15th, 16th, 17th) in English and many other languages.

Chancery/charge

A heraldic device emblazoned on the face of a shield.[3]

charter

A legal grant of authority or rights.

chirograph

1. A historical record that has been torn or cut into two pieces, sometimes with writing across the division, such that each piece serves to authenticate the other by exactly matching it; an indenture.[5]
2. Any handwritten document.[5]

chorography

The geographical description of regions, often with reference to their history and antiquities.

chronicle

A historical account of facts and events arranged in chronological order.

chronology

The study of the sequence of past events.

Classical antiquity/classical era, classical period, or classical civilisation.

The period of cultural history between the 8th century BC and the 6th century AD in the geographical area centred on the Mediterranean Sea, particularly relating to the contemporaneous civilisations of ancient Greece and ancient Rome, known as the Greco-Roman world, which flourished and wielded enormous influence across much of Europe, North Africa, and Western Asia during this time. Though its boundaries are imprecise, the classical period is traditionally considered to have begun with the earliest writings of the Greek poet Homer and ended with the fall of the Western Roman Empire and the decline of classical culture during Late antiquity and the Early Middle Ages.

Cimmerian Terranes/Also called Cimmeria.

An archipelago of small landmasses that developed in tropical and subtropical latitudes on the eastern side of Pangaea during the Triassic. Blocks that comprise it include what is now Turkey, Iran, Afghanistan, Tibet, and Malaysia.

Circa/Variously abbreviated c., ca., circ., or cca.

Approximately, about, around, near or in the vicinity of. A Latin term signifying approximation or uncertainty, usually by immediately preceding a date or a numerical measure. Circa is widely used in historical writing and genealogy when the dates of events are not accurately known. When used with date ranges, it or its abbreviation is applied before each approximate date, while dates without circa preceding them are generally assumed to be known with certainty.

citation

A reference to a published or unpublished source for an assertion or argument.

Classical tradition

classics/Also called classical studies.

The study of classical antiquity, particularly Ancient Greek and Latin literature and their respective languages, as well as Greco-Roman art, philosophy, history, mythology, and society.

cliometrics

The systematic application of economic theory, econometric techniques, and other formal or mathematical methods to the study of history; a quantitative economic

history./codex/(pl.) codices

A book constructed of several sheets of paper, vellum, papyrus, parchment, or similar materials, especially a manuscript book with handwritten contents and formatted so that individual pages are stacked and fixed to a spine along one edge.

codicology

The study of codices or manuscript books as physical objects, specifically the materials and techniques used to make books, including writing surfaces (such as parchment or vellum), pigments, inks, bindings, handwriting, marginalia, glosses, and so on.

coherence theory of truth

A theory that regards statements as accurate if they are coherent within some specified set of sentences, propositions, or beliefs.

Cold War/colonialism

The practice or policy by which one people or sovereignty exerts social, political, and/or economic control over other people or geographic areas, typically by establishing a colony whose administration is distinct from that of the colonisers' home territory and generally with the aim of economic dominance. Foreign administrators rule the colony in pursuit of their own interests, often imposing their language, religion, and culture on the colonised region while seeking to benefit from the exploitation of its people and resources. Colonialism is usually associated with, though distinct from, imperialism.

Common Era (CE)

comparative history

The comparison of different societies which existed during the same time period or shared similar cultural conditions.

computational history

Congo craton

A separate continental plate that rifted from the supercontinent Rodinia in the Late Precambrian. It contained a large part of what is now north-central Africa.

conjectural history/conjectural portrait/context

In archaeology, a discrete physical location, distinguishable from other contexts, which forms one of the units making up an overall archaeological site. The context in which an artefact is found provides essential evidence for its interpretation.

correspondence theory of truth

A theory that regards statements as accurate if they correspond to the world that we know by perception.

counterfactual history

A form of historiography that seeks to explore history by extrapolating a timeline in which key events happened in ways other than how they did in fact occur.

Cretaceous Western Interior Seaway/Western Interior Seaway.

The epicontinental sea formed as marine waters from the north spread over North America between approximately 130 and 70 million years ago (Ma). At its peak in the Middle Cretaceous (~90 Million Years Ago), it extended from present-day Utah to the Appalachians and from the Arctic to the Gulf of Mexico.

Crypto history

Cultural/ cultural history

The academic study of the origins and history of the culture and cultural practices (e.g. music, theatre, literature, fine art) of a particular group of people.[4]

Culture.

D

deep history

The study of the distant past of the human species, i.e. the earliest parts of human prehistory, or any other aspect of the time period during which the earliest humans existed (with "humans" usually meaning anatomically modern humans, as opposed to earlier hominid species). Deep history incorporates a wide range of methods from disciplines such as archaeology, primatology, anthropology, genetics, evolutionary biology, and linguistics to assemble a standard narrative about the origins and evolution of human populations before the beginning of recorded history, and also of correcting a perceived scholarly bias towards the study of more recent **historical periods.**

demographic history digital history

The use of digital media in the academic study of history aids historical analysis, research, or presentation, including digital archives, data visualisations, interactive maps and timelines, audio files, and virtual representations of historical periods and places, often in online formats. See also computational history.

diplomatics

The study and textual analysis of historical documents.

discipline

The study, or practice, of a specific subject using a particular set of methods, terms and approaches. History is a discipline, as are archaeology, chemistry, and biology.

dominant narrative

dossier

A group of documents deliberately assembled to provide information about a specific topic. The term often connotes information that has been purposefully collected from various sources, as opposed to documents that exist in an organic collection originating from a single source or resulting from routine activities.[5]

E

economic determinism

The socioeconomic theory posits that economic relationships have been the primary or sole driving force throughout human history.[4]

economic history

The study of economies or economic phenomena of the past.

Edwardian

1. The period of British history that spanned the reign of King Edward VII (1901–1910), or more generally, the period between the turn of the 20th century and the outbreak of the First World War in August 1914.
2. Of or related to this period; an adjective used to describe any person, object, event, idea, or concept characterising or associated with the Edwardian era, either by having originated or

flourished during the period or by retrospectively coming to represent it, especially in the United Kingdom but more broadly in any part of the British Empire.

Effect of reality

Elizabethan

1. The period of English history that spanned the reign of Elizabeth I, Queen of England and Ireland (1558–1603). Elizabeth was the last monarch of the Tudor period, and the Elizabethan era is often regarded as a golden age in English history, characterised by economic growth, naval supremacy, and national pride.

2. Of or related to this period; an adjective used to describe any person, object, event, idea, or concept characterising or associated with the Elizabethan era, either by having originated or flourished during the period or by retrospectively coming to represent it.

empire

A type of sovereign state made up of multiple territories and peoples subject to a single and supreme ruling authority, often an emperor or empress. Empires can be composed exclusively of contiguous territories, e.g. the Russian Empire, or may include territories which are remote from the empire's home territory or metropole, as with a colonial empire. The concept of an empire is often associated with the idea of imperialism. However, the latter also refers to a political policy or ideology that is not necessarily practised by empires and can be applied to many other forms of government.

Enlightenment

A cultural and intellectual movement of the late 17th to late 18th centuries that emphasised reason and individualism rather than faith and tradition, predominantly among Western European cultures but also in other parts of the world; or the time period itself during which this movement flourished.

environmental history

An approach to history that examines how nature and natural processes (i.e. plants, animals, geology, etc.) have shaped human agency and affairs, and conversely how humans have shaped nature.[4]

epigraphy

The study of ancient inscriptions.

episteme

The dominant mode of knowledge or understanding of a particular era is familiar to many, if not all, forms of knowledge produced at the time.[6]

epoch

An instant in time chosen (sometimes arbitrarily) as the origin or beginning of a particular calendar era, thereby serving as a reference point from which time is measured and by which historical events are temporally related.

era

Any span of time defined for chronology or historiography. In chronology, an era is the highest level of organisation for measuring time, as used in defining calendar eras for a given calendar and regnal eras in the history of a monarchy. The term is also used in geologic time, where an era is a subdivision of an aeon.

essentialize

To assume the existence of an inner "essence" or an essential character shared by all of the members of a group, which in reality is diverse, variable, and fluid.[4]

ethnohistory

A branch of history or an approach to historical scholarship which addresses the history of the native peoples of a particular place or region, in particular, the indigenous peoples of the Americas. Ethnohistory is an interdisciplinary approach that often supplements written historical documents with methods from anthropology, folklore, oral history, and archaeology.[4]

euhemerism

In mythology, the presumption that mythological accounts were based on or originated from real historical events or persons has accumulated elaborations and exaggerations over many generations of retelling until reaching their present form.

Euramerica

A supercontinent that existed in the Late Silurian through Devonian, formed by the collision of Baltica, Laurentia, and Avalonia. It included what is now North America, Greenland, Scandinavia, and Europe. It is also sometimes referred to as the "Old Red Continent" for the red colour of its oxidised deposits.

Eurocentrism

A worldview that is centred on Western civilisation or Western culture, particularly that originating in or associated with Western Europe, to the exclusion of or in a way that is biased against non-Western cultures. The term may also apply to the entire continent of Europe or beyond, to countries and cultures whose histories are closely tied to Western Europe through immigration, colonisation, or influence.

F

Fakelore/pseudo-folklore.

Inauthentic, manufactured folklore that is presented as if it were genuinely traditional. Compare invented tradition.

farm book/feudalism

The legal and social order prevailing through much of medieval Europe, in which society was structured around a set of reciprocal legal and military obligations.

fin de siècle/floruit (fl.)

Denoting a date or period during which a particular person or group is known to have been alive or active, or to which their works or contributions are dated (i.e. when they "flourished"), used especially when a person's dates of birth and death are not precisely known.

folklore

The expressive body of culture shared by a particular group of people, encompassing the oral traditions (e.g. tales, proverbs, and jokes) and the material culture as well as the customs, lore, folk beliefs, rituals, celebrations and ceremonies, holidays, and initiation rites practiced by that group, and in particular those cultural elements which are transmitted informally from one individual to another and from one generation to the next either through verbal instruction or demonstration.

fonds

In archival science, an aggregation of documents which all originate from the same source.

G

genealogy

The study of family relationships.

geological time

golden age

Gondwana

A supercontinent that existed from the Cambrian to Jurassic, mainly composed of what is now South America, Africa, Madagascar, India, Antarctica, and Australia.

great man theory

Gregorian calendar.

H

hagiography

A biography of a saint or saints, or more broadly, any biography in which the author is uncritical or reverential towards the subject.

hegemony

The political, economic, military, and/or cultural predominance of one state over other states, or more generally of any group or regime which exerts undue influence within a society.

heraldic badge/heraldry

The design, display, and study of armorial bearings and devices are often practised together with the study of ceremony, rank, and pedigree.

heritage tourism

Tourism involves the exploration and appreciation of a place's or a group of people's cultural, historical, or environmental heritage. The term encompasses both tangible and intangible aspects of history, including historic sites, monuments, and artefacts, as well as the traditions, customs, and practices associated with a particular culture or historical period.

hermeneutics

The theory and methodology of the interpretation of texts.

histoinformatics

histoire des mentalités

An approach to social or cultural history that attempts to describe and analyse how historical people thought about, interacted with, and classified the world around them, i.e., the mentalities, perspectives, or modes of thought through which they interpreted historical events as well as their own lives. This methodology thus aims to understand the psychology of people who lived in the past. It is often associated with the Annales school of historiography and with microhistory.

Histoire totale.

historian

A scholar who studies or writes about history.

Historical demography/ materialism

A branch of Marxism that posits the development of history is not determined by the subjective desires or actions of specific human beings, but is instead shaped by the objective facts of material existence. It views human history as unfolding in response to humans' attempts to alter the natural environment to meet their specific biological needs.[2]

historical method

The collection of techniques and guidelines that historians use to research and write histories of the past. The historical method involves the historian identifying and drawing upon primary sources, secondary sources, and material evidence, such as that derived from archaeology, evaluating the relative authority of these sources, and then combining their testimony appropriately to construct an accurate and reliable picture of past events and environments.

historical metrology/ negationism

Falsification or distortion of the historical record, especially by the practice of denialism. The term is sometimes used interchangeably with historical revisionism. Still, it may also be considered technically distinct, in that the latter can be applied to newly evidenced, well-reasoned reinterpretations of history. Historical negationism, by contrast, is always illegitimate in its attempts to revise the past because it is practised without impartiality or because it uses techniques that are inadmissible in proper academic discourse, such as presenting known forgeries as if they were genuine, inventing implausible reasons for distrusting genuine historical documents, and manipulating statistical figures to support a particular point of view.

historical realism

The view that there is a continuity and correspondence between the real world and the narration of that world in historians' narratives.[7]

historical record/reenactment/revisionism/significance/society

An organisation dedicated to preserving and promoting interest in the history of a particular place, time period, or subject, or of the study of history in general.[5]

historical source/historical thinking

The practice of critical thinking and literacy skills in evaluating and analysing primary source documents to construct a meaningful and reliable account of the past. See also historical method.

historical value/historicism

1. A mode of historical enquiry that insists that the past must be understood on its own terms, as opposed to trying to understand it from the perspectives permitted by modern knowledge, values, and beliefs, known as presentism.

2. A determinist philosophy of history which holds that the course of historical events is governed by discoverable laws or by some overarching theme or pattern to which historical trends must invariably adhere, permitting historians to predict the likely direction in which future events will unfold, generally by assuming that the trends of past events will recur in a predictable sequence or manner.[1]

historicity

The historical actuality or authenticity of persons or events in the past; the quality of being part of history instead of being a myth, legend, or fiction. The historicity of a claim about the past is its factual status.

historiography

1. The study of the methods, sources, and theoretical approaches used by historians in developing history as an academic discipline.
2. A body of historical work on a particular topic.
3. The history of historical writing about a particular topic.

Historism/history

The study of the past, as described in written documents, generally considers events occurring before the written record as prehistory. The term is also commonly used to refer to any set of events which happened earlier in time, written or otherwise. In academic study, history is considered the product of our attempts to understand the past, rather than the past itself. History encompasses past events, as well as the memory, discovery, collection, organisation, presentation, and interpretation of information about these events.

history of science/homily/human history

1. The complete narrative of humanity's past, generally as reckoned from the emergence of anatomically modern humans c. 300,000 years ago to the present day (though sometimes inclusive of much earlier periods in human evolution), and thereby encompassing both prehistory and written history.
2. The scientific study of this narrative, as it is understood through archaeology, anthropology, genetics, linguistics, and, since the advent of writing, from primary and secondary written sources.

humanism
An intellectual movement of the Renaissance associated with the rediscovery of classical ideas.

I

Iapetus Ocean
A relatively small ocean that existed between the continents of Laurentia, Baltica, and Avalonia from the Late Precambrian to the Devonian.

illuminated manuscript
A manuscript in which the addition of decoration supplements the text.

imperialism

impresa/ impress, heraldic badge, livery badge, personal device, and cognisance.

An emblem, badge, or para-heraldic device worn by nobility in the Middle Ages, usually accompanied by a motto in Latin and painted on shields or helmets in tournaments, embroidered on clothing or on equine caparisons, or embodied in standards, brooches, paintings, tapestries, or other works of art. These emblems were intended to express the character, aspirations, and achievements of a particular person, rather than an entire family or lineage, and were often designed anew for each occasion.[8]

incunabulum

A book, pamphlet, broadside, or other printed document that was produced during the earliest period of printing in Europe but before the widespread adoption of mass production techniques, i.e. generally in the few decades between the invention of the printing press and the year 1501.[9] In the following decades, it became increasingly common and inexpensive to print many copies of the exact text, such that incunabula from the period immediately preceding the beginning of the 16th century are disproportionately rare and valuable to historians. Incunabula are printed by definition, either as block books or with movable type, and thus are distinct from manuscripts, which are handwritten.

Industrial Age/information history/interdisciplinary

The study or practice of a subject which applies the methods and approaches of several disciplines. For instance, while history, literature and archaeology are separate disciplines, they may be combined in an interdisciplinary approach.

interpretation

The ensemble of procedures by which the historian, according to personal perspective, temperament, social conditioning, and conscious choice, imposes a pattern of meaning or significance on his subject; the process of selection, arrangement, accentuation, and synthesis of historical facts that establishes the personal stamp of an individual historian on an account of the past.[10]

interregnum

A gap or discontinuity in the rule, administration, or activity of a government, organization, or social institution, especially in the rule of a monarchical dynasty; i.e. the period of time between the end of the reign of one monarch and the beginning of the reign of the next monarch, during which a monarch belonging to a different dynasty reigned, or during which no monarch reigned. The term usually refers to the temporary dissolution, usurpation, or replacement of the ruling dynasty, or of the monarchy itself, with another dynasty or a different form of government entirely, followed by the eventual restoration of the original dynasty or government, and also generally implies a period of widespread social unrest, civil wars or wars of succession, or power vacuums in which foreign invaders come to prominence.

interwar period

In the 20th century, the period between the end of World War I on 11 November 1918 and the beginning of World War II on 1 September 1939 is generally referred to as the interwar period, which may also be used to describe the period between any two successive wars.

journal

A scholarly periodical devoted to publishing academic writings, often related to a particular historical theme.

Julian calendar.

L

lacuna

A gap in a manuscript, inscription, or text.

Landscape history/landscape archaeology.

The study of how humanity has altered the physical appearance and landscapes of its surrounding environment in the past, and how these changes continue to occur in the present.

late modern period

Laurasia

A supercontinent that existed from the Jurassic to Early Tertiary after splitting from Pangaea. It was composed of Laurentia, Baltica, and Avalonia (what is now North America, Scandinavia, Greenland, and Western and Central Europe), and eventually fragmented into Eurasia and North America in the Tertiary with the opening of the North Atlantic Ocean.

Laurentia

A separate continental plate existed from the Late Precambrian to the Silurian, comprising a significant portion of what is now North America, northwest Ireland, Scotland, Greenland, and parts of Norway and Russia.

legend

local history

The study of the history of a small geographical area, of a local community, or of the regional incidence of broader national or international trends. If undertaken to shed light on broader historical questions, local history may be regarded as a branch of microhistory.

longue durée

An approach to the study of history popularised by the French Annales School, which gives priority to long-term historical processes and phenomena, concentrating on all-but-permanent or slowly evolving structures from which broad patterns and trends can be interpreted, in contrast to the more traditional focus on the lives of specific individuals and specific events that occurred at particular points in time.

M

macrohistory

The study of significant, long-term trends in world history aims to uncover overarching patterns that transcend the more specific details of diverse historical cultures.

manuscript

Any document written by hand, as opposed to one that is printed, typed, or reproduced in some other way.

manuscriptology

The study of history and literature through the use and interpretation of handwritten documents. The term is similar to codicology but is primarily used among historians of South Asia, especially India, because many of the historical manuscripts produced there are not considered codices in the strictest sense of the term.

microhistory

The intensive historical investigation of a small and narrow unit of research (e.g., a specific event, community, person, object, or idea) is generally undertaken to shed light on broader historical questions. Local history may be considered a branch of microhistory.

The Middle Ages/also called the medieval period.

The period in the history of Europe and the Near East, lasting from approximately the 5th century to the 15th century AD, is usually considered to have begun with the collapse of the Western Roman Empire circa. AD 476 and to have ended with the transition to the Renaissance and the discovery of the Americas in the late 1400s. The Middle Ages can be seen as part of the broader post-classical period of world history, and as the middle of the three traditional divisions of Western history, preceded by classical antiquity and followed by the modern period. The medieval period itself is often subdivided into the Early, High, and Late Middle Ages.

migration

The movement of human beings from one place to another with the intention of settling, permanently or temporarily, at a new location. Human migrations have been defining components of the history of every settled place and a major driver of economic, cultural, and linguistic exchange between populations; therefore, historians often emphasise the importance of studying their causes, paths, and effects.

military history

The study of the history of armed conflict and its impact on society. It may range from the analysis of specific military actions and engagements to the much broader examination of warfare as a political tool.

modern history

modernity

1. The state of being modern, by any of various definitions of the term.[6]
2. The historical period defined by modern history, with various starting and ending points but sometimes inclusive of the present day (i.e. contemporary history), mainly when used generically to contrast the recent or current state of human civilisation with previous eras.

3. The ensemble of sociocultural norms, attitudes, practices, ideas, and beliefs associated with this period, often with an emphasis on those originating in the Renaissance, the Enlightenment, the Industrial Age, and/or the early modern period.

monograph

A piece of writing, especially a book or an essay, that is the product of detailed, specialised research, often by a single author, on a particular subject or an aspect of a subject, e.g. a specific historical phenomenon, person, place, or event.[6]

mythology

The collected body of myths shared by a culture or a group of people, or the academic study of such myths.

N

narrative history

The practice of writing about history in a story-like form, using literary elements commonly found in storytelling to relate the course of actual historical events, such as a central theme or narrative arc and a final climax or resolution. Real historical figures may be presented as "characters" identifiable as protagonists or antagonists.

national memory

A form of collective memory shared by the people of a particular country or nation and defined by their everyday experiences, history, ethnicity, society, or culture. The idea is closely tied to nationalism and is an integral part of national identity.

natural history

A domain of inquiry involving organisms, including animals, fungi, and plants, in their natural environments, which leans more towards observational than experimental methods of study.

notaphily

The study and collection of paper currency and banknotes.

numismatics

The study and collection of all forms of currency, including coins, tokens, paper money, medals, and other means of payment used to resolve debts and exchange goods.

O

official history

A work of history which is sponsored, authorised, or endorsed by its subject, such as an authorised biography; or a narrative which is the accepted or conventional interpretation of historical events as formally proclaimed or supported by a government or institution, particularly as it is distinguished from alternative narratives or interpretations.

one-place study

A type of family history, local history, or microhistory which describes and analyses the people or events living in or associated with a single place, such as a building, road, neighbourhood, village, or community, or any other geographic area, during a particular time period. This contrasts with studies united by different themes, such as a history of a specific family lineage, whose members may have been geographically dispersed, or of particular types of events which may have occurred in more than one place.

Onomastics/Also onomatology.

The study of the etymology, history, and use of proper names.

oral history

1. The collection and study of historical information obtained from individuals or families via some form of oral or verbal communication (e.g. planned interviews, public speeches, or everyday conversation, or audiotapes or videotapes of these events), as opposed to information obtained from written documents or

other non-verbal sources. Oral history strives to record and preserve knowledge that cannot be obtained in different ways (e.g., stories told by people who are illiterate, or passed down by cultures that do not have a written language), particularly from people who directly participated in or observed past events firsthand. Knowledge transmitted orally is unique in that it often shares the tacit or subconscious perspectives, thoughts, and opinions of the speaker, which might otherwise be excluded from written accounts, along with nuances particular to unplanned, off-the-cuff conversation, where the speaker has not had time to prepare their responses and is unable to change them after the fact.

2. Any information gathered in this manner, or any work of history, written or otherwise, which records transcripts of orally communicated accounts.

original order

A concept in archival theory that proposes maintaining a group of records in the same order in which they were created.

origo gentis

In medieval studies, the origin story of a particular person or group of people, as recounted and interpreted by the person or people themselves, often details their chronological history, sometimes by combining actual events with myths and folklore.

P

Palaeography/ Also palaeography.

The study of historical writing systems, especially ancient ones, and the deciphering, dating, and authentication of historical manuscripts, with a focus on the forms, processes, and methods of writing, particularly the analysis of handwriting, rather than the textual content of documents.

Paleo-Tethys Ocean

A large ocean that originated between eastern Gondwana, Siberia, Kazakhstan, and Baltica in the Ordovician and finally closed in the Jurassic. The Tethys Ocean replaced it as eastern Pangaea was assembled.

palimpsest

Pangaea

A supercontinent that existed from the end of the Permian to the Jurassic, it was assembled from large continents, such as Euramerica, Gondwana, and Siberia, as well as smaller landmasses, including the Cathaysian and Cimmerian Terranes. The name Pangaea is Greek for "all lands".

Pannotia

A supercontinent that existed in the Late Precambrian and gave rise to the continents of Gondwana, Laurentia, Siberia, and Baltica in the Cambrian.

Panthalassic Ocean/Also called the Panthalassa.

A vast ocean that existed from the Late Precambrian to the Jurassic, circling the globe and connecting to smaller oceans that developed throughout the Phanerozoic.

past

The entire set or any subset of events which happened previously in time.

people's history

Also called history from below.

1. A type of historical narrative which attempts to account for historical events from the perspective of ordinary people rather than leaders or authority figures, using a bottom-up approach that rejects elite perspectives, instead emphasising those of the poor, the disenfranchised, the oppressed, nonconformists, social or cultural minorities, and any group that otherwise exists on the margins of society.

2. History for and about the majority of the population, especially that which is highly accessible and relevant to the people as a whole,

as opposed to history that is intended for or only accessible to well-educated audiences or serious scholars.

periodization

The process or study of categorising the past into discrete, quantified, and named periods or blocks of time, e.g. the Bronze Age, the Middle Ages, the Victorian Era, etc. This is often done to facilitate the analysis of history and the causality that might have linked specific events, resulting in descriptive abstractions that provide convenient labels for periods of time with relatively unique or stable characteristics. However, the time periods represented by these labels often overlap because their beginnings and ends are imprecisely defined. In reality, history is continuous and not generalised; therefore, all systems of periodisation are more or less arbitrary.

phaleristics

The study of military orders, decorations, and medals.

philately

The study of postage stamps.

philology

The study of language in oral and written historical sources, particularly literary texts, involves establishing their authenticity and original form, as well as determining their meaning. The discipline lies at the intersection of textual criticism, literary criticism, history, and linguistics.

political history

The study of past events, ideas, movements, and leaders in politics.

Also, pre-literary history.

The period of human history between the use of the first stone tools by hominin apes (c. 3.3 million years ago) and the invention of the earliest forms of writing (c. 5,000 years ago), the latter of which marks the beginning of conventional history. The distinction between prehistory and history – i.e., between events that occurred before the advent of writing and those that occurred after – is important because the scientific study of prehistoric events relies on very different methods from those used to study historical events. In the absence of written records, prehistory can only be understood through the interpretation of physical artefacts, fossils, and preserved archaeological contexts, combined with inferences based on research from other natural sciences disciplines, particularly anthropology, evolutionary biology, and geology. The prehistoric period also lacks a universally consistent end date, as human populations invented or adopted writing at different times and in various places. See also protohistory.

presentism

The application of present-day ideas and perspectives to depictions or interpretations of the past.

primary source

Material from or directly related to the past. The term usually refers to written records and documents created during the period being studied, such as diaries, letters, legal documents, accounts, photographs, and news reports. Still, it may also, in the broadest sense, include cultural artefacts. Contrast the secondary source.

prosopography

The study of collective biography: the examination of a historical group of individuals, e.g. those in a common occupation, institution, or place, through a collective study of their lives.[6]

protohistory

1. A period between prehistory and history during which a particular civilisation or culture has not yet developed writing, but during which other contemporary cultures have already noted in their own writings the existence of the pre-literate culture. For example, the cultures of ancient Celtic and Germanic tribes are considered protohistoric

when they began appearing in contemporary Greek and Roman sources.

2. The transition period between the advent of literacy in a society and the earliest surviving writings of the first historians to emerge from that society.

provenance

The chronology of the ownership, custody, or location of a historical object, document, or group of records.

pseudohistory

A type of pseudoscholarship that attempts to distort or misrepresent the historical record, often using methods resembling those in legitimate historical research and frequently in service to a particular political, religious, or personal agenda. Works of pseudohistory share some features with other types of pseudoscience, such as treating myths, legends, and other unreliable sources as literal historical truth; emphasising historical sources that appear to support the pseudohistorical thesis while ignoring or dismissing those that contradict it; and conflating possibility with actuality, assuming that if something could have happened, then it did.

psychohistory

public history

A range of activities undertaken by people with some training in the discipline of history, but who are generally working outside of specialised academic settings.
Contents:

Q

quantitative history

An approach to historical research that makes use of quantitative, statistical, and computer-based tools.

R

radical history

History practised as a form of social protest; i.e. history written in conscious opposition to perceived social injustice and dedicated to the furtherance of progressive political and social change. Practitioners of radical history believe that historians are morally obligated to relate their research to the struggle for positive change and to use the study of the past for the betterment of the present and the future. From their standpoint, knowledge of the past is not valuable for its own sake but only insofar as it may be used to serve some social purpose.[10]

regnal year

A year of the reign of a particular sovereign or monarch, with the date considered as an ordinal rather than a cardinal number, e.g. "the third year in the reign of King Henry VIII". Regnal dating systems were widely used in historical times to date specific events and official records, including documents of parliamentary sessions in the United Kingdom until 1963, when the Gregorian calendar was instead adopted as the formal dating convention.

Renaissance

respect des fonds

An archival principle which proposes that collections of archival records should be ordered and preserved according to the administration, organisation, individual, or entity by which they were created or from which they were received.

revisionist history

Any approach to history in which a previously held interpretation of history or of a historical event is revised. In the most general usage, every original historian may be said to be a revisionist historian, because the simple act of generating a new understanding of the past necessarily challenges or re-interprets the body of historical knowledge about a subject, though the term may also refer more specifically to re-interpretations of the mainstream or "orthodox" views on a particular time period or event, a practice known as historical revisionism, or, with the much more negative connotation of distorting the historical record in service of a political agenda, to historical negationism.[4]

revolution

Rodinia

A supercontinent that existed during the Late Precambrian before the supercontinent Pannotia, and the oldest supercontinent for which scientists have a good record. The name Rodinia is derived from the Russian word for "homeland".

Romanticism

A cultural and intellectual movement of the late 18th to mid-19th centuries that emphasised emotion and sentiment rather than reason, predominantly among Western European cultures but also in other parts of the world.

S

saeculum

A length of time approximately equal to the potential lifetime of a human being or, equivalently, to the time it takes to regenerate a human population with new individuals completely – that is, the duration between the moment at which an event occurs (such as the founding of a city) and the point in time at which every individual who was alive at the first moment has died.

Scientific Revolution

seal

A device for making an impression, usually in wax, clay, or lead, or the impression so formed, which historically was commonly used to authenticate documents on the rationale that a carefully crafted symbol or image would be complex for counterfeiters

secondary source

Material created by somebody removed from the event being studied; i.e. someone who was contemporaneous with the event but not physically present to witness it, or who was working from a period of time after the event occurred. All historical textbooks, for example, are secondary sources. Contrast primary source.

sensory history

Siberia

A separate continental plate that existed from the Late Precambrian to the Carboniferous, comprising a large part of what is now central Russia, specifically the modern region of Siberia.

sigillography

The study of seals and symbols used to authenticate documents, which are variously made by impressing an image into wax, clay, lead, or another substance.

social history

A branch of history that studies human societies of the past, particularly their social structures, hierarchies, and expectations, and how these have changed over time, often by detailing the experiences of ordinary people in the past.

The study of the collection, organisation, and interpretation of (historical) data.

Stone Age

The first of the three periods into which prehistory is traditionally divided, during which stone was widely used by early hominins to make tools with an edge, a point, or a percussion surface. It preceded the Bronze Age and the Iron Age. Still, it spanned a period of time far more extended than either of them, usually considered to have begun as early as 3.4 million years ago and to have ended with the advent of metalworking and particularly copper smelting, which were adopted at different times in different parts of the world but generally between 4000 BCE and 2000 BCE, after which bronze became widespread and supplanted stone in many uses.

stratigraphy

In archaeology, a key concept in interpreting a site is establishing the relative chronology of its separate physical contexts.

subaltern

In postcolonial studies and critical theory, colonial populations that are socially, politically, and/or geographically excluded from the hierarchy of power in an imperial colony and from the metropolitan homeland of the colonial empire are often deliberately marginalised to deny them agency and voice in colonial politics.

T

teleology

A mode of historical interpretation that holds that events move towards a definite end state or goal.

terminus ante quem (TAQ)

The latest time at which a specific, punctual event could have occurred, as indicated by placing the event relative to any other events whose dates are known with certainty. The concept establishes a limit after which an event could not have occurred based on logical expectations about the progression of a chronology, e.g. the decree of a law that is known to have been decreed by a specific monarch could not have occurred after the monarch's death.

terminus post quem (TPQ)

The earliest time at which a specific, punctual event could have occurred, as indicated by placing the event relative to any other events whose dates are known with certainty. The concept establishes a limit before which an event could not have occurred based on logical expectations about the progression of a chronology, e.g. a battle in which a specific person is known to have been killed could not have happened before the person's date of birth (or any other securely dated event in the person's life).

Tethys Ocean

A small ocean that existed from the Triassic to the Jurassic. As Pangaea was split into Gondwana and Laurasia during the Jurassic, an arm of the ocean developed westward, known as the Tethys Seaway or Tethys Sea.

three-age system

The periodisation of human history into three time periods. The most common example is the division of prehistory into the Stone Age, Bronze Age, and Iron Age. However, the concept may also refer to other tripartite divisions of historic time periods.

time

The indefinite continued progress of existence and events that occur in an apparently irreversible succession from the past, through the present, and into the future.

timeline

A list of historical events presented in chronological order, typically of a tabular or graphical design, especially in the form of a line labeled with specific dates or ranges of dates and the contemporaneous events that occurred on those dates; often the length of the line scales to the duration of time it represents, allowing viewers to quickly and easily comprehend the order of events and the relative amounts of time between them.

timeliness

The quality of punctuality and proximity to a historical event is a means of assessing the reliability of a source. Timeliness is a crucial consideration in determining the reliability of historical records, as records produced contemporaneously with an event are generally considered more accurate than those produced at a later time.[5]

top-down approach

An approach to historical scholarship that emphasises the experiences and perspectives of elites and leaders, as opposed to those of average people.[4] Contrast the bottom-up approach.

toponymy

transhistoricity

The quality of a concept or entity that persists throughout human history and is not governed or defined by the frame of reference of a particular time and place.

translatio studii

An historiographical concept originating in the Middle Ages, in which history is viewed as a linear succession of knowledge and learning transfers from one place and time to another. For example, ancient Rome was commonly seen as having inherited the knowledge, ideas, and cultural values of the ancient Hellenistic civilisations that preceded it.

transnational history

typescript

A typewritten document, i.e. produced using a typewriter or a digital computer, as opposed to a manuscript, which is handwritten.[5]

typology

In archaeology, classifying artefacts, buildings, and field monuments according to their physical characteristics is an essential tool for managing large quantities of archaeological data.

U

universal history

A work that aims to present a complete history of all humanity as a whole, coherent unit, including all times, nations, peoples, and events in recorded history, insofar as a scientific treatment of them is possible.

unwitting testimony

Unintentional evidence provided by historical sources, e.g. by authors whose writings reveal the implicit or subconscious attitudes, beliefs, or preconceptions of the author or of the society or culture to which the author belongs, even when the author did not intend to do so. The interpretation of unwitting testimony by historians acknowledges that primary sources may contain valuable information about the past which is not explicit or deliberate.

Urban history.

V

Victorian.

W

Whig history

A mode of historical interpretation which presents the past as an inevitable progression towards ever greater liberty and enlightenment; or, more broadly, any teleological or goal-directed narrative that assumes the inevitability of progress in human civilisation.

women's history

The study of the role that women have played in history, with particular emphasis on the growth of women's rights, individual women and groups of women of historical significance, and the effects that historical events have had on women. Inherent in the discipline is the belief that more traditional approaches to history have minimised or ignored the contributions of women and the impacts of political, social, and technological change on women's lives; in this respect, women's history is often practised as a form of historical revisionism, seeking to challenge the orthodox historical consensus and make it more inclusive.

world history

written history

Y

Yuga

Index

American, 12, 26, 57, 78, 79, 80, 86, 90, 96, 97, 98, 101, 106, 107, 108, 109, 113, 114, 119, 127, 130, 133, 134, 138, 140, 142, 143, 144, 147, 150, 164, 184, 185, 186, 187, 189, 195, 196, 199, 204, 230, 231, 233, 287, 288, 305, 358, 386, 413, 420, 442, 447, 454, 457, 458, 461, 462, 468, 482, 490, 492, 515, 527, 528, 539, 541, 542, 563, 593, 594, 602

animals, 11, 45, 609, 615, 628, 646
British, 10, 11, 12, 29, 39, 54, 66, 115, 116, 117, 118, 120, 121, 123, 124, 132, 144, 158, 159, 162, 165, 176, 204, 219, 233, 234, 235, 249, 256, 260, 266, 267, 270, 271, 272, 276, 286, 287, 288, 293, 294, 295, 303, 315, 316, 320, 324, 329, 356, 367, 376, 378, 386, 400, 430, 433, 446, 455, 456, 461, 462, 508, 527, 528,

539, 541, 545, 547, 588, 591, 626
Detroit, 15
Empire, 12, 626
Force, 11, 158, 167, 186, 303, 320, 386, 496, 497, 545
Forgive, 9
French, 39, 63, 64, 65, 68, 158, 159, 160, 170, 179, 242, 244, 248, 253, 254, 263, 264, 265, 269, 274, 275, 276, 277, 278, 316, 320, 321, 322, 323, 342, 356, 375, 379, 400, 430, 441, 552, 591, 599, 610, 642
God, 9, 78, 85, 225, 370, 599, 600, 601
Hutchison, 13
IGCSE, 3, 10, 17, 115, 152, 299
ISRAELIS, 11
JARUZELSKI, 514
Julia, 12
Kennedy, 10, 90, 92, 94, 97, 101, 105, 109, 112, 113, 126, 127, 128, 130, 133, 134, 136, 137, 138, 139, 140, 141, 142, 143, 144, 145, 146, 147, 148, 149, 150, 151, 229, 385
KEY, 9
Khruschev, 10, 90
Ku Klux Klan, 153, 300, 406, 407, 411, 412, 414, 417, 465, 466, 467, 469, 471, 472, 474, 487, 499, 503
Lincoln, 226, 227, 506, 507, 509, 510, 511, 512, 513, 514, 525, 526, 529, 530, 531, 532, 533, 534, 535, 537, 538, 539, 540, 541, 542
Meagan, 12
Nazis, 11, 24, 41, 42, 55, 70, 72, 73, 197, 215, 236, 237, 238, 239, 281, 297, 304, 335, 361, 388, 398, 403, 404, 587
Norwegian, 261, 272, 277
Pope, 11, 50, 62, 63, 64, 243, 244, 245, 246, 328
research, 9
Russia, 25, 38, 56, 66, 67, 153, 185, 213, 214, 285, 291, 313, 314, 335, 362, 372, 376, 388, 396, 546, 567, 577, 614, 616, 642, 659
Shania, 14
treatise, 11
Treaty, 21, 42, 70, 157, 159, 169, 170, 210, 214, 254, 257, 258, 261, 262, 265, 266, 270, 275, 290, 302, 331, 334, 345, 357, 373, 374, 383,

441, 442, 448, 450, 452, 457, 461, 552
UNITED, 4, 25, 57, 153, 163, 217, 281, 291, 305, 336, 363, 389, 546, 549, 556, 559, 567, 570, 577, 580, 587, 590
Verdun, 23, 303, 323, 324, 379
Victorian, 665

Whig, 665
Wilson, 11, 21, 254, 331, 357, 375, 376, 440, 441, 442, 443, 444, 445, 448, 449, 450, 452, 453, 454, 455, 456, 457, 458, 459, 460, 461, 462
Yuga, 666
Zak, 15

www.ingramcontent.com/pod-product-compliance
Lightning Source LLC
Chambersburg PA
CBHW071352300426
44114CB00016B/2031